Statemei

"When Men Buy Sex: Who Really Pays?" provides a sober warning and clear depiction of the abject human rights failures and increased trafficking activity associated with a legalized or decriminalized sex industry.

Heinz and King leverage their lived experience to unveil the euphemisms and deceptions which continue to keep so many Indigenous and non-Indigenous Canadian girls and women enslaved in inequality.

Anyone sincerely concerned with the well-being of humanity will heed this book's call. A strong and universally applied approach to stem consumer demand is necessary to prevent Canada from becoming the world's brothel.

—Paul Brandt
Founder, #NotInMyCity
Former Chair, Alberta Human Trafficking Task Force

This book is fantastic and so needed.

Readers will be hard-pressed to find a more comprehensive analysis of the sex trade industry. While the buying and selling of sex, most often exploitative, have commonalities wherever they occur, this book fills a void on this topic in Canada. It is a must-read for anyone trying to understand the realities of prostitution and, in particular, who really pays when men buy sex. The voices and stories of experiential women ring out in this book, as they must for any reader seeking to learn more on this issue that affects primarily women and girls. The focus in the book, on the harms caused by buyers treating women and girls as commodities, is appropriate and essential when seeking to understand the sex trade.

Much appreciation to Andrea and Kathy for their tireless efforts in this movement.

—Glendyne Gerrard
Director of Defend Dignity, 2011-2023

*"**When Men Buy Sex: Who Really Pays?**" is an exceptional and insightful read. Heinz and King do an amazing job in elevating the voices of the exploited. This provides an unfettered understanding of sexual exploitation in Canada by providing real stories, taking away the "Pretty Woman" lie that is often furthered by Hollywood and media.*

The lie perpetuated in exploitation, that women like what they are doing, is exposed and debunked by the lived experiences highlighted here. The authors and contributors show the industry is not one of work but rather an industry of pain, suffering, and exploitation. Sex buyers need to read this to understand the negative impact of their actions on the exploited.

—Dan Jones
Associate Chair of Justice Studies, NorQuest College
Retired Police Officer

*"**When Men Buy Sex: Who Really Pays?**" is moving and weighty. Its impact comes from knowing that what you are reading has roots in the authors' personal lived experiences. Some of the content is tough to take in; it is raw, it is honest. The assessments and recommendations come from research and data, not sanitized and white-washed notions. The perspective of the "empowered sex worker" is effectively dismantled.*

This book provides a balanced and considered narrative of the social, personal, political, and emotional factors involved when a human being exchanges sexual access to their body for money. There is a call to the reader to be part of the solution, for us to do better, and to create a world where the inherent value and dignity of all people is recognized and upheld.

With passion and vulnerability, Andrea and Kathy present us with an alternate vision, one where the systemic objectification and exploitation of others for profit is unacceptable in a free world.

—Paul Lavergne
Registered Psychotherapist, Sexual Recovery Therapist, Trainer,
YouTube Interviewer
The Turning Point Counselling Services

This book is the next powerful tool in the fight to eliminate sexual exploitation. Andrea Heinz and Kathy King have executed the perfect merging of facts-based research and soul-filled anecdotes to reach all kinds, from active advocates to concerned citizens.

With a topic such as this one, it is not enough to only tell the reader of **what** is happening; it is imperative to also connect them with the **who** it is happening to. Heinz and King have expertly showcased the intricate web that has been weaved through decades of systemic oppression, patriarchal beliefs, and male entitlement that has entangled so many. And once you see it, you simply can't go back. *"When Men Buy Sex"* puts to bed the last vestiges of 'pro sex work' mentality and provides an unshakeable foundation from which to charge ahead and create an exploitation free world.

As someone who walked into the commercial sex industry believing myself to be an empowered feminist, only to find out I was actually a victim of trafficking, this book is a balm to my soul. It should be required reading for anyone who wants to claim the sex trade is empowering.

—Alexandra Stevenson
Trafficking Survivor and Founder of 'The Laughing Survivor'
B.A. in Criminology, post-secondary certification in Victimology,
M.S. in Psychology

"When Men Buy Sex: Who Really Pays?" is a question that challenged me since the 1990s. I was one of the people who "paid" for the impact of men cruising my neighborhood, seeking vulnerable youth and women to exploit. Even today, I am confronted with condoms thrown out the driver's side window of the cars that park outside my house. And yet those whose bodies are violated pay much more dearly than me and my neighbours.

Andrea, Kathy, and all who contributed to this book have cracked open many stories that need to be heard and acknowledged. This is a timely book. I hope readers can draw strength from it, contribute to debunking myths that glamorize the sex industry, and empathize in solidarity with all whose lives have been deeply impacted.

—Kate Quinn
Executive Director, Centre to End All Sexual Exploitation, 1996-2023
2012 Woman of Distinction Award for
Lifetime Achievement in fighting sexual exploitation
2022 Queen's Platinum Jubilee Medal recipient for
30 years of community advocacy

"When Men Buy Sex: Who Really Pays?" is a must read for all parents, youth, service providers, systems, and the general public. Sexual exploitation is a complex issue rooted in racism, sexism, and classism and it is a 100% preventable crime. Andrea Heinz and Kathy King share rare insights into this reality for all women, illustrate the unique challenges Indigenous women face, and, most importantly, offer solutions by honouring the voices of Survivors.

This book is educational, heart-wrenching at times, and inspiring. Readers will be forever changed and compelled to act. Our Indigenous teachings say that a warrior is defined and measured by how they protect the most vulnerable and stand up for what is right. Andrea and Kathy exemplify this. They are brave, show humility, love, and kindness, and their work is truly heart medicine work.

Meegwetch (thank you).

—Diane Redsky
Advocate for Indigenous Women, Girls, and 2SLGBTQQIA+ peoples' safety
Director, National Task Force on Sex Trafficking of
Women and Girls in Canada

The book is amazing, just amazing, with in-depth resources provided, experts consulted, and survivor stories that leave the reader in tears.

If there was ever a book published in Canada that tells the WHOLE story about the truth behind the commercial sex industry and its myths exposed, this is it. From the personal testimonies of courageous survivors who expose the willfully ignored dark culture of male entitlement to the bodies of girls and women, to the explanation of how this has been allowed to continue in an age where the equality of women is celebrated, the reader will not only be educated but stunned.

"When Men Buy Sex: Who Really Pays?" should be a mandatory read for all youth, a generation that is capable of shifting Canadian culture by demanding that buying sex be legally and socially abolished.

—Vancouver Collective Against Sexual Exploitation (VCASE)

*For far too long, Canadian sex buyers have benefited from anonymity and hiding in the shadows while their victims have suffered in silence. No more. **"When Men Buy Sex"** is an important and necessary volume of evidence and voices that unveil the significant harms of buying sex. Canada has a responsibility to protect those most at risk and hold accountable those who exploit them. I am grateful that Andrea Heinz and Kathy King have put together this book and confident that it will advance a national conversation to end exploitation.*

—Arnold Viersen
Member of Parliament for Peace River—Westlock
Co-chair of the All-Party Parliamentary Group
to End Modern Slavery and Human Trafficking

When Men Buy Sex: Who Really Pays?

Canadian Stories of Exploitation, Survival, and Advocacy

Andrea Heinz & Kathy King

 FriesenPress

One Printers Way
Altona, MB R0G 0B0
Canada

www.friesenpress.com

ISBN
978-1-03-916851-0 (Hardcover)
978-1-03-916850-3 (Paperback)
978-1-03-916852-7 (eBook)

1. SOCIAL SCIENCE, HUMAN TRAFFICKING

Distributed to the trade by The Ingram Book Company

ACKNOWLEDGEMENT

We acknowledge the land on which we are gathered as the ancestral home of many First Nations, Métis, and Inuit. As Canadians, we are all responsible for working toward the vision of equality and justice as the treaties promise.

We honour Elders past and present, those who walked this great land from the beginning of time, and those with whom we are now learning truth and reconciliation.

We honour the elements of Creation and the sacred role of women. We acknowledge the profound loss of many missing and murdered Indigenous women and girls; and we call on Canadians to speak out against violence, racism, and sexism.

DISCLAIMER

The material presented in this book may trigger memories of trauma or feelings of distress. Readers are encouraged to engage in self-care practices and access emotional support as needed.

All profits from the sale of this book will be donated to projects and initiatives supporting exit opportunities and the prevention of sexual exploitation in Canada.

DEDICATION

This book is dedicated to all our sisters, brothers, and children who were coerced or pimped/trafficked into sexual servitude. May we hear the depths of their trauma and respond with compassion, equality, justice, and freedom.

We acknowledge the minority of sex sellers who claim to choose involvement in the industry. May their demands for individual liberties be measured against documented collective harm.

PREFACE

As we invite readers to explore our perspectives of commercial sexual exploitation, we openly seek to infiltrate the undefined spaces between apathy and anger. Our goal is to enhance empathy by putting names and faces on the suffering inherent to sexual coercion and violence. We hope to inspire nuances of thought that will generate new alternatives for shaping freedom, respect, and equality in Canada and worldwide.

As Canadian authors, we track the complexities of human nature through a unique collection of personal and family narratives, Canadian history, statistical data, and legislation. Other exploration includes the roles of community engagement and political responses. Contrary to frequent discussions about sellers, our focus on the buyers of sex illuminates the often-obscured reality that there would be no sexual exploitation or human trafficking without consumers.

Our book functions like a kaleidoscope. Fragments of life remain consistent, although viewpoints change. Some men buy sex; reasons and prevalence are influenced by culture; laws and enforcement vary over time and place; women tend to be stigmatized; men continue to be enabled; demand generally exceeds supply; oppression and trafficking happen; the transactions harm countless women; a few claim their right to "work" for money; objectification is fundamental; social and economic inequalities contribute to exploitation. As each chapter turns to reveal a different context, readers are invited to examine their beliefs and attitudes.

Each chapter presents questions for consideration, our position statements (lest there be doubt), quotes from other authors, and discussion around the topic. Further sections include experiential voices of women who have survived commercial sexual exploitation, the personal reflections of an anonymous buyer, guest contributors who serve the cause of advocacy for abolition, and a review of non-State torture research.

TABLE OF CONTENTS

INTRODUCTIONS

Kathy King:

As the elder, I will begin.

My story dates back to the early 1990s when my then-teenage daughter, Cara, began experimenting with drugs and suffered recurring bouts of psychosis. It was a terrible time for both of us. As a single parent, I watched her life spiral out of control, unable to access adequate treatment or supportive housing. In the summer of 1997, Cara disappeared from the streets of Edmonton.

My incredible frustration with the myriad gaps in service at the time was overshadowed by indignation at media response when her body was found a month later. Cara was labelled and stigmatized, by words I refuse to repeat, because of what had been done to her rather than by her. I was horrified that a troubled and vulnerable young woman could be blamed for her own exploitation with no attention paid to her abusers.

Beyond my shock and horror was the numbing realization that we were not alone. Many women disappearing across Canada were dismissed in life and dishonoured in death. I vowed that Cara's story would not end in the field where she had been discarded. Although I had been unable to save my child, others in similar circumstances might still have a chance.

I have worked hard for over 25 years to transform my grief and helplessness. I am concerned that vulnerable persons worldwide continue to be groomed, exploited, and destroyed in the service of sexual consumers. I hope my daughter's tragic life and premature death can play some small part in expanding awareness and reducing demand. We must see the evil of commercial sexual exploitation and name it to save our children.

My first public censure appeared in the *Edmonton Sun* on Sept. 6, 1997, albeit relegated to page 21. I made a point of providing alternate media coverage following Cara's death and, in that interview, said, "Every drug dealer and john in the City of Edmonton has to share some responsibility."

Three years later (Aug. 14, 2000) CEASE, the Centre to End All Sexual Exploitation, conducted an inaugural memorial for women who had lost their lives due to commercial sexual exploitation. I was invited to share a family reflection and included the call to focus on consumers:

> We cannot overlook that the sex trade and the drug trade are funded and perpetuated by johns, men who are lining up all over the world to buy sex from disadvantaged women and children. We must question why our society continues to protect the identity of these men while young women are being exploited and killed. The sex trade is a consumer driven industry, and as long as there are consumers, there will be other greedy men finding a way to take advantage of the money exchanged.

Later, I learned that Sweden was the first country in the world to pass revolutionary legislation in 1999 that criminalized the purchase of sexual services.

Fast forward 20 years and sparks ignited flames across North America. In 2020, amid the global pandemic, the Coalition to End Sexual Exploitation hosted an online Global Summit July 18–28: "10 Days, 100 Speakers, 10,000 Abolitionists."

Less than one year later, the Canadian Sexual Exploitation Summit: Disrupt Demand (May 2021) drew more than 50 speakers from Canada and around the world. Over one thousand attendees gathered to share, listen, learn, and mobilize forces against the normalization of the sex industry.

It is encouraging and inspiring to know that I am not alone in my convictions. Although my passion was born from a deep and debilitating tragedy and many others share similar experiences of disconnection, abuse, and trauma, ordinary people provide hope and reassurance. Conscientious citizens, scholars, and lawyers have come to similar conclusions based on their observations, research, reflections, and spiritual awareness. I am proud to offer our book to support this community.

WHEN MEN BUY SEX: WHO REALLY PAYS?

Andrea Heinz:

In 2006, at the age of 22, I found myself approximately $60,000 in debt. I had endured nearly seven years of toxic romantic relationships with boyfriends who were emotionally, physically, and financially abusive. As well, I had, as Garth Brooks sings, several "friends in low places." I was convinced they could (and would) turn their lives around if only someone extended generosity and support their way. Pairing all of this with a complete lack of financial literacy, no viable education or skills, an empty fridge, and bills due, it didn't take much for an ad in the *Edmonton Sun* newspaper to capture my attention by promising women aged 18–30 $2000/week for "adult entertainment."

Having grown up in a remote urban service area (Fort McMurray, Alberta), the entire world of commercial sex was completely foreign to me aside from romanticized depictions in popular culture, such as the film *Pretty Woman* and sexualized musical acts like Madonna. I certainly didn't know enough about the sex trade to give what could be considered informed consent for my participation. I believed what so many young women do: "I'm having sex anyway, why not get paid money for it? What's the big deal?"

Falling victim to the brainwashing of liberal feminism's "sex positivity," I ended up selling sex more than 4,300 times over the course of seven years in Edmonton's licensed "body rub centres" (brothels). During the first three years, I operated out of as many different brothels, each involving traumatic experiences. I eventually convinced myself that the key to my longevity (mental survival) was to build my own brothel where women, myself included, could sell sex without direction or control placed upon them. I had accepted the "sex work" ideology that sex sellers could be happy, empowered, and liberated. I saw sex sellers as contracted employees, running a business where we were doing a "job like any other."

The house of cards eventually fell and, five years in, my delusions began to unravel. I realized I had been heavily dissociating in order to endure strange men spitting on me, slapping me, removing condoms without my consent, choking me, stalking me, and verbally degrading me. Locked into a commercial lease, I couldn't see my way out of the industry; I felt trapped. Guilt began to plague me when I recognized that I was not "helping" women, as I initially thought. Rather, I was enabling violent and misogynistic men to sexually abuse marginalized women for a mere $300 per hour ($50 of which went to my "business" for room rental fees). I stopped renting rooms but continued to sell sex in my brothel until such a time that a professed "happy hooker" bought me out (at a loss of $50,000).

Since exiting in December of 2012, I have dedicated myself to raising awareness about the impacts of being sexually objectified and used for men's pleasure and gratification. I have written several narrative and academic pieces to shift the conversation to one that is grounded in truth rather than palatable illusions and lies. I now understand the sex trade to be compensated sexual abuse.

Although our nation presently has what I feel is appropriate federal legislation in place to address sexual exploitation (*PCEPA: the Protection of Communities & Exploited Persons Act, 2014*), we still have a very long way to go in changing the minds and culture within Canada about women's equality and fundamental human rights. Several municipalities violate Canadian law by licensing brothels, strip clubs, and escort agencies, and many citizens unfortunately believe there is no harm in men using money to coerce young, impoverished women into performing sexual acts to survive.

With this book, I welcome you, the reader, to join us in examining what sex trade lobbyists don't want you to know. In doing so, I trust you too will become an ally in the fight against the commoditization of human sexuality, both in Canada and throughout the world.

REFLECTIONS ON PERSONAL COST

Kathy:

Early July 1997 was the last time I saw my daughter. Cara was staying with her boyfriend in a dingy basement apartment a few blocks north of Alberta Avenue in Edmonton, an area linked with sex visibly for sale. Neighbourhood residents had earlier petitioned the city to create one-way streets to minimize the disturbance of cruising john traffic.

A huge Rottweiler guarded the house, making me afraid to enter the yard. Cara loved that dog, as she did most animals, and simply hugged him with genuine affection while I navigated the short distance to her back door. When we visited my parents' farm, she reported, "The cats in the barn have lipstick all over them."

It had been a difficult year. Cara and her boyfriend had been together about two years, and both experimented with drug use. I knew there were times when she supported him, but there were also times when he cared for her through various illnesses. She started the year hospitalized in psychiatric care. She was discharged in March, supposedly with her consent, to the Women's Emergency Accommodation Centre. Over the next few months, while negotiating for anti-psychotic and contraceptive injections, I tried in vain to help her secure an appropriate supervised residence.

I always worried more when I was away from the city. Cara was very social and did not cope well alone during the day when her boyfriend held a legitimate job, as he did that summer.

With mixed feelings, I allowed myself a two-week vacation across Canada and, not surprisingly, could not make contact when I returned. Cara's boyfriend informed me he kicked her out because she resumed drug use. She finally called on Aug. 2. Unfortunately, I was occupied that day, and we planned to meet two days later. But I never saw her again.

The month became a nightmare as the silence grew with no contact. I called Cara's friends; her friends called me. I talked to Edmonton Police several times and called the various agencies that might be in contact. I made up a missing poster and left copies at several places.

It was just as well that I missed the news on the evening of Sept. 1. The first I heard of an unidentified body being found was when my radio wakened me for work the following morning. I rushed for the paper, and the front page showed four men in white hazmat suits carrying a white body bag from a field. I called the RCMP with details of my concern and went to work as usual because I didn't know what else to do.

That evening I saw a small group of people gather on my front sidewalk. They came to my door and my worst fears were confirmed. My beautiful, fun-loving, "high risk" daughter, age 22, had been identified through her dental records.

Twenty-five years later, I continue to tell Cara's story because she is one of many missing, murdered, and exploited women of Canada. They all deserve to be heard and honoured. I hope memories of their short lives can be used for good so others can enjoy the peace and freedom they were denied.

Edmonton Journal, B1, September 2, 1997
showed the removal of a body,
later identified as Cara King,
from a field near Sherwood Park.

The quest continues for justice, prevention,
sacredness, and equality.

Andrea:

I wrote this poem soon after exiting seven years in the commercial sex trade. It speaks to the moments where truth was evident but ignored by buyers under the facades of choice and free will. Upholding this illusion is a requirement of sex sellers; every buyer wants a smile.

InVISIBLE

I "work" at the brothel you go to.

Do you see me?

I line up with the other women. You look at me leeringly.
I'm apprehensive.

Do you see me?

You tell the boss I am "the one." The others are upset you chose me. I'm uneasy.

Do you see me?

We enter the room. You insist on a deal. I oblige. I
feel cheapened.

Do you see me?

I start to undress for you. I'm fearful. I'm ashamed.

Do you see me?

You touch me. My skin starts to crawl. I pull away for
a moment.

Do you see me?

You ask if I enjoy what you are doing to me. I smile. I say yes.
I lie.

Do you see me?

You finish. You tell me you had a great time. I say I did too.
Another lie.

Do you see me?

You ask if I like my job. I say I love my job. I'm lying again.

Do you see me?

I walk you out. It's awkward, uncomfortable. I feel objectified, dehumanized.

Do you see me?

You are gone. I meet the next man waiting. I wonder...

Did you see me?

> (First published July 11, 2021, by Nordic Model Now!)

PART ONE:
WHO PAYS?

WHAT IS SEX? A biological urge? A physiological release? A sensual experience? An act of love and intimacy between two people? An expression of caring? For some, acts of domination and control? For others, acts of submission? Is it work? A means of making a living? Are we destined to live with a plurality of understanding? Can we do so without animosity? Is there space for common understanding where women and men can unite?

In most discussions of commercial sexual exploitation, attention turns to the women. How can we support them? What if they are forced? What if they feel they have no options? What if they are addicted? What if selling sex is a conscious choice?

We are long overdue to turn attention to the buyers. What are their motives? Are they driven by curiosity or entitlement, healthy masculinity or compulsion? Must they be tolerated? What is healthy masculinity?

Why do some men choose to buy sex? Is the commercial sex industry an inevitable consequence of gender and economic inequality? What if buyers are addicted? Can any compensation justify the harm they inflict on those being purchased?

We categorically endorse the following statements: We support full equality, freedom of choice, and respect for all women. We advocate sex trade abolition, the elimination of sexual purchase, and the end of human trafficking. Shifting buyer mentality and reducing demand are the most effective ways of eliminating commercial sexual exploitation worldwide. We support an increased social network to eliminate the desperation that often drives decisions in the face of poverty and marginalization.

We support all survivors of the sex trade including those who consider themselves sex workers, but we don't believe that sex is work. Having to sell access to your body in order to survive is an experience of oppression not freedom (LIFT, May 14, 2021).

We cannot profess our solidarity with those who are oppressed when we are unwilling to confront the oppressor. Compassion without confrontation fades quickly into fruitless sentimental commiseration (Henri Nouwen Society, Jan. 10, 2018).

CHAPTER 1:

CONTINUUM OF CONSENT & LEGAL OPTIONS

WHO IS HARMED when sex is bought? What is the nature of that harm? Is "harm reduction" an oxymoron? Does harm reduction make a difference, or is it merely a reactive response? Must we settle for "less" harm over eradication and ongoing prevention?

Is there a difference between trafficked and licensed sellers? Could someone be both? Are health and safety significantly improved in a licensed system? Is it realistic to trust that all buyers would purposefully choose a licensed seller in a free market where trafficking could be prevalent? If so, how would a buyer determine who is trafficked and who is not?

Does the exchange of money justify the objectification, commodification, and degradation of sellers? Do licensed systems represent alternative playing fields where buyers demand less and pay more? Does a licensed system create an alternative to the "underground" economy where more desperate sellers perform more horrific acts for less compensation?

What about "survival sex," when women feel they have no other options to provide for themselves and their children? Does "survival sex" reflect society's failure to provide an adequate network of social services?

This book bears witness to evidence the world wants to ignore.

Readers will encounter narratives of suffering; we seek to generate awareness that will move others to action in confronting and working to eliminate the scourge of commercial sexual exploitation in Canada and worldwide. Testimonies of survivors expose the tragic consequences of being purchased for sexual services. The exploitation of women anywhere in the world represents a threat to women everywhere.

> Sexual exploitation encompasses a wide range of sexual abuse or utilitarian sexual uses of persons, regardless of age, including (but not limited to) sexual objectification, sexual violence, pornography, prostitution, sex trafficking, and child sexual abuse (Dawn Hawkins, CEO, National Coalition on Sexual Exploitation, 2021).

> To some, sex buying might seem like a harmless business transaction. Just a regular guy blowing off steam by paying someone for sex. But spend a day in the shoes of those being bought, tackling the trauma and physical and psychological harm that not one but [a] myriad of "regular guys" impart. They have endured years of sexual violence, harassment, brutalities, and dehumanization at the hands of these men (Chrissy Hemphill, human trafficking specialist, *Detroit News*, March 12, 2021).

$ $ $ $

Prostitution is generally understood as the exchange of sex for money. This academic definition, however, does not acknowledge the widespread abuse and exploitation inherent to the sex industry. Engaging in sexual activity for payment (of cash, rent, food, or drugs) implies informed consent. In reality, there are often considerable disparities in socioeconomic status, agency, and power between the buyer and the person bought. It would theoretically not be exploitive if such an exchange was truly informed and consensual between two parties of equal status. However, we need to be mindful that many of those bought for sex include trafficked, pimped, and abused women and children. Even those who profess to act independently often do so from a place of financial desperation and lack of options.

The reality of commercial sex forces us to examine the freedom of sexual expression within the context of human rights and equality. The heart of our discussion explores how we define ourselves relative to one another and the world. Personal and sexual freedom means we must recognize when mutuality and equality are compromised and acknowledge the damage caused by that imbalance. The issue of coerced "consent" is seldom brought to the forefront. We must understand how individuals, families, and communities have been and continue to be harmed by the inherent inequality perpetuated by commercial sexual exploitation.

Our vision is a world without human trafficking and sexual exploitation. Our mission is to increase awareness, eliminate buyer demand, and help expand economic and social supports for vulnerable and marginalized people. Heinz (2020b, p. 2) repeats an earlier proclamation that "the exchange of sexual services for payment between parties of unequal social or financial status is a human rights violation, often endangering the bodily integrity, dignity, and health of the providers, affecting their psychological, financial, and social well-being" (Dianne Post, 2011). Coercive sexual access is increasingly being recognized as an act of violence, which constitutes an offence against the person.

We use the term "sex sellers" when speaking of non-trafficked persons because it is familiar and encompasses a range of activities from webcamming to selling pictures of various parts of one's body to in-person touching and penetration. However, autonomy levels on the supply side exist on a spectrum ranging from being trafficked to being independent. Like Bagley et al. (2017), we are reluctant to dignify commercial sexual exploitation with the term "work." Accordingly, we use quotation marks when employing labour language.

We refer to sex sellers as she/her while acknowledging that many males and gender-diverse individuals are included in this population. We recognize that more research and awareness are needed. It is beyond this book's scope to explore the challenges of these groups.

Men who buy sex are termed customers or clients in a business/service industry model. Tricks, johns, or punters are colloquial terminology. Unless quoting an original source, we refer to men who buy sex as consumers, buyers, or purchasers (or intermittently as aggressors, offenders, oppressors, opportunists, perpetrators, predators, rapists, torturers, and violators) as we examine the impact of their individual and collective behaviour.

We humbly acknowledge the vulnerability and receptiveness of over 3,000 men who attended the STOP: Sex Trade Offender Program (aka john school) in Edmonton since 1996. Year after year, their unrehearsed appreciation and acknowledgement of what they learned through the program encourages us as STOP educators and affirms that our efforts have value.

Many people struggle with the concepts of "victim" and "survivor." We employ both terms throughout this book and understand them as follows: Victims represent passive recipients of adverse circumstances, such as child abuse, poverty, racism, bullying, or exploitation. Survivors are those who have overcome unfortunate events and no longer feel defined by them. Recovery involves shifting one's perception of a previous assault, destitution, discrimination, or oppression to no longer feel curtailed or limited by the experience.

The distinctions between victim and survivor are not intended to diminish the complexities of adjustment and adaptation. Rather they reflect the transition from passive "happening" to active recovery. A more universal term often employed by those with a history in the sex trade is "experiential." Not all women who sell or have sold sex identify as either victim or survivor, yet they are all experiential.

Rarely are sex trade experiences identical. Sexploitation includes a range of activities that exist on a spectrum of visibility. The nature of an iceberg allows a useful analogy for the activities we see and those we don't see (King, 2021).

VISIBLE
adult entertainment,
exotic dancers, escorts,
licensed "body-rub" facilities,
XXX porn rentals, online

SEMI-VISIBLE
street traffic, independents,
private clubs, phone lines, sugar daddies,
personal "dating" ads, survival sex

INVISIBLE/ "UNDERGROUND"
pimps, traffickers,
culture of commodification,
women reduced to objects to be purchased,
desperation fuelled by poverty and addictions
Exploitation of the marginalized, vulnerable, & traumatized
Underlying dynamic of inequality
Production of porn depicting slapping, spitting, brutality,
gagging, bestiality, racism, violence, torture, BDSM,
urination, defecation, degradation, submission
Vicious cycle of deviant association/ stimulation
leading to increasingly perverse demands,
"Suffering too painful for people to see" (Rebecca Mott)
Targeting of women & children in poverty-stricken countries,
sex tourism, Thailand, Cambodia, Germany, Puerto Rico,
dark web access to "live" action not even recorded
Evil exists: There will be victims if there are consumers.
Sex trafficking: 20 million women & children globally (2020 stats)

Another way to view commercial sexual exploitation is on a spectrum of consent from trafficked to fully autonomous involvement. This approach acknowledges that "agency and victimization are more accurately reflected as a continuum rather than as a dichotomy" (Gerassi & Nichols, 2017, p. 7).

Such a spectrum includes the extreme victimization of force, torture, and kidnapping through shades of coercion and desperation to voluntary participation. Overlap also exists. One example is a woman freed from trafficking but lacking the confidence or other skills to earn a living another way. Another example includes those who voluntarily participate for short-term monetary gain only to find themselves controlled by profiteers or caught in a downward spiral of debt and despair.

The public seems comfortable separating sellers into the two extremes of coerced versus consensual, or trafficked versus licensed, depending on the municipal jurisdiction. Unfortunately, a minority, who call themselves "sex workers" and argue for increased protection and respect "like any other job," often distract attention from more pervasive and hidden exploitation.

A study in the Harvard Law and International Development Society (2012) analyzed data from 116 countries and reviewed case studies from Denmark, Germany, and Switzerland. The study found that *"countries with legalized prostitution are associated with higher human trafficking inflows"* (emphasis added). Increased social and political acceptance of commercial sexual exploitation opens the door to further abuse of many while supposedly protecting a minority. Balancing individual rights against the risk of collective harm is a major challenge. We contend that collateral damage to individuals and communities from open sexual access must take precedence when initiating "harm reduction" for those who claim to be willful participants.

The spectrum of commercial sexual exploitation includes the pimped and controlled, the addicted, the coerced, and the financially desperate. It is a cruel twist of society that women in desperate economic circumstances, with limited means of survival or realistic alternatives, can be encouraged to sell sex. The saying "A blow job is better than no job" captures a blasé attitude toward the consequences of desperation for some women. Not only does such nonchalance speak to society's failure to provide adequate social support, but it also defends patriarchal structures. Only in a chauvinistic hierarchal society would sexual servitude be seen as an acceptable option for a woman to feed her family, pay her debt, or support a drug habit.

Regardless of the seller's circumstances, what is common from one end of the spectrum to the other are sexual consumers. As Melissa Farley (2021) notes, buyers are unconcerned about who is the neediest. On the contrary, they are concerned only with their purchasing power, or their right to buy access to a woman's body, regardless of her situation.

In 2016, about half of an estimated 40 million victims of human trafficking around the world were forced into sexual slavery (International Labour Organization, 2017). The magnitude of the problem reflects the tragic reality that there are not, and never will be, enough voluntary sellers to meet existing consumer demands for sexual "services." Often sex buyers are older males operating from a position of socioeconomic advantage, while those being bought are typically younger and vulnerable females, frequently racially marginalized, controlled, trafficked, or coerced into selling themselves.

The United Nations Global Report on Trafficking in Persons (Jan. 2021, p. 35) provides a more comprehensive breakdown of victim profiles: "In 2018, for every 10 victims detected globally, about five were adult women and two were girls." While the majority of victims were trafficked for sexual exploitation (50%), reports of forced labour have increased over the last decade (38%), as has criminal activity (6%), begging (1.5%), and forced marriages (1% overall). Other forms of trafficking include baby selling and organ removal.

Although labour (22%) and other (6%) forms of trafficking exist in North America, 72% of detected victims were exploited sexually (United Nations, 2021, p. 35). While all forms of human trafficking are deplorable and deserve intervention, our discussion of Canada focuses primarily on sexual exploitation.

Women who are coerced, pimped, and trafficked into sexual servitude are largely hidden from public view by the smoke screens of licensing (contrary to federal legislation since 2014 but municipally validated under various euphemisms) and the "sex work" lobby. Even when the polarities are acknowledged, there appears to be little room in public perception for the vast middle ground of unhappiness and submission.

$$\$ \quad \$ \quad \$ \quad \$$$

Many legal options are quoted by advocates of various positions regarding the best response to commercial sex. We review the implications of various legal models and the importance of a balanced approach, such as the Nordic Equality Model provides (Nordic Model Now! July 4, 2017a). While some models claim similar goals, there are considerable opinions about how the goals can best be achieved.

Considerations across models include:
- Ensuring sex sellers have full access to health services and protection from infectious conditions;
- Breaking down stigma, restoration of human dignity;
- Recognition of human rights, including access to the criminal justice system.

Prohibition Model:
- All aspects of prostitution are criminalized;
- Seeks to deter both parties, although traditionally women have been targeted;
- All activities are illegal and considered "underground," whether as a pimp, trafficker, seller, or buyer.

Abolition/Equality Model:
- Focus is on demand, and purchase is criminalized;
- Providers are exempt from prosecution in most circumstances, and buyers are targeted for intervention;

- Public education and exit services for sellers are included.

Legalization Model:
- Regulation includes work permits, licensing, and designated tolerance zones;
- No penalties for sellers or buyers within regulated terms;
- Business rules apply—advertising, profit, taxes, etc.

When prostitution is legalized, brothels become big business, owners are entrepreneurs, and tax revenues are generated. Advertising is everywhere. "Menu" services are expanded, costs become competitive, and practices become more dangerous with less protection for sellers. Limited resources create increased competition. Those sold become a resource to be used as efficiently as possible for profit. For example, Germany became a sex tourist destination in 2002, with over 1 million men now buying sex every day. Ingeborg Kraus, clinical psychologist and trauma specialist, describes the situation as "hell on earth" (2021).

Decriminalization Model:
- Removal of all penalties, normalizes male entitlement;
- "Sex work" is recognized as legitimate employment;
- Harm reduction is offered to sellers, discretion to buyers.

In a decriminalized state, all players in the sex trade, including pimps, brothel keepers, and profiteers, operate outside of criminal regulation. For example, after decriminalizing "sex work" with its passage of the *Prostitution Reform Act (PRA) 2003*, New Zealand became a more favorable destination for sex tourists despite its relatively isolated geographic location. Although the initial intent was to improve circumstances for women, "violence from sex buyers, pimp control, and social stigma do not decrease" when prostitution is normalized (Moran & Farley, 2019).

In summary, the unfortunate impact of both legalization and decriminalization includes:
- Increased prostitution. What is tolerated then increases. Buyers are protected as sources of revenue.

- Sex trafficking increases to fill the extra demand. There are never enough willing sellers. Children are at increased risk of being groomed.
- Less overview from police means more illegal activity. That includes human trafficking. Networks develop unimpeded.
- Pay and conditions for women deteriorate. Brothel owners become businesspersons competing for profit.
- The status of all women is negatively impacted when women are defined by sexual accessibility. Indigenous and minority women are at increased risk of exploitation.
- Funding for exit services and recovery becomes more difficult when "sex work" is normalized. Commodification becomes the new norm.

$ $ $ $

An impassioned global letter from over 200 women representing human rights organizations around the world was posted by CATW (Coalition Against Trafficking in Women) Australia (Aug. 27, 2021), condemning proposed decriminalization in Australia. It was noted that Victoria's *Prostitution Control Act 1994*, also known as the *Sex Work Act 1994*, failed miserably at regulating brothels and bringing prostitution "above ground." Some of the points made by the women in opposition to decriminalization are worth repeating:

- Twenty-seven years of legalization expanded the sex trade as opposed to managing it. For every registered brothel, there were over five unlicensed "parlours" with many foreign women.
- "Prostitution is a system of complex exploitation for the profit of brothel owners and other exploiters enriched by sex buyers."
- "You cannot control the sex trade, a multi-billion-dollar global illegal enterprise, through decriminalization; it controls you."
- Women's journeys into prostitution include "histories of childhood sexual abuse, poverty, state residential homes,

displacement, intergenerational abuse, and systemic inequalities, all vulnerabilities that lead to sexual exploitation. And regardless of their race, sex, gender, or ethnicity, sex buyers reduce them to commodities for sale."

- "Society avoids addressing these abuses by weaving narratives of 'consent'," which even if rarely true, are irrelevant under the law and human rights principles in situations of exploitation or sexual violence.

$ $ $ $

Personal reflection, Andrea:

The hypocrisy of the world of commercial sexual exploitation is illustrated by an incident that happened while I was still in the industry. I was invited to fly to the United States as a companion with one of my "regulars," a well-respected surgeon. We were questioned by Border Security, and he admitted to purchasing my time. Officers called ahead to hold his plane because he was scheduled to attend an important conference. In the meantime, I was interrogated for several hours, labelled a "prostitute" by U. S. Customs & Border Protection, and denied future entry to the United States for at least 10 years.

$ $ $ $

Under Canadian legislation since 2014, the tables would be turned. Buyers are criminalized, while sellers (mostly) are immune from prosecution. We have written this book supporting an Equality Model that holds buyers responsible for the harm they perpetrate and removes stigma from sellers. We call on readers to recognize the gender and economic imbalances prevalent in the sex trade and to challenge the entitlement of sexual consumers.

CHAPTER 2:

INHERENT TRAUMA OF BEING SOLD

ARE WE ALL AT RISK if some humans are relegated to commodity status? Do buyers create a double standard? Does society have a responsibility to protect all citizens from objectification? Is it possible to mitigate trauma in the commercial sex industry?

Why do we resist hearing the voices of women who have been coerced into or trafficked within a life of sexual servitude? Is their silence interpreted as consent? Is it easier for observers to absolve themselves of compassion or responsibility if they assume the women being bought and sold somehow contribute to their exploitation?

Historically, in most cultures, groups of women have been shamed or criminalized for their exploitation. Women have been forced to provide sex during times of war and in positions of servitude. Children have been groomed and raped in sadistic homes, past residential schools, or economically deprived economies.

Our trauma is not locked into one culture, one country,
or even enclosed in cities—our trauma is everywhere but
made nowhere.

It is the trauma of living inside torture.

It is the trauma of having no access to full humanity.

It is the trauma of serial raping.

It is the trauma of being silenced.

It is the trauma of being denied basic human rights.

It is the trauma of no protection from society or laws.

That is just the surface of our trauma ...

(Rebecca Mott, March 29, 2021)

$ $ $ $

Selling sex is an extremely dangerous activity. Individuals in the industry are regularly exposed to serious harm, such as drug culture, disease, violence, discrimination, degradation, debt bondage, criminalization, and exploitation.

Melissa Farley, researcher and author, has been a strong advocate for women for several decades. She explains the harm of prostitution is largely invisible in society and in law (Farley, 2003). The interconnection of racism, colonialism, and child sexual abuse have created conditions of oppression where the basic conditions for genuine consent—safety, equal power, and real alternatives—are absent. Her early warning that "Until there is recognition that prostitution harms women, application of appropriate law will be impossible" (2003, p. 29) still holds true today. Her declaration that gender equality, race discrimination, and poverty must be eliminated also underline the social challenges facing marginalized populations.

Farley (2004) asserts that the decriminalization or legalization of male predatory behaviour trivializes violence against women. Exploited women develop serious health problems and experience emotional devastation and death rates many times higher than is common in the general population. Buyers who use women, groups that promote full decriminalization or legalization, and governments that support the sex industry all endanger women.

> Prostitution is an institution that systematically discriminates against women, against the young, against the poor, and against ethnically subordinated groups ... It is a particularly vicious institution of

inequality of the sexes ... The silence of most of those [involved] ... is a result of intimidation, terror, disso-ciation, and shame. Their silence, like the silence of battered women, should not be misinterpreted, ever, as their consent (Farley, 2004, p. 1117).

Norma Ramos (2012), then executive director of the Coalition Against Trafficking in Women, claims prostitution teaches men and boys that women and girls can be rendered into commodities for sexual use and abuse. As she explains in "Legal Prostitution Can Never Be Safe" (*New York Times*, Apr. 19, 2012), it creates a callous-ness among men that undermines the human rights of all women and girls. Objectification results from disempowerment, stemming from the seller's limited choices for securing a living and the buyer's sense of entitlement to degrade his "purchase" and treat her vio-lently for sexual stimulation and release.

Rachel Moran (2013) articulates the traumatic depths and nuances of her former life in the sex industry. In her powerful memoir, *Paid For: My Journey Through Prostitution*, she describes how suffering invades the physical, mental, emotional, spiritual, and economic levels of a seller's life and impairs their sense of identity. Moran argues against reframing such atrocities as "work" because providing sex in exchange for money implies tolerance, not consent.

It was necessary for us to believe that we were in control because to accept that the opposite was true would have been to internalize the full awfulness of our present situation, and the conditions of prostitu-tion are damaging enough without a deep and thor-ough acknowledgment of their character. It is enough to feel them without accrediting them with the full-ness of their destructive power. Ignoring them, shut-ting out the viciousness of their nature, is perhaps the prostitute's primary policy of defense; her prin-cipal survival strategy (Moran, 2013, pp. 133–134).

Survivor stories are seldom told because much of the "business" must be concealed and denied for it to continue. Public relation campaigns do not mention the torment and suffering of sex sellers,

nor the high rates of suicide and murder. Profiteers deny information on the ordeals of those being sold to the public to protect the
monstrous profits of pimps and traffickers (Farley, 2006). Only in
speaking the unspeakable can we render culturally visible the disgusting abuse sellers face daily.

Prostitution Narratives: Stories of Survival in the Sex Trade
(Norma & Tankard Reist, Eds. 2016) includes first-person narratives
of 22 women. One survivor wants the sordid context of the word
"prostitution" to be fully understood by readers:

> When you are in prostitution you internalise the
> violence.... Realising the truth is so depleting. You
> dissociate yourself from the men and their actions,
> because no one has the psyche to be present in the
> acts of violence....
>
> When you understand the complexity of violence,
> then you understand that prostitution can never be
> recognised as a profession, but that the only thing
> to do is to criminalise those who organize, maintain,
> and exploit people... This obviously includes those
> who pay for the sexual violence, which the buying of
> sex is....
>
> People always ask me how criminalisation of buyers
> would have helped me... My answer is this: If it had
> been a crime to buy women for sexual pleasure
> then I would have known that what these men were
> doing was wrong. For a long time, I blamed myself,
> thinking that it was my own fault.... But I am sure I
> would have left prostitution much earlier if the law
> had been on my side.... There was no support or help
> to get out.... There is no social or political support
> for recognising prostitution as being violent and
> harmful (Tanja Rahm, "Internalizing the Violence" in
> *Prostitution Narratives*, pp. 80–82).

Nicole Bell founded a survivor support group, LIFT: Living in
Freedom Together, in Worcester, Massachusetts, USA. She describes
similar sentiments in "A Survivor's Story" (2016):

> I was a victim of sexual exploitation as a teen and most of my adult life. I spent the majority of my adulthood between street corners and jail cells. Before the exploitation, I had hopes and dreams like every young girl … and those weren't them…. Before learning that I was a victim and that I did not choose this life for myself, most nights were filled with self-hatred and blame. [I] thought all the dreams that I had as a young girl would be just that … dreams.

Bell does not believe full recovery is possible. Instead, she tries to provide through LIFT what others gave her, which is a glimpse of hope in a safe, non-judgmental environment.

Heinz describes the raw reality of selling "services" when interviewed for *The Advocate* (King, 2020). Although her entry was voluntary, it was based on financial constraints. According to Heinz, commercial sexual exploitation is insidious and pervasive, the physical and emotional equivalent of being sexually violated several times a day. In addition to repeated sexual assaults, she, as a seller, needed to be continually on guard and mentally brace herself for humiliation by buyers. Acts of degradation included being short-changed, filmed without her knowledge or consent, and dealing with disgusting and repulsive requests.

Even after a seller is able to exit the industry, as Heinz did, there are often many challenges. She may have bills and expenses and lack education or employable skills. Sellers who want to exit but cannot obtain alternate financial resources risk becoming numb. They may completely dissociate from a sense of themselves and spiral into despair. Heinz admits the period before her successful exit was frightening; she recalls being so dead inside that she didn't feel "real." She often fantasized about suicide as a way to end her daily pain and struggle.

Heinz, in an earlier publication (2020b), identifies herself as part of a quasi-autonomous group during her time in the sex industry. The InSTEP Model's optimal intervention points were developed based on that segment of the seller population. She describes her observations of the continuum of agency among sex sellers as:

- 'Level 1,' a large generally unseen trafficked portion of victims;
- 'Level 2,' a quasi-autonomous population, "quasi" because financial distress influences their "choice" to participate; and
- 'Level 3,' an exceptionally vocal group with other economic options who claim to enjoy monetized sexual servility.

The Entry phase for the quasi-autonomous is a time when monetary rewards are high enough that other economic options pale in comparison (Heinz, 2020b). The perks of being "self-employed" with flexible hours, paying debts, and enjoying a new standard of living make selling sex seem "worth the sacrifice" despite the resultant turmoil or harm. The tipping point is signified by an internal shift when the monetary rewards no longer justify the cost. This can happen gradually; some women avoid it by "numbing out" with drugs or dissociation. Increasingly negative feelings take an emotional toll and lead to feeling trapped.

Sellers typically struggle with continued denial of the harm they are experiencing (Stage 1) before actively seeking an alternative (Stage 2). At that point, sellers are open to interventions and services that could help them transition out of the sex trade.

Money continues to be a major concern when considering exiting and after exiting. Lacking employable skills, surviving on reduced income, and remaining out of debt are all obstacles. Women often experience a distorted sense of self and identity, addiction issues, and physical illness beyond the accumulated trauma they have experienced.

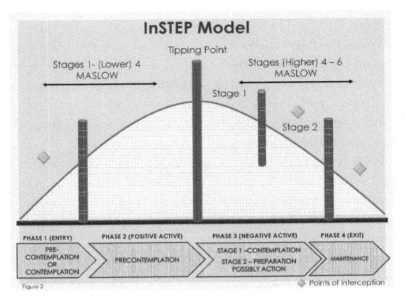

On Exiting from Commercial Sexual Exploitation: Insights from Sex Trade Experienced Persons (Heinz, 2020b)

The InSTEP Model illustrates the shifting perspectives of quasi-autonomous sellers. Exited women's voices are important because, once removed from the influence of fast money, they can better reflect on the circumstances of their involvement. The priority of sellers shifts if they attain financial stability and can explore who they are outside of their previous singular identity.

$$\$ \; \$ \; \$ \; \$$

The subculture of the sex industry is often not understood by those who are not involved or directly impacted. Economic survival typically depends on buyers' accolades, affirmations, and positive referrals through online "review boards." Sellers are always conscious of having to "perform" well enough to receive repeated positive endorsements. While such performance feedback loops are consistent with many "professional" services, the pressure of pretending to be happily engaged is extremely difficult once the tipping point has passed.

Gone are the days when most sex trade activity was visible to the public, with sex sold on street corners. With the rise of the internet, even the more marginalized sellers and their exploiters operate online, using smartphones to post ads and attract buyers. Craigslist.com and, later, Backpage.com operated for many years as sites for sourcing sex on demand.

More recently, Leolist.cc emerged as "the" prominent website for these activities. Leolist.cc is very "mainstream" and can be accessed on any home computer with the click of an "I agree" button, indicating the viewer is over 18. Leolist.cc is the shopping equivalent of a big box store like Walmart or Superstore.

There are also personal and unique "mom and pop" shops known as Escort Review Boards. These "discreet" sites require visitors to sign up. They are populated by sex buyers known as "hobbyists" and "pooners" (or "punters" in Europe). This online community of men cold-heartedly rate and cruelly dissect the women they abuse, sharing tips with fellow opportunists.

Escort Review Boards profit by charging the women (sellers) or their handlers (brothel/agency owners) membership and advertising fees, sometimes thousands of dollars annually. The websites also generate ad revenue through pornography, online stores selling sex toys, and "businesses" facilitating meetups.

Reviews posted by buyers on "the boards" represent some of the most heartless if not sociopathic pieces of writing online. The self-titled "hobbyists" are not only overtly narcissistic and self-centred but also reek of extremely inept critical analysis skills. Their comments tend to be a play-by-play of which sexual acts were performed, the seller's attitude, and detailed graphic comments on the seller's physical features. The evaluative measures are called "LAS ratings"—Looks, Attitude, and Service. The buyers state how much they paid for the sex acts received.

The boards are a major source of embarrassment, shame, hurt, anger, and trauma for many women. Some people believe the myth that normalizing sex buying will reduce "stigma" and improve the treatment of women by the buyers. Review boards reflect the terrible cost of objectifying and dehumanizing women.

We choose not to share access to review boards, as we do not want to give them a platform for greater exposure. Unfortunately, thousands, maybe tens of thousands, of such reviews can be found online with relative ease. The following example is a partially abridged version posted by a website user in 2021 on a Canadian board.

> Booked a session with 18-year-old [name deleted] from Leolist... We booked for half an hour and I wanted to make sure BBBJ [bareback blowjob—no condom] was still on the menu... When I found the location, I'm standing outside for at least 15–20 minutes before she came down to greet me ...

> She didn't seem at all very friendly when she greeted me... In fact, she didn't even say one word to me. As we were walking down the hall, she was walking so fast I could barely even keep up with her. When we got inside, I gave her the donation ($). In her text, she told me I could even COF [cum on her face] for an extra $50 so I gave her $250. Then she asked me if it was ok if she smoked a blunt... She asked me if I wanted to have a hit and I said, no, I don't do drugs.

> Now she's asking me instead of a blowjob could she just give me a hand-job? I politely said no the agreement was BBBJ and an extra $50 for COF. She was a cute young girl, very petite, and her eyes looked kind of messed up due to the fact she was high as a kite, I'm sure. So now she's trying to tell me that she had some kind of allergic reaction to something and that neither one of us is going to enjoy her giving me a BBBJ.

> So, she's trying to get out of it... We're now going to the bedroom, and I asked her if she would like a massage and she was very much into this. One thing that I like doing is giving girls really nice body massages. Now she's asking me if she could just do a

CBJ [covered blow job using condom] and next time she will do BBBJ ...

I said to her, "do you wanna just do doggy style?" and she agreed to it, so we did it. After giving it to her I pulled out and came on her nice tight ass! And then she kind of rudely said "you didn't have to get it all over me" and she right away went to the bathroom to clean herself up.

When she came out, she didn't hardly say one word to me. She just got dressed, said "have a good night," and I left. I felt like she didn't have a good time and I didn't really have a good time either... She's not into this at all, at least with me she wasn't, and we didn't ever do the COF for extra $50. Maybe I should've asked for that $50 back?

She's a nice girl and all. Sort of shy and she's only been doing this for a few months now so I guess I should maybe give her a break but I just don't like it when people are advertising stuff and then when I see them, they're trying to get out of it. I didn't get any blowjob whatsoever... I'm 99 percent sure her blowjob skills would've sucked because she just wasn't into it at all.

So that's my review. I won't repeat.

Review boards make it necessary for those being coerced to appear ready to perform and to seem welcoming and enthusiastic about their pending abuse and violations. Such expectations strengthen the case that while money may create the illusion of consent, it does not negate the harm or revulsion experienced.

Predatory and opportunistic sex buyers don't just limit their comradery to the review boards; some even go so far as starting public blogs to offer "tips" to other men on how to more effectively exploit women in the industry.

The following is an excerpt from one buyer's Feb. 2023 blog post where he shares "how to raw-dog your favourite hooker":

Over time I have developed a set of methods I use to gain compliance from these women... If I am paying for sex, I'm getting it raw. I don't care what they say or how much they protest... I have a weightlifter's physique. Anyone who looks at me knows I am strong. Whenever I'm in the room with a girl, the power dynamic always shifts to my favor. She knows I am stronger than her. That makes a difference when you are asking her to comply with a bare request. She's way more willing to submit to a guy who looks like he can kill her than a middle-aged soylent-chugging finance bro or a mega-rich landwhale.

He continues by stating that personal hygiene will make a woman believe a man is free of sexually transmitted infections, describes the right "type" of woman to "target," offers manipulative language to convince her to have intercourse without a condom, and pointers on how to coerce her financially through threats of walking away, knowing she is in need of the agreed upon money. He finishes his article by sharing a photo of a woman, presumably unaware that she has been posted to his blog, saying, "I've got a date planned this weekend with a nursing student. I'll be fucking her raw."

$ $ $ $

"Sex work" is strategically used by advantaged sellers and the sub-culture of profiteers and handlers. It has been adopted as benign in mainstream language and popular culture, creating the illusion of consensual participation. However, the extent to which consent exists in a patriarchal system depends on myriad variables, including opportunity, constraint, poverty, racism, histories of sexual and substance abuse, pimping, and grooming (Dines, May 7, 2021).

Rachel Moran's revolutionary voice cuts through sanitized discourse and confronts those who favour cultural and legal means of normalizing prostitution. Mianti (2017) cites Moran's explanation of the sexual violence inherent in prostitution:

> I understood it by feeling my body used as a mastur-batory object by thousands of men who, of course, know that the sex they buy is unwanted. Otherwise,

25

they wouldn't pay for it. Using cash to buy someone's entrance into the body is an act of sexual violence in itself, per se. I know because I've lived through it and saw it happen to many others, and not all have survived. I am obliged to tell the truth about the harm men do to women.... These men know perfectly well the evil they're committing. That's why none of them want their mothers, sisters, and daughters going to work in brothels.

[Money] works as a silencer, and anyone who is involved is well aware of it. Money is the compensation for unwanted sex, and when you have been compensated, you have no right to complain. Sex in prostitution is not only abusive, but it is abuse that must be ignored, by contract. Money has a symbolic role but also has the function of reducing it to silence. In this sense, shame for the culpability is added to the original wound.

Ingeborg Kraus explains (June 6, 2021) that when a woman allows strangers to penetrate her body, she must extinguish natural responses such as fear, shame, disgust, contempt, and self-blame. The resulting dissociation causes body numbness and distortions in memory and awareness. Revulsion is replaced with feigned indifference and neutrality in return for compensation. Long-term consequences to sellers include addictions, depression, isolation, fear, or trauma bonding with their offenders.

Survivor Rebecca Mott in a webinar (June 6, 2021) describes trauma as a shadow in her life and a feeling that she doesn't deserve happiness. Learning to feel, accepting her memory fragments, and living with her trauma were some of her biggest challenges during recovery.

Below is an excerpt from Heinz's reflections, adapted from *Nordic Model Now! Supporting Students Impacted by the Sex Industry ... A Handbook for Universities*, which was released Nov. 17, 2021:

"It's a job like any other," I was told.

The first man I saw forced sex acts on me that I wasn't comfortable with.

Most of the men were married with children and were two, if not three (or four) times my age.

Men were repulsively unhygienic—refusing to shower beforehand, wanting to finger me with dirty long nails, breathing rancid breath two inches from my face as the smell of their body odour filled the room.

Men would arrive with skin tags, warts, ringworm, oozing sores, and other unknown rashes or bumps. They'd try to conceal it with dim lighting or excuse it as "irritation from shaving."

Men frequently tried to remove condoms; there was no shortage pressuring me for a blow job without a condom. That happened daily.

Men would film me and photograph me without my consent.

Men would choke me regularly.

Men would frequently make sexual references to children. "You're a good girl" was repeated countless times, and a schoolgirl outfit was a top request.

Men would make sexual references to animals and request urine/fecal play.

The dehumanizing and demeaning remarks were so hard on my spirit that I learned to dissociate as soon as my clothes came off. Many nights I would cry in my bed before falling asleep.

The *Nordic Model Now! Handbook* (Nov. 17, 2021) claims that it is important to separate offers of support from political motivations, so the voices of abused, marginalized, and vulnerable people are not lost in the "cacophony" of the political sphere. The book refers to survivor "Dana" as an example of a woman who felt politicized rather than helped:

It is indeed important to not be judgmental toward women in the sex trade. Blaming them for their situation or inability to exit are examples of toxic judgment. But saying, "Do what's right for you" to a woman at the bottom of the social ladder can seem more like indifference than a lack of judgment.

Many women in the sex trade suffer from poor self-esteem and low self-efficacy. They need someone to believe in them, someone who sees in them a human being. They need someone who has confidence in their ability and can offer practical advice and help. Rather than reassuring them that they are doing what is right for them, it is better to tell them that they deserve more.

Decades after I got out of prostitution, I still remember someone telling me, "You deserve more." It really shook me at the time, but it gave me the strength to get out. I have no respect for those who said it was my "right" to sell sex and that it is just a "business." They know very well that sucking a dick to pay the bills is not something they want to do or see their children doing.

$ $ $ $

The harm suffered by some who have been pimped, trafficked, or abused can only be described as torture. Jeanne Sarson and Linda MacDonald are nurses and educators from Nova Scotia. Since 1993, they have worked to support women worldwide in recovery from torture, trafficking, sexualized exploitation within intimate relationships, prostitution, and pornographic victimization. They began their work after meeting a young woman who had been systemically tortured by her family (Barnard, 2021).

Torture is defined (merriam-webster.com) as the "infliction of intense pain to punish, coerce, or afford sadistic pleasure." Within sexual exploitation, torture is often used to break a person's resistance and force compliance with buyer demands. The sadistic activities of some perpetrators for sexual release are over and above tactics used by traffickers to dominate and control.

As hard as it is to imagine sanctioned military (State) torture, it is even more upsetting to imagine torture as an instrument of sexual trafficking. Using a list developed by Amnesty International to track the atrocities to which state prisoners were subjected, Sarson and MacDonald (May 7, 2021) found in a study of 30 women tortured in prostitution, many had been brutalized in similar ways. The authors contend that victims will exhibit PTSR, a post-traumatic "response," a condition more appropriately named than PTSD, a "disorder."

Adequate legal recourses rarely exist for women who escape torture and want to charge their traffickers, as there are no criminal charges that address their experience. The *Criminal Code* does not recognize offenders who torture women and children outside of political authorization. A possible "aggravated assault" charge does not fully encompass the ritual horror and cumulative cruelty many women have suffered. The most common tortures include rape, rape with guns or other objects, death threats, savage repeated beatings, gang rapes, pornographic photography, and being forcibly drugged with pills or alcohol.

Some buyers actively seek to torture women simply because they enjoy doing so. Transgressions reported by victimized women include stalking, sleep deprivation for days at a time, being woken during sleep, repeated rapes including by large groups, being hung by the neck, and being trained to be a slave.

Sarson and MacDonald break the silence around what they call "non-State" torture with their daring exposé, *Women Unsilenced: Our Refusal to Let Torturer-Traffickers Win* (2021). The forms of violence against women can be grouped into three categories: (1) "classic" from war literature, (2) commercial-based crimes, and (3) forms of violence declared by the United Nations as torture. All types are inflicted against millions of women and girls around the world. Women who have survived insist the torture they endured must be named to socially and legally acknowledge the violations of their human rights and dignity. Not being heard or believed understandably increases emotional pain. Victims who have suffered the dehumanization of torture deserve additional therapeutic and legal options. There also must be a concerted effort to eliminate such brutality.

The research of Sarson and MacDonald is further testimony to silenced victims who experience unspeakable horrors as part of their exploitation. A review of the authors' innovative work on non-State torture is presented in Part Seven.

CHAPTER 3:
THE PRICE OF SILENCE: HUMAN TRAFFICKING

WHAT HAPPENS to a child or young person forced into sexual activity? What is the impact on their sense of worth, their self-esteem? What if they are told it is an easy way to make money? What if they are supporting their family? Is the money ever worth the cost?

How does a child recover or sustain themselves after repeated violation by a series of strangers? What is social complicity? See no evil? Hear no evil? Is human trafficking the price of silence?

There are many other people to consider for every woman or child caught in sexual exploitation. Without perpetrators or consumers, there would be no exploitation. A whole network of enablers also provides grooming, transportation, accommodation, and advertising.

Some parents may fail to protect their children because of trauma they have suffered. Community members may be complicit through denial or lack of knowledge in allowing or sanctioning the exploitation of vulnerable children. Family and acquaintances of buyers may feel embarrassed and betrayed by the behaviour of their kin or colleagues.

Some well-intentioned legislators and politicians provide the illusion of acceptability for the commodification and abuse of victims by believing they can "prevent harm" in the sex industry.

> Honor killings, sexual slavery, and genital cutting may seem to Western readers to be tragic but inevitable in a world far, far away. In much the same way, slavery was once widely viewed by many decent Europeans and Americans as a regrettable but ineluctable feature of human life. But then in the 1780s a few indignant Britons, led by William Wilberforce, decided that slavery was so offensive that they had to abolish it. And they did. Today we see the seed of something similar: a global movement to emancipate women and girls (Nicholas D. Kristof and Sheryl WuDunn, 2010, xxii).

> The moral issue of the subjugation of women isn't frivolous today any more than slavery was in the 1790s. Decades from now, people will look back and wonder how societies in the twenty-first century could have acquiesced in a sex slave trade that, as we've seen, is bigger than the transatlantic slave trade was in the nineteenth (Kristof & WuDunn, 2010, p. 237).

$ $ $ $

The challenge of the 21st century is recognizing the tragic circumstances under which many of the world's females are forced to survive (or not) and alleviating such conditions. Authors Kristof and WuDunn in *Half the Sky: Turning Oppression into Opportunity for Women Worldwide* (2010) survey conditions around the world. They describe India as a country with millions of girls and women kidnapped or born into brothels, many beaten, starved, or drugged to ensure compliance. China's estimate was even higher, at 10 million or more. The implicit social expectation of upper-class girls to preserve their virtue meant that uneducated and lower-caste girls were targeted for exploitation. In many countries, such as Brazil and most of Africa, where women are driven into brothels by economic pressure, their horrific conditions can properly be labelled slavery (p. 9). It is unfair to consider economic desperation a "grey zone" of tolerance.

It is significant to note that Nicholas Kristof (Dec. 4, 2020) also helped expose Canadian abuses with "The Children of Pornhub: Why does Canada allow this company to profit off videos of exploitation and assault?" printed in the *New York Times*. The lack of political will noted earlier (Kristof & WuDunn, 2010) continues to be exemplified by narrow government thinking that the sex industry could be made "safe" and by a vocal minority that promotes decriminalization of sex buying.

The gender inequality associated with child "marriage" is still common in many countries. Melinda Gates (2019) asserts that the younger and more powerless a girl, the more appeal she has as an obedient and defenceless servant. It seems these same qualities are attractive to pimps and consumers.

A distressing example of the exploitation of girls due to poverty appeared in the *National Post* (Farmer, Nov. 3, 2021). The headline read: "Desperate Afghans sell daughters to avoid starvation." It told the story of poverty-stricken parents selling their nine-year-old daughter to a 55-year-old man as his bride. The father explained that he had little choice because he wanted to keep his other eight family members alive. He apparently could not find work, had already sold his 12-year-old daughter months earlier, and betrothed his three-year-old daughter. This speaks not only to the desperation of poverty but also to the perception of female children as disposable.

$ $ $ $

Who buys little children? Why do some men visit poverty-stricken countries to take advantage of children who endure terrible things to survive? How do we protect the impoverished and marginalized children of the world from men who pay to rape and abuse them?

Sex tourism involves travelling to another country to buy sexual "services." This happens in countries where "sex work" is common-place (with traffickers flooding the market) and poor countries where people are desperate for financial relief. A major concern is the trafficking of children and minors. While sex tourism is a multi-billion-dollar industry directly utilizing a large "workforce" of millions and indirectly benefiting service industries such as airlines and hotels, it is not without a moral cost. Developing nations are marginalized, as are their citizens, reinforcing ethnic stereotypes. Unfortunately, websites continue to advertise popular destinations, and governments generally do not place a high priority on the enforcement of consent or protection of minors. Sex tourism is a buyers' buffet, a pedophiles' paradise. The lust of perverts defies containment.

An especially poignant story comes from Victor Malarek (2010). He tells of an undercover investigator posing as a lone middle-aged White man in Svay Park, Cambodia:

> From the shadows, four small figures emerge.... A boy, no older than fourteen, asks the man in broken English, "You want girls? You want fuck girls?"
>
> The man asks about younger girls.
>
> The young hustler smiles knowingly. "You want small? I can get small-small."
>
> The boy quickly leads him down a path past a warren of run-down clapboard and metal shacks. The man is ushered into one and introduced to the mamasan, who sizes him up and then calls out to three girls. They patter into the room in bare feet, wearing only paisley-print pajamas. They are between the ages of five and nine. They smile as if on command, but the deadness in their brown eyes is heart-wrenching. The cost is thirty dollars for "yum yum" (oral sex), the madam says, stressing, "No boom boom" (intercourse). The man points to his video camera and she nods her approval for him to record his sexual feats (p. 162-163).

It is shocking that amidst global tragedies, there are people who further exploit homeless children by selling them into forced labour or sexual slavery. It is even more incomprehensible that there are buyers for those children. What needs to happen to challenge the heart of humanity to see all children as precious resources to be protected rather than exploited?

$ $ $ $

Why are some men attracted to children? And even if they cannot help their attraction, how can they not see beyond their own fixation to honour and protect the innocence of a child? Are offenders so abused or neglected in their early lives that they are incapable of basic sensitivity to others? Or are they born damaged?

Sadly, many children are not safe in their own homes. Instead of receiving love and protection, they are exploited sexually and sometimes groomed for sale. Incest became an issue of social awareness in the 1980s with many books and articles on the subject.

One distressing story is that of Jacqueline Lynn, who was born in Saskatchewan and grew up in Vancouver. She shared the trauma of her painful history in *Prostitution Narratives: Stories of Survival in the Sex Trade* (Norma & Tankard Reist, Eds. 2016):

> Andrea Dworkin once said that incest is the boot camp for prostitution. Deep in my bones, I know this to be true. I was my stepfather's fuck-doll albeit a frozen one. I moved in all the right places. I said all the right things. I moaned. I groaned. I gave sexual performances worthy of Oscars. I told my stepfather how good a cock he had every time he raped me. He trained me for every trick I would turn in my life. All those men needed to be reassured that their cocks were the very best too. Do you have any idea of all the orgasms I've faked in my life? Countless! At what cost to me? It's inestimable.
>
> The first trick I turned was old, fat, and white, just like my stepfather. Turning this trick was no different from being raped by him. I performed. I did

all the things to this trick that I had been trained to do to my stepfather. Within minutes, it was all over. I left the room with money in hand. I thought this was "easy" money. I felt free, unencumbered. I had a sense of pseudo-sexual empowerment. At least, I didn't have to pretend I was in love. I was not trapped in an ongoing abusive relationship, or so I thought (p. 165).

It is not uncommon for those who have been abused as children to feel "empowered" by receiving money because it gives them some control over what was previously taken from them.

Public attitudes change slowly and with them, the language we use. For example, in 1999, Alberta proclaimed the *Protection of Children Involved in Prostitution Act* to ensure that children under 18 were recognized as victims who could not be considered as having made a "lifestyle choice." This legislation was appropriately renamed the *Protection of Sexually Exploited Children Act* in 2007. Services were extended for youth to age 22. While many children are exploited for sexual purposes, the term "child prostitute" embodies an oxymoron that obscures the reality and responsibility of perpetrators. It is important that children not be blamed or stigmatized for the actions of adults in their lives.

$ $ $ $

Paul Rubner, a former member of the Calgary Police Service, speaks of his work with children under the provincial legislation unique to Alberta. His story "Changing Perspectives" is found in Part Six, Guest Contributors.

$ $ $ $

Despite various child protection legislation in Canada, there is a huge demand for child sexual abuse material (CSAM), commonly referred to as "child porn." Some children are introduced to exploitation in their own homes, yet the sexual exploitation of children happens far beyond incest. Perpetrators, pimps, and traffickers look for vulnerable and lonely children who can be easily controlled and manipulated outside of protective relationships. Exploited youth are often trafficked by gangs, compounded with peer-to-peer recruitment. Seemingly "ordinary" men buy trafficked children.

Although child sexual exploitation is consumer driven, it is enabled by many levels of collusion, from active traffickers to those who turn a blind eye. Three levels of victimization are intertwined:

- Perpetrators who partake in sex tourism and sexual activity of minors;
- Vendors who procure and trade children as commodities; and
- Facilitators who allow it through poverty, corruption, lack of due diligence, lack of legislation, and lack of enforcement.

$ $ $ $

How often does sexual exploitation happen to boys? Who are their predators? Why is it more difficult for young men to come forward? How does being forced to be sexual with older men impact boys? Where and when are boys more at risk?

Such predators often remain protected through a culture of secrecy, shame, and silence when they prey on children, regardless of the gender of their victims. Although not commercially sexually exploited, former NHL players Theoren Fleury (born 1968) and Sheldon Kennedy (born 1969) can be credited with disclosing the demand for young boys by some men. In 1996, Kennedy revealed his earlier sexual abuse by a junior hockey coach and in-line skated across Canada to raise awareness. Kennedy published *Why I Didn't Say Anything: The Sheldon Kennedy Story* in 2006. In his book *Playing with Fire* (2009), Fleury disclosed his abuse (at the hands of the same man who abused Kennedy) and the devastating impact on his life.

$ $ $ $

What unique challenges do the gender-diverse face? Are they more vulnerable to being denied traditional employment and housing?

Gender-diverse people are described by the Missing and Murdered Women and Girls Inquiry as 2SLGBTQQIA+, which includes Two Spirited, Lesbian, Gay, Bisexual, Transgendered, Queer, Questioning, Intersexual, Asexual, plus others. They are recognized as a vulnerable population who experience higher rates of suicide, addictions, poverty, and murder. Unfortunately, some seek respite in the sex industry when they face barriers and stigma to finding employment or housing in mainstream society.

> Most of the research on LGBTQI+ persons' vulnerability to trafficking has been conducted in North America, and, to a lesser extent in Europe and Latin America. The limited studies available reveal the need for increased research at a global level, especially in countries with strong social stigma and severe laws criminalizing same-sex relationships and/or transgender identities (United Nations Office on Drugs and Crime, 2021, p. 38).

$ \$ \ \$ \ \$ \ \$ $

Trafficking in Persons Report:

The Trafficking in Persons Report, 20th Edition (US Department of State, June 2020) declares, "Traffickers are denying nearly 25 million people their fundamental right to freedom, forcing them to live enslaved." There are no breakdowns per country.

The first TIP report in 2001 included data from 82 countries. By 2011, 179 countries were represented. The analysis is based on the principles of prosecution, protection, and prevention. Countries are ranked on a four-tier list according to the extent of government efforts to eliminate human trafficking. The United States considers "trafficking in persons," "human trafficking," and "modern-day slavery" to be interchangeable umbrella terms that refer to both sex and labour trafficking.

The June 2020 Trafficking in Persons Report (p. 43) states that in 2019, there were 11,841 international prosecutions related to trafficking, resulting in 9,548 convictions. However, of the 118,932 victims identified, only 13,875 (12%) were labour related. Presumably, most of the other 88% were related to sex trafficking.

The 118,932 victims counted by TIP were a far cry from the estimated 25 million trafficked people mentioned in their introduction. One wonders why there is not more information about the projected harm, although most readers realize crime statistics are poor reflections of social reality given the challenges of disclosure, investigation, and evidence.

The TIP Report (2020) concludes with the words of US Secretary of State, Michael Pompeo:

> To turn the tide, action must accompany words.... We are leading by example as we encourage governments, survivors, NGOs, industry leaders, communities of faith, and advocates in every country to remain steadfast in the protection of human dignity and the pursuit of freedom. Let's all continue this fight together.

The United States places itself, with Canada, as a Tier 1 country in fully meeting minimum standards. However, Canada was temporarily downgraded to Tier 2 in 2003 for not fully complying (Perrin, 2011).

Much of our review focuses on recommendations within Canada, hoping that we can be a leader in world response. Canada was credited in 2021 with increased funding for victim services and launching a five-year public awareness campaign. However, comprehensive data, efforts to identify victims, protection for all victims, and investigation and prosecution were deemed inadequate: "The range, quality, and timely delivery of trafficking-specific services varied nationwide, and service providers reported a shortage of victim services, including emergency shelters and longer-term housing" (TIP, July 2021). We believe Canada can do better than simply meeting "minimum" standards.

United Nations Global Report on Trafficking in Persons:

The United Nations Global Report on Trafficking in Persons 2020 (January 2021) draws on data from 148 countries and makes the significant statement:

> Although found in every country and every region, trafficking in persons remains a hidden crime, with perpetrators operating in the dark corners of the internet and the underbelly of the global economy to entrap victims for sexual exploitation, forced labour, domestic servitude, and other forms of exploitation (p. 4).

As previously mentioned, the report states that for every ten victims detected globally, five are adult women, and two are girls mainly trafficked for sexual exploitation. The report notes that "traffickers prey upon the marginalized and impoverished" (p. 4).

Of the women trafficked, 77% were for sexual exploitation, with 72% of the girl victims. Of the men trafficked, 17% were for sexual exploitation, with 23% of the boys. With a world population of about 7.8 billion, that would equate to over 15 million women and 5 million girls trafficked for sexual exploitation, and over a million men and an equal number of boys (United Nations Office on Drugs and Crime, 2021).

International Labour Office:

The International Labour Office (2014) estimated that 22% of the 20.9 million people in forced labour globally were trafficked for sexual exploitation; that would be 4.5 million, mostly women and girls. It was noted that the Asia-Pacific region and Africa accounted for the highest forced labourers. At the same time, cross-border movement was strongly associated with forced sexual exploitation.

A common feature of sexual exploitation was that victims were unaware of the monies being paid. With migrant victims, "debt bondage" was often created by a chain of traffickers and exploiters who charge recruitment, travel expenses, and advertising beyond the profit of brothel managers. The profit made from pornography was even more difficult to estimate.

Although forced sexual exploitation generated an estimated US $99 billion profit, the ILO did not endorse or legitimize "sex work." It was also noted that "profits" were higher in Asia because of the large number of victims but higher per capita in Developed Economies (capitals in original) due to the high average price of sexual encounters.

A further report from the ILO Global Estimates of Modern Slavery (2017, p. 5) portrays more dramatic figures, indicating that numbers had almost doubled in five years:

- On any given day in 2016, 40.3 million people were victims of modern slavery.
- There were 5.9 adult victims for every 1,000 adults in the world and 4.4 child victims for every 1,000 children in the world.
- Women and girls accounted for 71% of modern slavery victims, including those in forced marriages.

As well, "an estimated 3.8 million adults were victims of forced sexual exploitation and 1.0 million children were victims of sexual exploitation. The vast majority of victims (99 per cent) were women and girls" (p. 9). The majority were exploited in Asia/Pacific, with 4% in the Americas. Methodology included drawing on several data sources from 2012 to 2016.

Private sector expert Carmen Niethammer (Feb. 2, 2020) further interpreted the above numbers. She reported that human trafficking was a $150 billion annually global industry and required a public-private partnership to crack the business. Traffickers use banks to funnel money and hotels to book customers. She also suggested that health care providers need to be more aware of possible victims.

A Canadian Perspective:

Benjamin Perrin notes in his major exposé *Invisible Chains* (2011) that before 2005, there was no *Criminal Code* offence of human trafficking. This absence was despite Canada's Liberal government's 2002 endorsement of the 2000 United Nations Palermo *Protocol on Human Trafficking to Prevent, Suppress, and Punish Trafficking in Persons, Especially Women and Children*. Even with comprehensive child sex tourism legislation, only one individual was convicted between 1997 and 2007, and his exploits were discovered by accident. A second offender pled guilty to several charges in 2010 after losing his challenge against sex tourism legislation.

Benjamin Perrin worked previously in Cambodia with human rights investigators to help rescue children from sex tourism. He notes Canada was very slow to recognize human trafficking:

> The first major report by the RCMP, *Project Surrender* (2004), estimated that approximately 600 foreign nationals are brought to Canada for sex trafficking each year, with an additional 200 being brought for forced labour trafficking annually (2011, p. 29).

Canadian statistics are also confusing. The Global Slavery Index website (2018) estimates that "on any given day in 2016, 17,000 people were living in conditions of modern slavery in Canada, a prevalence of 0.5 victims for every thousand people in the country." As of Nov. 2017, 433 of the 455 human trafficking victims identified were for sexual exploitation, the remaining for forced labour. It was also noted that 93% of those identified as sex trafficking victims were Canadians rather than foreign citizens.

Statistics Canada (Ibrahim, 2019) states that the number of police-reported human trafficking incidents in 2019 was 511, culminating in over 2,400 incidents in the 11 years since that data became available. About two-thirds were violations of the *Criminal Code*, while the other third was against the *Immigration and Refugee Protection Act*. The vast majority of identified victims were women and girls. Prosecution is another story. In 2018–2019, most human trafficking charges (89%) were stayed, withdrawn, dismissed, or discharged.

In 2019, the Government of Canada announced a five-year plan, The National Strategy to Combat Human Trafficking (Cotter, 2020). According to Public Safety Canada, the Strategy is based on five key pillars:

- preventing human trafficking in Canada and internationally;
- protecting victims and potential victims;

- improving the capacity to identify and prosecute human trafficking cases;
- partnering with provincial, territorial, national, and international stakeholders to better collaborate and coordinate; and
- empowering victims and survivors of human trafficking.

Significantly, Canada's National Strategy (2019) notes that 26% of all the victims of human trafficking were girls under 18, while 44% were between the ages of 18 and 24. That confirms what most people already know: Girls and young women are common targets of sexual exploitation.

Although the number of reports is increasing, Megan Walker, former director of the London Abused Women's Centre, feels they are simply the tip of the iceberg (Statistics Canada, 2021). She saw 481 women and girls through her agency alone from 2015 to 2020. She felt there were many reasons most women and girls do not report their exploitation to the police, including the lack of both meaningful outcomes and support throughout the process.

Julia Drydyk, executive director of the Canadian Centre to End Human Trafficking, agrees new data demonstrates the need for more support (Raman-Wilks, 2021). Increased access to services has empowered many victims to come forward to report their situations. Drydyk asserts, "This increase demonstrates that victim-centred services have to be in place to help victims ready to exit their horrifying human trafficking situation."

Status of Women Committee:

The numbers quoted by Canadian politicians, following the declaration of the National Human Trafficking Awareness Day in 2021, come from the Status of Women Committee and were based on 2018 Statistics Canada data, which reported 1,708 incidents of trafficking (Cotter, 2020). Of those, 90% occurred in the metropolitan areas, 97% were women and girls, 45% were between ages 18 and 24, and 28% were under 18. These statistics emphasize the predominance of young female victims.

The committee acknowledges that Human Trafficking is difficult to detect and is subject to underreporting. Of the 582 cases that made it to adult criminal court, 81% of the persons accused were men, and only 38% of cases made it through the system to sentencing.

The vast majority, 92% of victims, knew the person accused of trafficking them. For 31%, it was a so-called friend or acquaintance. A boyfriend or an intimate partner trafficked another 29%. Sadly, many young women are enticed and groomed by promises of love and security, then encouraged to participate in providing income or forced to pay back what they have allegedly already received. The introduction of drugs often complicates the situations.

$ $ $ $

While the percentages above may be accurate, we know the real numbers of trafficked persons are much higher. Globally, 40 million victims, over half of whom are used for sexual exploitation, are believed to be trafficked in a multi-billion-dollar industry. Based on very limited statistics, 15-20% of U. S. men are sexual consumers (ProCon.org, June 1, 2011). If we were to apply this globally, a world population of 7.8 billion (x 50% male x 75% age 18–75 x 15%) would generate over 400 million buyers. Using very rough estimates, if 20 million victims are trafficked for sexual exploitation, at least 20 consumers abuse each victim. It may be a male fantasy to have access to multiple partners; it is not a common female desire to be required to service multiple men.

Canada is recognized as a source, transport, and destination country. A country with Canada's population (0.5% of the world) could potentially be harbouring 200,000 trafficked victims. Consider the numbers another way. Based on Canada's population of 38 million, over 100,000 sex sellers would be required to meet the sexual demands of over 2 million sex consumers. (Again, this is based on 38 million population x 50% male x 75% adult x 15%. One victim for every 20 offenders means over 100,000 trafficked women or children.) These numbers will be discussed in more detail in Chapter 5.

Although a vocal minority of "sex workers" claim to provide consensual services, many vulnerable women and children in Canada and around the world are left without a voice or a choice. We are long overdue in giving these unrecognized victims full recognition. If monied men with sexual appetites are responsible for providing a significant social net, the impoverished of the world are at risk. Society must protect all vulnerable citizens' dignity and sacred nature.

$ $ $ $

Coco (not her real name) in "Triumph over Tragedy" describes a horrific history of being abused and groomed for probably 50,000 opportunists to take advantage of her body during her tragic childhood, youth, and young adult life. Her story can be found in Part Five, Experiential Voices.

"Why are there whores?" asks Jessica. Her "WHY?" poem, also in Experiential Voices, reflects the cynicism of a woman who endured many entrapments of a patriarchal system at the price of "empowerment."

Harm extends far beyond those directly involved. The impact of street activity on an inner-city community is explored by Kylee Nixon in "Making Sense of the Inertia." Her article appears in Part Six, Guest Contributors.

Readers are also invited to follow the archetypal nightmare of a young woman tricked, manipulated, and trapped in a web of circumstances beyond her control. "Along Came a Spider..." is presented in Part Six by guest contributor Megan Walker.

CHAPTER 4:
VOCAL MINORITY VS. COMMON GOOD

WHAT HAS CAUSED such a painful polarity among women of the world that while most want freedom from objectification and commodification, others claim empowerment within those same conditions?

What is the equality and mutuality we seek? Is it possible for women to live their best lives while complicit with commercial sexual dalliances or oppression? Is there a meeting place where we can agree that a woman's right to freedom is respected?

Robert Jensen, a former professor of journalism at the University of Texas in Austin, has studied and written extensively about controversial subjects such as media law, ethics, politics, White supremacy, institutionalized racism, patriarchy, capitalism, sexualization, feminism, masculinity, and pornography. He posed questions similar to those above in *The End of Patriarchy* (2017):

> Is it possible to imagine any society achieving a meaningful level of any kind of justice if people from one sex/gender class can be routinely bought and sold for sexual services by people of another sex/gender class? If one class of people were defined as 'available to be bought and sold for sexual services', is there any way that class of people would not be assigned subordinate status to the dominant class that does the buying? Is justice possible when the most intimate spaces of the bodies of people in

one group can be purchased routinely by people in another group?

Same question, stated differently: If we lived in an egalitarian society with sex/gender justice, would the idea of buying and selling people for sexual services likely emerge at all? If we lived in a society that put the dignity of all people at the center of its mission, would anyone imagine 'sex work'? (p. 97).

Economic coercion is not sexual consent.

Included in the misguided category are a segment of advocates who call themselves "feminists" by declaring that women can be "empowered" through payment for sexual exploitation. The vocal minority claiming such a "choice" diminishes the dignity of all women by validating the buying power of men.

Choice Feminism is a hyper-individualized belief that any choice a woman makes is inherently feminist.

If we accept that "sex is work," the poor, low-educated, disabled, mentally-ill, addicted, migrants, refugees, homeless, victims of domestic violence, and all those who already fall through the cracks of our brutal unequal societies, are going to be further pushed into prostitution whitewashed as "stable employment" (LucianN @ Fourth Wave, Nov. 7, 2021).

There is not now, never has been, and never will be a feminist case for men to commercialize the bodies of women (Rachel Moran quoted by Alexandria Slater in "The Irony of Choice Feminism" March, 2021).

The Choice Feminism movement promotes the belief that any decision made by a woman is inherently feminist because they've exercised their right to freedom of choice. This may be true for the privileged few, however, it fails to consider the way society has conditioned a lot of our choices, or how racial and socioeconomic barriers limit the number of opportunities available for some women (Alexandria Slater, March 2021).

$ $ $ $

A hypothetical conversation:

We will call her Lola. She is a composite character drawn from three considerations: partly a pseudo-name CBC gave a woman who spoke about founding a new sex-worker support agency in Alberta, partly from attempted personal communication with a "sex work" advocate, and partly from their campaign material.

Lola, a brothel owner, said she "feared for her safety" because of stigma within the industry. She created a website funded by the federal government to illustrate her point. Images and stories of several missing and murdered women across Canada were used to illustrate that they were (supposedly) killed by stigma rather than spiteful or malicious men. No one consulted with family members of the deceased victims. And if you could follow that logic, there was a constitutional challenge to support. We choose not to advertise the website as we consider the material presented to be erroneous and fallacious.

At the press conference announcing her agency, I might have attempted to ask a few questions.

"Hi, Lola. My name is Kathy. You seem to represent a very strong opinion. I'm trying to understand if there might be a middle ground to protect individuals in the sex trade."

"Who are you with?" Lola demands.

"Well, I like to consider myself an independent thinker, and I'm trying to understand both sides. I thought the *PCEPA* legislation was a shift away from stigmatizing women."

"I recognize your name," she snaps. "You're with that End Demand organization. I don't know why you are even talking to me. Surely you know what a carceral and prohibitionist approach sex trade abolition is and all the harm it causes for those working in the industry."

Choosing not to respond to her vitriol, I simply reply, "I know several women who identify as survivors. My concern is that the discussion seems to have become polarized, and I am sincerely trying to explore if there can be a middle ground."

To myself, I think, *Carceral? Does she feel imprisoned?* Well, I suppose that is her point. Because *PCEPA* legislation criminalizes sex buyers, she is still operating in a criminal context, even though sellers are largely exempt from prosecution.

After a few moments of contemplation, I clear my head and try again. "Lola, I didn't come here to argue. I came to see if I can better understand your perspective. I agree that women should not be stigmatized, that there needs to be more outreach and support, that the public needs to be more aware of sex trafficking, that health services need to be available for women experiencing physical and emotional distress, and that poverty relief needs to be available. It seems, though, that we disagree on how all of those can be best achieved."

Lola's look of contempt is not subdued. She repeats, "The obvious solution, if you care to open your mind, is to remove the stigma of sex work by decriminalizing it."

I quickly interject, "You are equating stigma with criminalization. How does holding sex buyers accountable cause stigma for women?"

Lola looks at me as if she just stepped in dog sh*t. "That is precisely the problem. You have no right to judge the work I do. And you have no right to suggest that my customers are immoral or criminal. That is what causes the stigma. And that is what we are fighting to change. Now, if you will excuse me, I have a campaign to run. The important thing for you to keep in mind is that I am working WITH people in the industry, and WE know best what we need for ourselves, with NO *help* from outsiders like you with judgmental *opinions*."

With that, Lola sweeps out of the room and away from lingering reporters.

Another conversation continues ...

KK: Well, that was interesting. She wants johns decriminalized so that sellers are not parties to criminal offences. I wonder why the johns are not rising in protest. Oh, but they have always hidden behind anonymity, and now they have sellers advocating on their behalf.

AH: Yes, it's frustrating. Women like Lola are mules for the patriarchy. They are not feminists. In their world, exploiters are legitimatized as "business people," brothels as legitimate "businesses." Of course, the City of Edmonton already allows that. I keep hoping that if the *PCEPA* legislation is ever taken seriously, we could work on reducing demand.

KK: That reminds me of another point. The city claims licensing brothels is part of harm reduction, like user sites for drug injection. Nobody seriously believes building more and more user sites prevents increased drug use, so why are they satisfied to claim that licensing brothels prevents exploitation?

AH: There is another point that the city is missing. While part of harm reduction is about meeting people where they are, as Lola mentioned, another principle addresses the structural sources of potential harm. The city is ignoring that part.

KK: That seems to be the biggest difference between the so-called camps. The decriminalization people want no restrictions. The pro-*PCEPA* people want to address demand because we see men's insistence on access to women's bodies as the underlying cause of sexual exploitation, compounded, of course, by systemic factors of racism and unequal socioeconomic status.

AH: It also upsets me that the decriminalization movement dismisses the voices of exited survivors. Luckily, there are more and more strong outspoken women around the world who were able to leave the sex industry. From our experience, we know how demoralizing and dangerous it can be, so we are willing to speak up in support of the Equality Model legislation.

KK: This is so discouraging sometimes. I'm sad that some women choose to be sexually monetized, although I can understand how financial circumstances might drive them. They deserve more options.

AH: Yes, it is sad proof of the social conditioning at play. Still, despite Lola's declarations, there will never be enough "happy hookers" to make the sex industry ethical.

KK: The world's free thinkers need to speak in solidarity with exploited women.

AH: Agreed. The vocal minority seem to speak only for themselves with little awareness of or concern for the plight of their sisters around the world.

KK: And don't even get me started about that horrible and insulting video of women who supposedly died of "stigma" because they were killed by murderous predators.

AH: Yes, that was despicably low. The bottom line is that sex purchasers need to be held accountable, and attitudes need to shift.

Once again, we repeat: Commercial sexual exploitation is detrimental to society for many reasons. Reducing the demand is one of the most effective ways of containment and prevention. Reducing demand includes changing public attitudes around consumer impunity while, more importantly, building a more supportive social net to mitigate gendered poverty.

$ $ $ $

One of the most fundamental issues in any society is the balance between individual rights and the collective good. While we recognize such fundamentals as the right to life, liberty, health, work, and freedom of expression, all of these are subject to greater principles of morality, public order, and the general welfare in a democratic society. While the able-bodied are entitled, or even expected, to earn a living, "employments" such as hitmen, drug dealing, theft, Ponzi schemes, and trafficking are considered illegal because harm to the common good outweighs the benefit to the so-called entrepreneur.

In earlier times and more simple societies, work was more easily defined. People built houses for shelter, harvested crops, and tended animals for food and clothing. As society developed, roles of transportation and communication became more complex, along with exploration, industry and development, leisure, and entertainment. Work became more abstract for many citizens. As commerce became more competitive, collaboration gave way to control and oppression.

Commercial sex continues to exist in a grey social area for many. While we agree that sellers should not be stigmatized or criminalized, we must not ignore the evidence of social harm caused by those who propagate the market, including pimps and traffickers. Even the vocal minority, who claim to be consensually involved, are not exempt from physical and emotional trauma. The primary social damage stems from perpetuating degradation and commodification based on gender inequality and objectification. Claiming a "feminist" right to economic empowerment, or quoting historical inevitability, does *not* change the bigger picture.

Questions raised contain both philosophical and political dimensions. We need to ask ourselves: What are the basic values of our society, and how do we want to define relationships? If we accept the principle that dignity, respect, equality, and freedom are fundamental rights for all human beings, how do those play out in our social roles?

Jensen in his presentation to the Disrupt Demand conference (May 7, 2021) suggests we go back to basics in our analysis. Although we are part of the animal kingdom and reproduce sexually, we are also *homo sapiens*, humans with knowledge and wisdom. Roles of gender are changeable and may vary from culture to culture, yet sexuality is essential to our survival. At the same time, sexuality is much more than a means of reproduction or an act to experience pleasure. Sexual behaviour can be part of building and maintaining a healthy and creative intimacy between people. It can be an exploration and celebration of ourselves and one another as we work together to construct an equitable and just society.

Traditionally defined by the male father-figure's supremacy, patriarchy is a system in which men hold primary power in roles such as political leadership, moral authority, social privilege, control of property, and private domestic relations. It is a social construct that, like White supremacy, capitalism, imperialism, and colonialism, has turned differences into male dominance and hierarchal systems. Over thousands of years, societies have developed justifications for blocking the racialized, the poor, the labourers, the conquered, and women from full participation.

Patriarchy functions as a system in which cultural and institutional beliefs, policies, and practices reproduce the domination of women and younger men by older, more powerful men. Patriarchy accounts for the dominance of men in government, the military, commerce, universities, and exploration. Over the centuries, in different ways and in many other cultures, women have had to fight for the right to vote, the right to an equal wage for equal work, the right to family planning, and the right to equal settlements after divorce. The subjugation of women and children has been linked to wife beating, child abuse, and rape culture.

American playwright Eve Ensler, known for *The Vagina Monologues*, now identifies as V (2021). She describes patriarchy as a criminal mindset that has taught men to conquer, claim, own, extract, dominate, occupy, and take what is not theirs. She argues that when someone enters a woman's body, they enter her in spirit as well as physically. The sexual violation of a woman changes her sense of self, separates her from her body, and takes her away from her community. In her conversation with Gabor Maté, V observes, "Patriarchy is like a fish in water; it is taken for granted, not even seen." Those who experience privilege and power, such as maleness and Whiteness, tend not to see it except as a given. Patriarchy is tied to racism and capitalism. Our challenge is to turn it around.

Consent was explained on Health Media (Santos-Longhurst, 2019) following the #MeToo movement. "If clear, voluntary, coherent, and ongoing consent is not given by all participants, it's sexual assault. There's no room for ambiguity or assumptions." Clear means active permission expressed through words or actions that are mutually understandable, not implied by silence. Voluntary means given freely and willingly, not through manipulation, coercion, threats, or power imbalance. Coherent means capable of granting consent, not if asleep, incapacitated, or intoxicated. Ongoing means at every stage of an activity, without assumptions. It's unfathomable that myopic buyers could take advantage of underage, high, or incapacitated victims or convince themselves that some kind of payment (especially to a pimp/trafficker) would absolve them of responsibility.

$ $ $ $

Personal reflection, Kathy:

I was fortunate to grow up with examples of gracious civility. My English paternal grandparents were homesteaders in Alberta. Although their chores were divided by gender—my grandfather tended the fields and livestock, while my grandmother tended the home and gardens—their relationship was based on love and equality. Over and above an ethic of conscientious work and mutual respect, a culture of healthy leisure was exemplified, with the front prairie yard rolled smooth in summer and chalked to create a tennis court.

My first ideological allegiance was to humanism, a philosophical stance that emphasizes all human beings' potential development and where human interests and values are affirmed. Humanism is motivated by compassion, human rights, and social justice; principles are founded on equality and respect, selfless service, the welfare of humankind, long-term health, and happiness, with limitless opportunities for creativity, companionship, and joy. I believe that we as individuals are called to collective responsibility, to lead lives of personal value that aspire to the common good of our social family.

Such an idealistic universe values mutuality over dominance, celebrates the unique capacity of every child, and provides supportive structures for everyone to express their full potential. Humanism recognizes that both men and women can be harmed by traditional gender socialization. There is little room in a world of mutual respect for ready access to women's bodies through commercial transactions.

$ $ $ $

Feminism evolved as a range of social and political movements and ideologies aimed at establishing equality of the sexes. Where humanism assumes equality, feminism directly challenges gendered roles and stereotypes that deny parity.

Feminist views on sexuality have varied, with opinions regarding the sex industry being particularly controversial. Radical feminists oppose the sexual objectification of women and so are critical of the sex industry. They see its exploitative nature as complicit in male sexual entitlement, rape, and sexual harassment. Alternatively, other self-proclaimed feminists distort sex positivity to argue that the sex industry can be a means for women to take control of their sexuality within an unequal system. What is confusing is that both views are presented and promoted under a feminist lens.

Radical feminist thinking recognizes that the majority of women in prostitution are forced by trafficking, poverty, drug addiction, trauma, lower socioeconomic status, educational disadvantages, and racial or ethnic minority status. The money exchanged is seen as a means of coercion rather than consent. Commercialized sex negatively impacts all women by reinforcing the patriarchal view that women are required to serve men sexually. Similarly, pornography is abusive because it reduces women to sexual objects for men to use and abuse.

This radical way of thinking has been eclipsed in recent years by "choice" feminism, which claims women can achieve equality within existing structures and institutions by monetizing their bodies.

Choice feminists claim there is no exploitation if women willfully sell their bodies and benefit from the transaction. Unfortunately, whatever the motivation of any individual woman, such decisions normalize the concept of objectification for sexual pleasure. This perspective does not reflect the degree to which many women are still oppressed by men.

Gail Dines is a professor of sociology who has studied pornography for over 30 years. She makes the point (May 6, 2021) that girls are socialized to be "porn ready" through the social emphasis on thin, toned, and sexualized images. Learning to self-objectify can lead to increased anxiety, depression, and body-loathing among girls. As they see themselves as desirable sex objects, conforming to pornified images, their *en masse* cultural grooming enables an infestation of predatory opportunists.

Dines (Oct. 26, 2021) is concerned that parents underestimate how much children watch pornography and how aggressive mainstream pornography has become. Boys and girls grow up with distorted expectations of how people behave in relationships. Cell phone use, often outside of parental knowledge, contributes to pornography marketing, including CSAM. With over 93 million selfies taken each day, a new generation of narcissistic children focused on their bodies is evolving. Not only that, but markets exist with incentives for teens to make money from their images through "content creation."

Robert Jensen, a former journalism professor, speaks passionately about the need to end patriarchy as part of the liberation of sexual pleasure from objectification. "If our goal is to maintain stable decent human societies that are defined more by mutuality rather than by dominance, we can ask does the sexual exploitation industry foster or impede our efforts" (Jensen, May 7, 2021). Rejection of exploitation is not about restraining sexual expression but about creating conditions for meaningful sexual freedom. Of course, it must happen within a context of social and economic equality so that financial coercion is not a consideration.

Heinz, in "A Mule for the Patriarchy: Waking Up to the Harm of Prostitution to Wives and Families" (2020a), expands her understanding of the damage to include how she, as a seller, harmed others by "championing and perpetuating the objectification of women, the exploitation of our sexuality, and the distortion of consent" (p. 3). By doing so, she felt she betrayed those who fight daily for genuine equality.

Wives and partners of sex buyers are described as "shadow women" by Ingeborg Kraus (2020). Very little attention has been paid to the collateral damage they experience. Over and above the possibility of acquiring sexually transmitted infections, they are often impacted by family debt or shame that they were not considered "enough" for their husband or partner.

> When sex sellers, as part of their learned and prescribed role, gleefully pander to men's desire for sexual access on demand, men's general perceptions of women change. Misogynistic and sexist views of women are reinforced, and suddenly all women are considered procurable pawns. Some women become "worthy" of payment for their sexual availability, and others not (Heinz, 2020a, p. 5).

Heinz explains that she believes sexual access is an intimacy best earned through trust, respect, and mutuality. Women as a group deserve solidarity. When circumvented consent becomes sanitized as "work," it negates the harm to all the women involved, the sellers themselves, the buyer's partner, and women as a whole. If sex is a "job like any other" and men are merely accessing a service rather than cheating on another relationship, women are commodified, objectified, and dehumanized.

One cannot overlook the hidden power sellers hold over sex buyers by an unspoken agreement to maintain their anonymity. Abusers and exploiters do not deserve anonymity. Buyers hide in plain sight, but often they are not really hiding because no one is looking for them. This can also lead to increased feelings of invisibility and worthlessness among those being sold who feel what is happening to them is accepted by society.

If sellers were able to band together to expose their buyers' information, there would be a seismic impact. Those who are trafficked and pimped often have no access to the identities of their abusers or the money exchanged. The vocal minority maintains discretion as part of their livelihood. Even years after they leave the industry, some exited women have reason to fear for their lives if they reveal the names of their exploiters. Others remain loyal to the code of silence as insurance if they should find themselves destitute enough to consider re-entering the industry. We can only imagine the potential outcomes if women broke their code of silence.

> **"When a woman is poor and hungry, the humane thing to do is put food in her mouth, not your dick."**
>
> **Rachel Moran**

PART TWO:
BUYERS & SUPPLIERS

WHO CAUSES THE HARM? *Do men really believe women are happy to share themselves intimately for payment? Do men think women eagerly submit to demeaning and humiliating behaviours?*

Do buyers even care? What would such men hope to achieve? Why do some men avoid respectful and loving relationships with women in their lives? Does sexual arousal ever justify violence, pain, torture, and degradation?

What else allows trafficking to flourish? Is paying for sex a learned behaviour or an uncontrollable urge?

> There is no issue as contentious among feminists, liberals, and human rights defenders as the sex trade. Radical feminists tend to argue that prostitution is both a cause and consequence of male supremacy, and that if women and men are ever to become equal, prostitution must not exist. But for liberals who believe in an essential freedom to buy and sell sex, or for human rights campaigners who see access to sex as a human right, abolition is simply not an option. While acceptance of the sex trade has become mainstream, the idea of ending it has become even harder to imagine (Julie Bindel, *The Pimping of Prostitution: Abolishing the Sex Work Myth*, 2017, xxvii).

Stigma has been used historically to suppress women's voices. Survivor literature consistently exposes the dynamics of abuse, trauma, racism, poverty, trafficking, and pornography that are part of women's experiences in commercial sexual exploitation. Stories from trafficked women worldwide share similarities because trafficking is a crime stemming from and maintained by universal misogyny.

A countermovement driven by a vocal minority suggests that buying sex is acceptable because sex is a normal masculine need.

Such claims excuse male privilege; deny gender, racial, and economic inequalities; and normalize violence against women. Proponents of "sex work" suggest that stigma is caused by criminalization rather than by dehumanization and that danger could be reduced with increased acceptability.

CHAPTER 5:

SYSTEMIC DRIVERS OF OPPRESSION

WHY DOES "DISCRETION" for consumers seem to be a common courtesy when commercial sex is openly advertised and readily accessible? Why does a culture of acceptability deny the industry's blatant abuse and degradation? Is it even possible to determine how many sex sellers operate voluntarily?

What does it mean for vulnerable people of the world when the demands of sex buyers far outnumber the availability of willing sellers? What are the implications for all people if we sanction the treatment of some people as though they are not human?

What is privilege? What does it mean to be a man with money? What percentage of men are buyers, and why is it important to focus on them?

We cannot overlook that the sex trade is funded and perpetuated by sexual predators and opportunists; men line up all over the world to pay for sexual access to disadvantaged women and children, many of whom seldom see the money exchanged. The sex trade, the commercialization of sexual exploitation, is a consumer-driven industry. As long as there are consumers, there will be greedy profiteers. Victims remain hidden when offenders are either invisible or protected.

Trauma is an invisible force that shapes the lives of all who are impacted. No society can understand itself without looking at its shadow side.

> [It is] men who perpetuate the harms of prostitu-
> tion—aided and abetted by the pimps, brothel owners,
> strip clubs, and the porn trade—against women and
> girls. It is they who carry ultimate responsibility for
> its crime (Norma & Tankard Reist, Eds. 2016, p. 20).

> What does it take to enable a sexual predator? It
> takes a village, as it turns out. If the predator is a
> wealthy and well-connected man, that is, and his
> victims are girls and young women who have neither
> wealth nor influence. It takes a village to raise
> children; it can also take a village to destroy them
> (Elizabeth Renzetti, July 24, 2021).

$$\$ \ \$ \ \$ \ \$$$

The following chart depicts "The Percentage of Men (by Country) Who Paid for Sex at Least Once: The Johns Chart" (ProCon.org, June 1, 2011). Information about male buyers worldwide was consolidated from 21 studies conducted between 1994 and 2010. Countries were excluded if information was available only for the previous year. Researchers reported difficulty finding reliable data because of the scarcity of prior research, variations in sample size, and possible underreporting by survey responders.

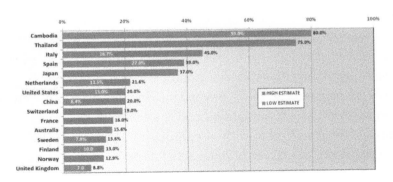

Image credit: ProCon.org, June 1, 2011

What are the raw numbers? Conservative estimates are that 15–20% of North American men—that is one in seven—are sexual consumers based on the statistics for the United States, as shown above. Numbers, not surprisingly, are higher in countries where commercial sexual exploitation is more accepted. That also raises the question of how much buying results from sex tourism rather than nationals.

The male fantasy of a legal sexual buffet is incongruent with the reality of teens exploited as children, troubled backgrounds, poverty, and other contributing circumstances. Do all men wear such blinders, or are some restrained by their conscience? We would like to believe that world consciousness can evolve to the point that sex trafficking of women and children is not an acceptable occurrence, regardless of male desires.

The numbers introduced in Chapter 3 are explored further. Conservative projections based on 2021 population estimates assume approximately half the population is male, and 75% are adults (between ages 18 to 75). If 15% of males buy sex, then:

World population of 7.87 billion/over 400,000,000 sexual consumers,

Canadian population of 38 million/over 2 million sexual consumers,

Alberta population of 4.4 million/about 250,000 consumers,

Metro Edmonton population of 1.49 million/84,000 consumers.

We know consumer traffic increases where "services" are more readily available because of poverty or a lack of restrictions. No wonder survivors' voices are lost, especially when many men vote, represent economic investments, and hold political offices.

What do perpetrators buy? Beyond specific sex acts, most buyers want a performance of enjoyment and the ability to assume a power position. "What's Wrong with Prostitution?" (Nordic Model Now! 2017b) itemizes the buyer purchase as follows:

(1) He buys the use of her body including her vagina, rectum, mouth, and breasts. He rents the use of her body.

(2) He buys her compliance. She must pretend she is enjoying the activity and that he is great—while she acts out his fantasy. That is part of the deal.

(3) He buys the freedom to say whatever he wants, no matter how insulting. Verbal abuse and degradation are also part of the deal.

(4) He buys the freedom to be in control, often demanding that she have a sexual response. She is expected to look and act like a willing participant, behaviour he interprets as evidence of her free choice.

Closer to home, it would take 100,000 potential sellers to serve the estimated 2 million consumers in Canada (including 12,500 for 250,000 Alberta consumers and 4,200 for 84,000 Edmonton consumers). Undeniably, there is money to be made by willing sellers, reluctant participants, or unscrupulous traffickers. Even if some "sex workers" across Canada sell "consensually" as lobbyists claim, the numbers indicate that many others do not engage on such terms and would rather be free.

Still, many Edmonton city administrators fail to see that licensed brothels do not align with their "safer cities" initiative. They perpetuate the myth that licensing commercial sex is sufficient to reduce harm. While licensed sellers may have some degree of pseudo-protection, their buyers are protected from arrest. In the meantime, increased demand intensifies the risk for more vulnerable populations.

Another complicating factor is the "marketability" of those sold. While exploitation often begins in childhood, the perceived worth of those sold diminishes considerably with age. As previously mentioned, the National Strategy (2019) noted that 26% of trafficked girls were underage, and 44% were 18 to 24. This increases the risk for and danger to younger women who are less likely to be educated or have secure careers.

Rachel Moran (2013) explains that "to work as a prostitute is to exist in an ever-present atmosphere of sexual violation" (p. 102). She identifies three basic types of violators. Some prefer to believe that violation does not exist; others know it exists, but knowledge is not enough to alter their behaviour. A third group is well aware and derives a great deal of sexual pleasure from violation. Those offenders tend to emit a "dark and evil frequency" (p. 103). Moran (2013) explains that violations can be overt or subtle:

> Some of the less overt violators would not need to physically feel a woman struggle against hands gripping her breasts so hard she thought they'd burst; some would gently stroke her breasts and feel her involuntarily shrinking from their touch, and they'd get off on that, for some that would be enough. There is clearly a difference in magnitude, but for me it does not alter the nature of the offence (p. 140).

Heinz (2020b) echoes the perception of three types of buyers, using her categories of the ignorant, the hurting, and the sadistic. She also notes (2021) that sex buyers are an under-studied population because of the anonymity innate to the industry. Burner phones and alibi networks contribute to the secrecy.

Programs for arrested buyers are discussed in Chapter 8 with reference to Edmonton's STOP: Sex Trade Offender Program. From a prevention or treatment perspective, separating offenders from their offences is important. For buyers to change in a pro-social way, they must develop an adequate sense of self-worth and view themselves as capable of change.

$$\$ \ \$ \ \$ \ \$$$

It is important to consider systemic inequities that allow buyers sexual access to marginalized women. Segments of society that are denied full participation in economic prosperity create pools of desperation to which buyers are attracted. Commercial sexual exploitation is anchored in misogyny, racism, capitalism, colonialism, ableism, and social/economic disparity.

Systemic drivers of oppression, economic, social, and racial inequality are evident in exploited groups worldwide, including the Black population in America, MMIWG (Missing and Murdered Indigenous Women and Girls) in Canada, and Asians exploited through sex tourism in their home countries and abroad. Various minorities have been targeted historically and geographically; no race or ethnic group has ever been exempt from unnatural, degrading, senseless, and evil luring. Many targeted young people are already distressed because of racial and economic disadvantages.

Melinda Gates (2019) describes the far-reaching effects of patriarchy in creating marginalization across societies:

> One of the most common signs of an abusive culture is the false hierarchy that puts women below men. [...] Gender and racial diversity are essential for a healthy society. When one group marginalizes others and decides on its own what will be pursued and prioritized, its decisions will reflect its values, its mindsets, and its blind spots (pp. 221, 225).

Esperanza Fonseca (2020) comes to a similar conclusion from a financial perspective, noting the association of prostitution with economic survival:

> Throughout all of history, when economic conditions worsen, prostitution increases [...] because people are more desperate to survive... From understanding the historical and material origins of prostitution, we see that violence is part and parcel of what is definitively a vestige of slavery, patriarchy, feudalism, and class war. **Prostitution has never existed without violence, slavery, patriarchy, and class oppression** (emphasis in original).

$ $ $ $

Misogynistic racism is also a factor among sex buyers. An unfortunate example was the massacre of eight people, including six Asian women, in the Atlanta "massage parlours" in March of 2021.

> Racists target the humanity of those they attack.... The violence, racism, and misogyny targeting Asians in North American public spaces is distilled and intensified in the racism of sex buyers at massage brothels where sex buyers are shielded from public view and protected by public authorities. These men are paying for the women to gratify the men's racist and misogynist stereotypes of Asian women as submissive, exotic, or hypersexual in a setting where the women's lack of power is all too real (Lee, Jay, & Farley, March 25, 2021).

The above authors noted that city officials in Atlanta colluded in the pretense of "spa" facilities being legitimate businesses, even though the three targeted were in the recognized red-light zone and had been reviewed on an online site called RubMaps.

Nicole Bell was among those who expressed outrage about the March 2021 murders:

> We are saddened by the loss of the eight people in Atlanta, and we are angry.... These murders were the result of racism, misogyny, and our cultural acceptance of violence against women, particularly prostituted women. It is evident many of these women were being sold for sex in brothels operating under the facade of a "day spa."

> Hate crimes against Asian Americans have increased exponentially since COVID. But let us not forget, every day in this country Asian women are fetishized and sold for sex....

> Women are exploited simply because they are women.... This is not a woman's issue—this is a societal issue. Equality should not be our fight, alone. Ending the sex trade should not be our fight, alone (Nicole Bell, LIFT, March 19, 2021 on Twitter).

Alice Lee and Suzanne Jay, with Asian Women for Equality in Vancouver, British Columbia, work as victim advocates for exploited and trafficked Asian women. Asian-themed brothels often display red flags that indicate trafficking: (1) passport confiscation, (2) use of debt bondage, (3) provision of drugs for control, (4) constant sur-veillance with restricted movement, (5) denial of options to leave, (6) pimps creating emotional dependency, and (7) pimps limiting the women's social contacts. Authors Lee, Jay, and Farley (2021) suggest that city officials anywhere could investigate these warning signs if they were serious about freeing trafficked women instead of protecting sex buyers.

Asian women trafficked from Korea, Vietnam, and China are fetishized to fit various sexualized views. They are frequently mar-keted as geisha, Japanese school girls, fresh off the boat, China dolls, and "mama-san" for men wanting to buy a racialized sexual experience (Jay, May 6, 2021).

Whatever their motivation, buyers are responsible for their behaviour. They need to understand the far-reaching effects of their actions on the people they buy. As Perrin (2011) describes:

> By confronting the demand for paid sex, we can ensure that purchasers are held accountable for the tremendous harm that they inflict on their victims, both directly through their individual acts of abuse and, together with other purchasers, indirectly by contributing to the entire process of victimization. Seen in that light, the purchasers of sex acts are as morally responsible for the suffering of their victims as are the traffickers who meet their demands (p. 161).

All buyers contribute to commodification, and those being sold deserve better options. Trafficking is not always obvious. In fact, recognition is often obscured by a vocal minority who claim they are being falsely victimized. Under the 2014 *PCEPA* legislation, with sexual purchase illegal, the need to discern the agency of those being sold is removed.

$ $ $ $

When confronted with despicable behaviour from sexually addicted men, it may be hard to remember that every sex buyer was once an innocent child. Gabor Maté (2009) attributes addictions to a lack of connection. We are all impacted by adverse childhood experiences. Those who do not learn resourceful resilience turn to other means to numb their pain. This may be the case for many caught in the cycles of pornography and exploitation.

Sexual addiction can have devastating effects on perpetrators and their victims. Shallow relationships can be one way of avoiding personal trauma. Pornography can short-circuit relationships by introducing toxic fantasies. Growing demand impacts consumer requests and perpetuates exploitation. The association of sexual stimulation with degradation and violence creates unrealistic relationship expectations.

Matt Cline (June 2021), with Restored Ministries, speaks compassionately about those struggling with pornography addiction. During his seven years of experience, addicted men attributed their behaviour to myriad feelings, including lack of connection, brokenness, self-worth, unresolved trauma, loneliness, and a sense of being unfulfilled. The men he deals with use pornography to escape "heart issues" such as guilt and pain. Any activity can be considered addictive if it is habitual and the person cannot stop. Pornography is unhealthy because it impairs brain development patterns and short-circuits the dopamine cycle, causing a "porn high" that can last for hours. Pornography may also rob users of other significant experiences by hampering creativity and interfering with forming and maintaining meaningful relationships. Demand for pornography is also associated with human trafficking.

Sex trade abolitionists advocate a sense of community over consumerism, connection over commodification, belongingness over betrayal, respect over objectification, peace and purpose over power, freedom over fear, hope over despair, joy over sadness, vitality over stagnation, and caring over anger. Men who aspire to these positive standards become allies in our quest for equality and respect.

International cooperation and coordination are vital to the fight against human trafficking. We need accurate data, political will, and a collective agreement that all people are created equal and deserve the opportunity to reach their full potential. Such engagement is a tall order when many countries are at war internally and with other nations.

We need a dramatic socio-cultural revolution to recognize the dignity and equality of all genders and races worldwide. We must ensure that all people are treated with respect and that social and economic institutions are altered to recognize human rights. Utopia? Perhaps. But we believe that human beings deserve to live in a world where all persons are free from purchase and slavery by others. We all have the right to personal integrity and relationships based on equality and consent.

The following story reviews the harm perpetrated by different kinds of buyers. Heinz's reflections, earlier shared in *Prostitution Narratives* (2016), were adapted by King as "Kendra's story" on Nov. 9, World Freedom Day, in *Autumn: Survivor Stories* at MissingCara. ca (2018). This excerpt focuses on buyers and the harm they cause:

> The seven years I spent in brothels were the most horrific and disgusting of my life. Many times men forced themselves on me, others stalked me in public. I've been violently sodomized, choked, filmed without my consent, and bled for days from my vagina and rectum. I learned to control my gag reflex, one time swallowing my own vomit.
>
> "Who are these men?" you may ask. Let me tell you about the types of consumers in hopes of dispelling the myth that the purchase of sexual services is a victimless crime.
>
> First, there are the lonely. These are rather sad men, incapable of forming real relationships, who console themselves with buying sexual satisfaction. They usually mean no harm although some become infatuated, thinking their attachment is mutual.
>
> Of course, selling a lie is part of the business. I had to say, "I'm so glad to see you; you're my favorite client" because if I told the truth, that the thought of them touching me made my skin crawl, I would like to believe they would not have returned.

Some of the lonely were otherwise seemingly nice guys, probably ignorant of the harm they caused. Unfortunately, however, this group also includes the unwashed, the old, the infirm, the morbidly obese, the pathetic, and the generally unattractive as well as those cheating on spouses and partners for any number of professed reasons.

Secondly, there are the uncommitted and sexually addicted who want a variety of sexual activities without emotional investment. They may be guys out on the town for what they see as casual fun without any strings. Ironically, this includes those in otherwise stable relationships who "don't want to cheat" because paying for sex "doesn't count."

The objectification inherent in purchased sexual access allows men complete emotional detachment. One example is an obnoxious celebrity who gloated that he did not pay women for sex, he paid them to leave. And don't even get me started on the overachievers who proclaim, "I'm so good you should be paying me."

Thirdly, the most disturbing group are the sadistic and perverse. These are men who enjoy the power they wield, subjecting women to cruel and painful acts, while insulting and degrading them. They are men who ask for nauseating performances, pornographic simulations, and acts involving animals, blood, feces, or urine.

Approaches rooted in legalization or decriminalization unfortunately open the door to increased prevalence of aberrant and deviant sexual activity. This is evident in Germany where consumers can preorder from brothel menus offering a wide range of licking, swallowing, and penetration, while ignoring the probability that many providers are trafficked. Whether benign or vicious, friendly or antagonistic, all consumers share the common trait of buying a lie, the lie that their requests are welcome, albeit for a price.

I calculated that in seven years, I "serviced" men over 4300 times. Each one of those times took away a piece of my soul. And not only did a part of me disappear each time, but the hole was also replaced with the negativity and revulsion I experienced. Even though I've been out of the business for many years now, I still feel contaminated, as if 4300 is branded on my forehead forever.

All sexual consumers must hear and understand that their purchase represents the objectification and commodification of another human being. I am slowly rebuilding with the help of family and friends. I challenge consumers to look at their choices and find a way of treating everyone in their life with dignity, equality, and respect.

CHAPTER 6:
DISSECTING THE DEMAND

IS THERE A DIFFERENCE between pimping and trafficking? What motivates some people to sell other human beings, and why is there a ready market?

Are all buyers blind or in denial about the harm they perpetrate? Will our evolution as humans move beyond capturing, trapping, enslaving, and selling others?

Who are the traffickers? How do they groom others, young males as well as females, through seduction as well as force? What do we need to do to free our world from such devastation? Is it enough to identify and prosecute traffickers? Do we not also need to deal with buyer demand?

A vocal minority of women who claim to be empowered by sex as "work" subscribes to the familiar arguments related to the "harm-reduction-through-licensing" model supported by Edmonton City Council and other municipalities. However, as previously mentioned, there will never be enough providers to voluntarily meet consumer demands. That is why trafficking happens. The freedom and safety of all women is important. We must not let the licensing model detract from the greater harm happening to more vulnerable populations.

In the world of economics, there is no market without buyers. Although we support all women, any endorsement of "sex worker" rights implies acceptance of buyer entitlement. We know that increased tolerance fuels demand. Conversely, as acknowledged in the preamble to Bill C-36, the *Protection of Communities and Exploited Persons Act, 2014*, "It is important to continue to denounce and prohibit the purchase of sexual services because it creates a demand for prostitution."

> One of the biggest impediments to anti-trafficking efforts is a lack of understanding of the issue.... It must be emphasized that the essence of trafficking is the forced exploitation of individuals by those in the position to exert power over them [...] Despite the similarities between the organized trafficking of drugs, arms, and humans ... we commit a grave injustice against the victims of human slavery if we reduce them in our minds to the status of commodities (Ruth Dearnley, 2013).

> Pimps know exactly what they are doing. Buyers will go where conditions are most favorable. The biggest gift to a pimp is to protect him from consequences (Rachel Moran, June 7, 2021).

$ $ $ $

At the STOP: Sex Trade Offender Program in Edmonton (see Chapter 8), participants are asked to provide feedback about what they learned at the end of the day. One year, a young man commented that we were too hard on pimps; "They are just guys trying to make a living," he said. After a day of education similar to the contents of this book, he still failed to grasp the harm of objectification. Fortunately, he was an exception, and most STOP attendees express appreciation for the deeper understanding they receive.

The problem of human trafficking is enormous. We have already touched on the numbers, but they are worth repeating. The figure commonly used by anti-trafficking educators is 40 million victims worldwide, with over half for sexual exploitation. Why? Trafficking for sexual exploitation exists because at least 15–20% of men are sexual consumers.

Is it any wonder politicians are reluctant to look at the numbers? There are probably over 2 million sexual consumers in Canada, over 250,000 in Alberta, and over 80,000 in Edmonton. Mostly, these men are otherwise responsible citizens who represent financial interests, pay taxes, and vote. Perhaps some politicians and other community leaders are included in the consumer population, pushing to have their selfish agendas validated.

Human trafficking in 2020 was reported to be a $150B "industry" with new young bodies always in demand. Simple math suggests each victim could generate tens of thousands, if not hundreds of thousands, of dollars annually. It was estimated that one victim controlled for one year in Canada could "earn" traffickers over $280,000 (CISC, 2008, p. 5). Exploitation is difficult to track, since most consumers access a variety of those recruited to be sold, and "novelty" is part of their game. The numbers are probably much higher than reported.

The tendency for sellers to acquire "regulars" or temporary "exclusive" agreements may be more characteristic of high-end brothels. However, even those buyers tend to push for new experiences. Based on survivors' stories, the consensus is that because "new" girls are in demand, they are often moved to different locations.

The myth of protection within legalization is addressed by Stella Marr (2012), who co-founded Survivors Connect as an on-line forum:

> Well-meaning people who've never been commercially sexually exploited think that legal brothels will protect the women in prostitution from pimps and violent johns. They are mistaken.... Pimps don't stop being pimps when you legalize what they do. If we legalize brothels, we'll only be giving these predators more power while we help them protect their cash.

Unfortunately, there seems to be an unlimited number of pimps, buyers, traffickers, pornographers, profiteers, and even some "workers" who attempt to marginalize research, lie, discredit, and silence abolition efforts. For every step forward, there is a constant pushback. As Farley (March 29, 2021) notes, "Pimps are not nice when you get between them and their money." It is a victory for the profiteers when sellers join them in the name of feminism, claiming to accept the inherent atrocities in the name of "work."

Ingeborg Kraus in a press release (October 18, 2021) quotes a police statement that illustrates the impact of legalization in Germany:

> In Germany, so-called voluntary prostitution is legal, but in fact forced prostitution is part of everyday life. Investigators assume that 96 to 98 percent of women in prostitution in Germany are controlled by others … 80 percent of women are migrants and come from the newly affiliated Eastern European countries….
>
> The transition between forced prostitution and "voluntary" prostitution is mostly fluid, so it is difficult to clearly separate these two terms and treat them separately.… Prostitution, as it takes place in Germany today, is predominantly forced and poverty prostitution from which third parties mainly benefit.

Ruth Dearnley, CEO of Stop the Traffik in London, United Kingdom, makes the point that preventing human trafficking cannot be tackled in a vacuum. Anti-trafficking strategies need to be embedded in all policy areas. "We cannot allow ourselves to marginalize the issue of trafficking, viewing it as something that can be ended with a few extra taskforces or dedicated units" (June 27, 2013).

One possible deterrent would be that all buyers charged with soliciting sex be required to give a DNA sample because they come from a pool of potential rapists and killers. Society's protection of buyers' anonymity exemplifies patriarchy at work. Similarly, a newspaper editor once refused to publish names of arrested buyers, arguing that enforcement was not the role of a newspaper. It has been a long and steady battle, but at least the media have responded to the call to refrain from sensationalizing and stigmatizing the murdered victims.

The downside of more compassionate reporting is that accuracy can also be distorted. For example, a young Alberta woman, murdered with her child, was identified as a single mom. The man charged, however, was reported to be her "boyfriend" rather than her pimp. By attempting to remove stigma from the victim, the actions of her accused trafficker were inadvertently minimized.

In "A Socialist, Feminist, and Transgender Analysis of 'Sex Work'" (2020), Esperanza Fonseca writes as a survivor of the sex trade. She understands feeling empowered by prostitution because that was where she could make her own money after being cut off from jobs, housing, and community. However, her involvement quickly became a trap of continual abuse and sadness, a soul-killing experience. She speaks of recognizing and moving through her "flames of trauma."

Fonseca (2020) suggests that selling sex in the context of class privilege is a game of "compensated dating." Those not forced to sell their bodies as an economic necessity should not be allowed to speak on behalf of oppressed women in the sex trade. Those in the latter category, who are there due to economic and social pressures, demonstrate that financial coercion is the driving force behind their involvement.

> Consent does not exist in a vacuum, sealed off from other conditions of society. To decontextualize consent from the broader structures of the economy and society, which both create the options we are able to choose from and apply pressure for us to choose certain options over others, is to only understand consent in its more superficial meaning.

> Under capitalism, workers are forced to sell the only commodity they have, namely their labour-power, in order to survive. **Those of us cut out from the formal economy, unable to sell our labour-power, are forced to sell the only thing we have left: our bodies** (emphasis in original).

> The sex trade under market forces will always result in the degradation of conditions for those trapped within it. You want to demand higher rates? Too bad, a woman from the lower strata of the sex trade will do it cheaper. You want to demand safer conditions? A more exploited woman is available elsewhere,

whether in poorer neighbourhoods at home or abroad in the peripheries of imperialism. With the decriminalization of pimps and johns, the global sex trade increases. And with that increase, the market becomes saturated and prices and conditions for prostituted women decline.

According to Fonseca, real power does not come from associations of collective workers asking abusers for less sadistic treatment. Rather, real power comes from abolishing the conditions causing exploitation, the market that trades women and girls. Pimps and johns do not see sex sellers as human but as commodities to be dismembered and reviewed based on their component parts. No person has the right to be a pimp, and there needs to be a mechanism to repress them. Decriminalizing buyers and pimps may allow the minority of privileged "sex workers" a more open market. Still, it makes life considerably more difficult for the majority who have no choice.

Similar concerns are expressed at the international level. Valiant Richey is the Special Representative and Coordinator for Combatting Trafficking in Human Beings with the Organization for Security and Co-operation in Europe (OSCE), a membership of 57 states. Richey (2021) summarizes the reasons we must address buyer demand as part of ending trafficking:

(1) Trafficking is financially motivated. Money is paid directly to traffickers by consumers.
(2) Multiple layers of harm are often intensified with violence.
(3) Sex trafficking is a highly gendered crime with 92–97% female victims.
(4) Racial minorities are disproportionally affected.
(5) International law requires demonstrated efforts to disrupt demand.

The United Nations Palermo *Protocol*, ratified by Canada in 2002, article 9(5) states that countries should take measures to "discourage the demand that fosters all forms of exploitation of persons, especially women and children, that leads to trafficking." Demand is recognized as a root cause. Most buyers do not care nor want to know if women are trafficked. The *Protocol* requires countries to have other interventions if they do not criminalize.

Prevention and criminalization of buying are two possible actions to reduce the demand. Prevention encompasses social, educational, and cultural components. Education ideally has multiple focuses, including high school education, college education, social media advertising, the medical sector, codes of conduct through employment policies, public awareness, search-engine advertising, chat-box disruption, and STOP (Sex Trade Offender Program) equivalents to reduce recidivism, websites, and review boards.

Criminalization sets a clear societal norm, discourages sex buyers' activity, holds them accountable for the harm they cause, and incentivizes law enforcement to scrutinize the industry. Richey claims that 15–20% of adult men are sexual consumers. He suggests, minimally, that criminalizing the use of trafficked victims in legalized markets would theoretically put more onus on buyers to be aware.

Richey's (2021) core recommendations include:

(1) Highlight our international obligations.
(2) Adopt a holistic response with multiple sectors.
(3) Build a strategy of complementary measures at a national level.
(4) Evaluate and measure initiatives.
(5) Criminalize more broadly.
(6) Ensure support and exit services for women. We know that "rescue" can be the easy part. Coping with trauma and recovery takes time and requires funding.

As the Canadian Centre to End Human Trafficking posted (Froutan, 2021), concern is not enough. We need education, empathy, and collaboration to propel change. According to a 2021 study, 57% of Canadians were unaware of sex trafficking in their community, and even fewer (15%) believed Canadian citizens were victims. The data demonstrate the need for continual educational information, prevention, and policing as traffickers continue to prey on the most vulnerable in our communities.

Grace Hawthorn, a British writer, summarizes the incongruity experienced by many women. She describes herself as a wayward feminist. She created a blog, *Grace Notes,* in 2017 where she regularly reflects on the duality of society. The following excerpt from July 31, 2019 (grace-notes.blog) embodies some of the questions many women ask about male sexuality:

> Dear men,
>
> I look at men, and the world men have built, and it is all built around your orgasms....
>
> You have built social systems of objectifying women and girls, grooming us from an early age to fit your fantasies and preparing us for how you intend to use us. How we look, how we inhabit our bodies, how we must be penetrable, how we must be ready for you, how we must please you, how we must turn you on, how the greatest compliment you can give us is that we are sexy and approved....
>
> You have built legal systems that legitimate and protect you, that ensure your entitlement to orgasms remain the central and most important concern....
>
> You have built economic systems where women are kept poor, so you can make us facilitate you sexually; you keep women without resources so you can coerce us and force us to let you masturbate on us and in us....
>
> Women and girls are injured, traumatised, and hurt over and over again in your pursuit of orgasm.
>
> You have built systems of pornography, and the technologies to distribute that pornography, in the interests of your masturbatory orgasms. There is no other purpose for porn and it is a mammoth industry.... The money involved in this industry is immense, and bleeds everywhere, into economies at every level, into politics, into policing, into media and

advertising, into tourism, into fashion, into business practices, into workplaces.

You have built systems of prostitution.... These systems are global, involving complicated logistics, bureaucracy, administration, involvement with state systems nationally and internationally. You have worked hard to make it seem like access to the bodies of others for your orgasms is a human rights issue....

It's endless, the damage you have wrought. You have defined sex itself as starting and ending with your orgasms. And we have not begun to talk about the violence, about how sexually exciting you find the violence. The upskirting, the peeping, the voyeurism, the following, the hissing, the groping, the touching, the flashing, the violent sex, the strangulation, the assaulting, the raping, in porn and in real. All of it, evidently, sexually incredibly exciting and giving you orgasms. Globally. Your excitement and orgasm to our humiliation and degradation.

So, what are they like these orgasms that are worth all this pain and all this destruction? What are they like that you have organised the whole entire world around this level of dehumanising damage? What is the benefit to you when the costs to us are so immeasurably high? What are they like, that this death-cult is what you value above all else?

Dear men, we need to talk about your orgasms.

CHAPTER 7:

PORNOGRAPHY AS MARKETING

WHAT IS SO UNIQUE about the male sexual experience that some men utilize increasingly graphic and vulgar means of stimulation rather than develop mutually satisfying relationships? Do they feel unworthy and project their feelings of inferiority onto others? Is that easier than facing their fears of not being enough?

What about the subjects, the so-called porn stars? Do masturbating observers really believe women enjoy being mass-exposed and objectified? How can viewers dissociate so completely from the sufferings, discomfort, and humiliation of others? Do we care about the women abused on screen? What are their stories? What happens when the short-term gain of the viewer's release requires further intensified sadistic stimulation?

The depths of human depravity cannot be underestimated. We cannot overlook that sexual exploitation is amplified by an insidious pornography industry. As images become more graphic, degrading, and violent, there is growing demand by perpetrators to have these illusions acted out, and the cycle of exploitation continues. Pornography is a channel for degradation and violence against women and children that would not be tolerated anywhere in the "real" world, thereby creating a disturbing fantasy mentality in viewers. Pornography is essentially a hate crime against women.

Men are not born with unhealthy attitudes toward women. These attitudes are learned by a hypersexualized culture that treats women as objects.... There is also an elephant in the room here that is clearly a root cause of violence toward women—the prevalence of pornography in our society.... There is a clear connection between human trafficking and online pornography. There is a lot of science suggesting a connection between exposure to violent pornography and aggressive behavior in men. A culture of men who consume this kind of material will lead to the kind of violence against women that we are seeing today. It's time we take a good hard look at this and start seriously regulating and restricting access to pornography (Tamara Jansen, Member of Parliament for Cloverdale—Langley City, March 26, 2021).

Pornography is the essential sexuality of male power, of hate, of ownership, of hierarchy, of sadism, of dominance (Andrea Dworkin quoted by Alexandria Slater, March 15, 2021).

$ $ $ $

The insidious influence of pornography creeps through the consciousness of society and into susceptible young minds, suggesting that brutality and objectification rather than mutuality and intimacy are norms for human behaviour. Pornography destroys the fundamental fabric of society by creating such distortions in both men and women, to the point that repeated use can lead to performance anxiety and diminished enjoyment.

As noted in the documentary *Raised on Porn* (Exodus Cry, 2021), once people experience the parallel universe of pornography, reality is not the same. The earlier someone is exposed, the more likely they are to become addicted. This is because the adolescent brain is not prepared to contextualize the complexity of sexual arousal. The adolescent brain is excited by stimulation, the content becomes intertwined with pleasure, and orgasm overrides the prefrontal, not-yet-developed rational brain. "Gonzo," or aggressive pornography, which is easily accessible, represents women as compliant and desirable objects. Unfortunately, as tolerance to stimulation increases, users seek more dangerous or darker venues to satisfy their arousal.

From the perspective of the subject, usually female, participation in pornography causes an added dimension of violation:

> Women who are filmed during prostitution for porn have more PTSD than non-filmed women. This means you never exit porn because the images never go away. The fear that these images will surface is lifelong. And the thought of men masturbating to your rape is intolerable (Gail Dines, quoting Melissa Farley, May 7, 2021).

Although programs exist for exited women, the struggles of pornography survivors are more difficult because their images may last forever, rarely affording a clean break from their past.

Many clinicians and educators warn of the dangers of pornography, naming it a public health crisis because of the normalization of violence and objectification. Pornography, unfortunately, also feeds racial stereotypes, misogyny, and sexual exploitation; this dynamic tends to be ignored by those who suggest that "freedom of expression" cancels the cost of the victimization of "performers." The capacity for reciprocity and authentic communication between persons is largely overlooked in favour of sexual entitlement and physical release. In fact, a pornified culture can leave countless youth blinded to the richness and diversity of full personhood and mutual relationships that can develop uniquely over time.

Another danger of pornography is that men overwhelmingly control the content (Dines, Oct. 26, 2021). Women are not saying, "This is how I want to be perceived" but rather "I will accept payment for your definition." Women in pornography, unfortunately, fall into the same continuum of exploitation as women in prostitution. Some women develop pornified views of themselves, as women tend to want to please their male partners. We need to help women, as well as men, negotiate new expectations.

Women are dehumanized as pornography moves away from the emotional and spiritual levels required for loving and nurturing relationships. As Gail Dines (2010) explains, dehumanizing a group to justify cruelty against individual members is not new to the pornography industry. It has been used through history by oppressors, racists, and homophobes:

> Once the humanness of these individuals is collectively rendered invisible by their membership in a socially denigrated group, then it is that much easier to commit acts of violence against them.

> In porn, the woman's lack of human qualities often results in men's inability to see just how violent the sex act is.... That these women are acting and may have come to porn not so much through choice but due to a lack of alternatives is rarely considered because this premise threatens to puncture the fantasy world created by both pornographer and user (p. 65).

Robert Jensen (May 6, 2021) suggests that men are so "intensely socialized to run away from the vulnerability that comes with intimacy that they find comfort in the illusory control over women that porn offers." Pornography may offer a temporary sense of power but not the real human connection one would hope most people desire. Valuing dominance over mutuality, and superficial stimulation over intimacy, makes the world a more dangerous place for women and children.

Pornography is not just "sex on film" as some may claim. It is a distortion of human sexuality. As a form of mass media, the two main components are production and reception. Pornography portrays what consumers think they want. It is produced under coercive conditions with injury sustained by participants.

Sexually explicit imagery, designed to produce sexual arousal, has become more "innovative" over the decades in the name of profit. Scenarios too upsetting to articulate would be denounced in any other forum. They are described as brutal, cruel, body-punishing, dehumanizing, often portraying male dominance and female submission, racist language, and pseudo-child enactments, all of which have become mainstream.

Jensen (May 6, 2021) suggests that the themes of pornography remain consistent:

(1) All women always want sex from all men,
(2) Women like all sexual acts that men ask or demand of them, and
(3) Any woman who initially resists porn will be sexually aroused.

Although both men and women are typically portrayed as hyper-sexual, men usually control the action and dictate the terms, while women are treated as objects.

Pornography is sometimes used as a means of control by traffickers, who take photos of victims and threaten to shame them by exposing those images. Traffickers also produce pornography of victims to diversify their profit and to advertise victims.

Over and above commercial exploitation, online users are often groomed or coerced to generate their own sexualized content. The expectation of pornography actresses and actors to appear as though they are consenting constitutes an additional barrier in determining consent versus coercion within explicit content. Participating in sadism for "entertainment" adds an additional layer of violation to women already used viciously for the pleasure of punters (Moran, June 7, 2021).

Our current Western culture, unfortunately, primes girls to believe they are disposable sex objects. It is incomprehensible that one could truly consent to losing control of the most intimate images of their body, with no recourse to have the images removed, their body exposed to millions of pornography users who view them with derogatory names, being attacked on social media and living in fear of loved ones seeing those images.

Pornography is killing us as a culture. As more and more young men masturbate to pornography, their capacity for empathy is diminished (Dines, Oct 26, 2021). Images of pornography bypass the frontal (thinking) area of the brain and are stored in the body as memories of sexual pleasure. Dines describes pornography as "making hate to women." She adds that in all her years of being sexually active, she never imagined "accidently dying" from "rough sex."

Pornography requires dissociation from love and spirituality. How do we reconcile the hate crime of pornography? Although pornography can be a huge pleasuring tool among anonymous men, we must understand that men are much more than their drive for orgasm. In reality, feminists are men's friends because we believe men are capable of moral and emotional humanity.

Child sexual abuse material (CSAM) aka "child porn" is another disturbing dimension of sexual exploitation. We acknowledge the worldwide epidemic, whether fuelled by pedophiles or other users descending into further depths of depravity for "edgier" stimulation. However, CSAM is beyond the scope of this book.

Laila Mickelwait is the founder of the global #Traffickinghub movement and the president/founder of the Justice Defense Fund. She has been combatting the injustice of sex trafficking for over a decade, focusing on criminal exploitation in the Big Porn industry. Mickelwait has presented in numerous countries, and her articles have been featured around the globe.

Pornography is not "adult entertainment" but a criminal realm that needs to be shut down. Big Porn is a global industry, run by a small group of titans, and distributed through tube-sites (Mickelwait, 2021). Pornhub was the world's largest conglomerate with an estimated 42 billion visits per year and most of the content user-generated. Real crime-scene footage is rampant with videos of rape, non-consensual acts performed on drunk or unconscious women, sexual abuse of children and minors, a wide spectrum of violence, and spy-cam scenes from changing rooms and toilets. Most videos are offered for free and monetized through advertising, thereby subsidizing criminal activity.

In "The Children of Pornhub" (Dec. 4, 2020), Nicholas Kristof asked, "Why does Canada allow this company to profit off videos of exploitation and assault?" Pornhub has a format like YouTube in that anyone can post their own videos and, until recently, viewers could download videos directly from their website.

> The issue isn't pornography but rape. It is not prudishness to feel revulsion at global companies that monetize sexual assaults on children; it's compassion.... We can also do much more to support children to make them less vulnerable to exploitation. That means ... tackling unconscionable levels of child poverty (Kristoff, 2020).

Although it is beyond our ability to comment on their marketing strategies, an investigative report on Pornhub was featured on CTV's *W5* (first aired April 3–4, 2021). It showcased the story of a 14-year-old girl who had been directed on Skype to remove her clothes and perform sexual acts. She later found her video had been posted on social media and several pornography sites, including Pornhub. The report told of her difficult struggle to have the video removed. Because her full name was posted, she still received calls from men who wanted to contact and abuse her 10 years later. We thank CTV for their revelations about the scope and perversion of such commercialization and the insidious social damage of such a movement.

Pornhub was reported by *W5* to receive up to 115 million daily visits. Ninety per cent of their scenes contained at least one act of aggression against women, such as gagging, strangulation, rough anal sex, hair pulling, spanking, and spitting on her face.

The infiltration of Pornhub into mainstream culture was demonstrated by an ad circulating on social media before Christmas 2021, albeit produced in 2015. A young man is shown presenting a gift to a lonely older gentleman, possibly a grandfather, thereby creating a tender bonding moment. One can only imagine the later delight of Grandpa alone in his recliner, patting his crotch while fixated on the results of his Pornhub gift card. At the same time, other family members question whether to leave children unattended in his presence. Is this seriously what we want for our senior generation?

Fortunately, the media also captured the story of Grammy-winning singer and songwriter Billie Eilish, who revealed that she regretted watching porn at a young age because it "destroyed her brain." Nineteen-year-old Eilish began watching when she was age 11 and said pornography distorted her view of sex and what she thought she was supposed to be attracted to. She added, "I'm so angry that porn is so loved, and I'm so angry at myself for thinking that it was OK" (Fieldstadt, Dec. 15, 2021).

In a letter to the RCMP dated March 15, 2021, more than 70 parliamentarians from all parties in Canada called for a full criminal investigation into Pornhub's parent company. The 53 MPs and 20 senators who signed the letter accused MindGeek of failing to report cases of child pornography to appropriate child protection authorities between 2011 and 2020. This came two weeks after a similar request from more than 100 victims claiming exploitive content, including CSAM and sexual assault videos, were posted to websites owned by MindGeek. MindGeek was reported to draw 170 million visitors daily, including 4 million Canadians, and generate $469 million in annual revenue. Though legally headquartered in Luxembourg, the company's main office was in Montreal (Reynolds, 2021).

On April 16, 2021, PayPal confirmed they were cutting off payments for X-videos because the site was used to monetize and distribute content depicting child sex trafficking, rape, and other sex crimes. PayPal cut off Pornhub for the same reasons in the fall of 2019. Thanks to the courageous journalists who elevated the voices of survivors and allowed victims of these sites to share their stories with the world. This is a welcome example of accountability in action (Mickelwait, 2021).

Several companies, including MindGeek, were accused of profiting from exploiting underage and non-consenting young women for years through selling ads and subscriptions. This should not be allowed. When Visa and Mastercard threatened to terminate their relationship with Pornhub, the company took down 80% of its video content, almost 10 million videos. This action suggested that most of the site's content had a questionable origin, or that Pornhub could not verify the age or consent for more than three-quarters of what they were selling.

W5 claimed that many would not have been in question if the sites had been adequately moderated. MindGeek issued a formal statement that they had "no tolerance" for non-consensual videos or exploitation of minors. While several class-action lawsuits work their way through the courts, MindGeek continues to control at least 20 porn "properties."

Shannon Stubbs, Member of Parliament for Lakeland, Alberta, and Arnold Viersen, Member of Parliament for Peace River—Westlock, joined forces Jan. 5, 2021, with an article in the *Toronto Sun*. Referring to MindGeek and Pornhub, "What other industry," they asked, "would be allowed to regulate itself after such a staggering display of negligence that it removed 80 per cent of its videos?"

A sign that public protest can be effective was reflected in a tweet from Laila Mickelwait:

> MindGeek owner of Pornhub with a monopoly on global porn told New Yorker their sites had 54 TRILLION visits in 2020—double Facebook/ Google combined.
>
> Two years later 80% of the tube content is gone & they're on the verge of being shut down for organized crime, child abuse & trafficking [@LailaMickelwait] (June 13, 2022).

$ $ $ $

Personal reflection, Kathy:

I reached the limit of my endurance even researching the depravity of pornography. It is a dark and horrible place I do not wish to visit, even from a distance. I cannot visualize much of what I have read nor bring myself to describe the degradation. I am appalled and humbled by the fact that many women walking the streets of Edmonton, some of whom I call my friends, have endured such unspeakable acts. I applaud those who have risen above their shame at having endured such atrocities, shame that was never theirs to claim, and who speak to educate and spare others.

I am extremely grateful for educators like Gail Dines and Robert Jensen for having the courage to bring the subject of pornography to the light of day on campuses across America. The fetishizing of control, dehumanizing, and objectifying must be recognized for what it is, so that social deterioration can be replaced with healthy values. As Dawn Hawkins, CEO of the National Center on Sexual Exploitation, declared, "Pornography's negative influence on the lives of those who watch … cannot be understated" (Nov. 8, 2021). Responsibility must shift from individuals to the forces who generate and distribute the material. Pornography is incompatible with human love, connection, and equality.

CHAPTER 8:

FOCUS ON OFFENDERS: JOHN SCHOOLS MAKE A DIFFERENCE

WHAT IS SEXUALITY? What is the range of "normal" expression between partners? How do we ensure mutuality and consent?

It is fair to say most people wish to be respected and cherished in their relationships with family, friends, and community. The monetization and degradation of what could be an act of intimacy creates a spiritual void.

Victor Malarek, in the foreword to *The Johns* (2010), asserts that the world of men fuels the demand for commercial sex:

> We will not be able to successfully eradicate sex trafficking without fundamentally challenging the demand for commercial sexual exploitation.... Ending demand cannot be achieved without the eradication of male privilege, which lies at the heart of the commercial sexual exploitation of human beings. This remains one of the most urgent under-addressed social injustices of our time (vii).

Paul H. Boge echoes Malarek's point in *The True Story of Canadian Trafficking* (2018) when he quotes a rescued teen victim:

> The johns make it all possible. Their minds are all screwed up. They believe the stupidest lies. It's like inside their heads they have to justify what they're

doing. I mean, get serious. What self-respecting fifteen-year-old is going to willingly have sex in an apartment? But they get around that by assuming every girl is 18. Then, they figure, it's just money. It's helping her. It's all a lie, but they'll convince themselves of anything because they want the sex so badly. Their minds just go crazy....

So, you have the traffickers lying to us girls because they want money. And you have us girls forming a trauma bond with our traffickers because we want the love so badly and want to stay alive. And the johns convince themselves it's not hurting anyone, because they want to do it with a young girl. And that's the whole cycle. A cycle of lying. Everyone being deceived. Pretty sick, don't you think? (p. 24).

$ $ $ $

The horror and scale of trafficking is mind-numbing. Victor Malarek's 2003 book, *The Natashas: Inside the New Global Sex Trade*, documents hundreds of thousands of women from Russia, Ukraine, Moldova, and Romania who were sold into sexual slavery in the previous decade. The worldwide sex industry was then estimated at 2 million victims. The incomprehensible tragedy of our times is that number exploded to 20 million in less than 20 years.

Some Canadians may find it hard to believe so much poverty and corruption exists in Eastern Europe that many young women accept such terrible risks in seeking livelihood away from their homeland. And yet we are also oblivious to such crimes in our own country.

Victor Malarek was the keynote speaker in Edmonton at a 2009 fundraising event for an anti-human trafficking group building a safe house in Ukraine. Nobody speaks his truth as eloquently as Malarek, as reported in the *Edmonton Journal* (Oct. 19, 2009):

There is a lot of "wink, wink, nudge, nudge" still in our police forces, all the way up to the Crowns (prosecutors) and into the courts. That horse-blinder thinking has got to stop. We have to start looking at the reality that is out there, and the reality is that these women are being prostituted worldwide....

They are the victims of a system that is in place for men, so that you have to decriminalize the women and criminalize the men. Once you do that, you send out the message it is men who are responsible, and you will see things start to change (Florence Loyie, A7).

What will it take to shake the world into awareness? Exploited women are crying to be heard while police, politicians, and even ordinary citizens are placated by "harm reduction" rhetoric. Conspiracy exists worldwide against the young, poor, and ethnically subordinated groups. The sex trade is a vicious, demeaning, and degrading institution of inequality that can never be sanitized by legalizing or decriminalizing it.

Malarek's book, *The Johns: Sex for Sale and the Men Who Buy It,* was released in 2010. It is difficult reading due to the depravity of the customers exposed. On a more positive note, we include Malarek's recommendations for change:

The truth is simple.... If men the world over did not demand paid sex, there would be no need to corral, break, and submit millions of women and children to this dehumanizing existence.

What have these women and children endured to be with these men? The violation of their bodies and the denial of their essence as human beings. What has it cost the "clients," the johns? Nothing more than a few dollars.

Now multiply that by tens of millions of johns the world over. With billions of dollars streaming in, the profits are enormous. To ensure future profits, there must always be enough women willing to enter this so-called profession to satisfy the bottomless demand. Trouble is there never are ... and never will be. The vast majority of women don't relish selling their bodies to survive.

Enter the traffickers, who through brute force ensure that there is an endless supply ready to satisfy the burgeoning demand—women of all ages, ethnicities, shapes, and sizes, women trained to submit to the full range of what johns demand. There's no question about it: the skyrocketing demand has contributed to global sex trafficking...." (pp. 293-294, emphasis added).

So what are we to do? Malarek's suggestions (2010) are simple and straightforward:

(1) **Target the johns:** Teach them what is at stake and hold them accountable for their actions.

(2) **Abandon the fantasy of legalization:** Government-sanctioned "respectability" will never sanitize the violence and degradation women endure.

(3) **Change societal attitudes:** Society must confront how damaged masculinity has become.

(4) **Start young:** We must prevent and re-educate young minds distorted by pornography.

(5) **Educate boys:** They must be taught loving relationships based on respect.

(6) **Enforce the laws:** Pimps and traffickers need to be prosecuted and contained.

(7) **Help the women:** The only avenue of escape is a real job. Society needs to address the economic and social inequities. (pp. 295–297).

Malarek provides a final summation:

This entire social tragedy boils down to one word: *dignity*—the dignity of women and girls worldwide. In prostitution, there is no dignity, no empowerment, or equality in any form. True equality between men and women will always be beyond reach as long as men feel they have the right to rent a woman's body. It is not a right, and it never should be. We need to do everything we can to abolish prostitution (p. 298).

$ $ $ $

STOP, Edmonton's Sex Trade Offender Program, aka john school, began in 1996 from the clear perspective that sexual exploitation harmed individuals, families, and communities. The program began through the collaboration of community mobilization, a responsive police service, and a receptive political structure. Citizens of Edmonton recognized that consumer-driven activity exploited a vulnerable and disadvantaged population. The program hypothesized that if sex-trade buyers were educated about the negative consequences of their actions, some would voluntarily change their behaviour.

Kate Quinn, Executive Director of CEASE: Centre to End All Sexual Exploitation, at a 25th anniversary recognition of STOP, acknowledged the many stakeholders involved:

> May 26, 2021 marked the 25th anniversary of the first STOP (previously known as POP: Prostitution Offender Program) in Edmonton. I would like to honour … the parents and peer educators, the neighbourhood speakers, and the leaders from those years—the Chief Crown Prosecutor, the Police Chief and "Vice" Detectives (now ALERT Human Trafficking Counter Exploitation), the Assistant Deputy Minister of Justice, Alberta Health Services, the Mayor, and City Councillors who approved the POP as a Safer Cities Initiative—and all those who helped get this program up and running in under three months! It was Edmonton's great way of working together to respond to serious community issues that affected so many people, families, and communities.

In 1985, "public communication" replaced "solicitation" as an offence under section 213 of the *Criminal Code*. That legal change extended liability for the first time to both the buyers and sellers of sex. Although provisions existed (from 1892) to protect women from being coerced, and although many "street walkers" were pimped, women bore the brunt of the stigma, arrests, and convictions. After 1985, men in Canada could be charged, providing the opportunity for offender programs. In Edmonton, men facing a first charge of "communicating" (public solicitation) had the option of attending an educational curriculum designed to educate them about the consequences of their actions.

The morning agenda of STOP, the Sex Trade Offender Program, includes information about vice laws and street facts, the ugly reality of pimping, and health risks around sexually transmitted infections. The exchange of money for sex may sound like a victimless transaction, assuming both parties are of legal age, fully informed, and consenting. That scenario, however, is far from the case in most situations. Women are frequently coerced to "work" from circumstances of abuse and desperation and are further brutalized and degraded by buyers.

During education on health hazards, illustrations of cauliflower-shaped growths and open sores are enough to cause even the most careful to cringe in horror and commit to prevention. The point is that both parties are at risk when precautions are not taken. Confidential testing for sexually transmitted infections is provided to participants as part of the program.

The afternoon curriculum moves to the symptoms of sexual addiction and the impact of buyers on community residents and merchants. Volunteers share stories of vehicles cruising around their neighbourhood, needles tossed in their yards, young girls being harassed at bus stops, children playing with freshly used condoms, and parents having to initiate extra safety education in schools to help protect students from these dangers. A volunteer from one of the local Sex Anonymous groups tells his story of addiction and recovery and explains the various support groups available. The day ends with personal stories from previous sellers who describe their harsh and disturbing experiences of exploitation, and from parents who share the anguish of losing children to the street.

All monies raised from program fees in Edmonton are returned to the community, via CEASE: Centre to End All Sexual Exploitation, to help repair the harm caused. Three main support pillars for victimized women are poverty relief, trauma recovery, and education.

Emergency assistance provides support not covered by existing agencies. Counselling programs have been developed, and bursary programs help exited women improve their education.

The good news is that few sex buyers who attend the offender program are charged again with a similar offence. Many men express remorse at the end of the day and appear genuinely grateful for the opportunity to learn a new perspective. They often apologize, admit they were thinking with the "wrong head," confess they now realize the harm of their behaviour, and promise they will never again attempt to buy sex. Some commit to educating their peers, others to seeking treatment, and others to building better relationships with their families.

Thousands of men in Edmonton have been educated over the last 20 years, one classroom at a time. The downside is a continual surge of new arrests. We need more tools to take the message to the larger community. Unfortunately, mixed messaging is created when municipal bylaws are used to circumvent federal legislation, as in several cities across Canada.

Malarek (2010) acknowledges that considerable skepticism exists about whether a one-day course could achieve a difference. To evaluate the program in San Francisco, a research team reviewed two decades of data in California, ten years before and after its inception. The first Prostitution Offender Program began in 1996 and was replicated in other American cities and other countries.

Researchers found that arrest rates after implementation of the program dropped in half and stayed at that level over subsequent years. The program's success was credited to two factors: (1) self-interest of the participants regarding the possibility of health problems, relationship issues, legal consequences, and victimization, and (2) appeal to altruism where empathy for the women is a motivation for change.

After the surprising results of the San Francisco study, the research team turned their attention to San Diego, where a program had been implemented in 2000. Similar results of a sudden drop in arrests were found. Criminologist Michael Shively, primary author of the study, concludes, "The collective evidence strongly supports the conclusion that the john school significantly discourages johns from reoffending." Shively adds:

> I'm in a strange position as a researcher because we usually tend to be skeptical and objective. But when you get results that are extremely positive, you end up sounding like an advocate. I've been doing research for twenty years, and I've never seen a program that works as well as this (Malarek, 2010, p. 266).

Of course, saying the program works assumes that a reduction in demand is seen as a positive consequence. Such an attitude does not necessarily seem to be shared by those who cannot see beyond licensing as "harm reduction." Although a more complete response to sexual exploitation and human trafficking is needed, john schools can be valuable in preventing first-time offenders from becoming habitual users of prostitution (Perrin, 2011).

CEASE provided the STOP intervention 140 times to over 3,200 participants from 1996 to 2021. Of those men, less than 3% were re-arrested (personal communication with Kate Quinn).

It must be noted, however, that with a projected population of 35,000 to 84,000 sexual consumers over those years in Edmonton, the arrest rate represents only a minuscule fraction of probable offenders. As well, only first-time arrestees are eligible for the STOP, although many admit to extensive buying before their arrest. Men savvy enough to use licensed facilities would avoid "stings." An unanswered question is whether regular users in licensed facilities represent a different clientele than those taking their chances on the street or via Internet ads.

Heinz's impression, based on lived experience from 2006 to 2013 within high-end studios, was that her buyers were mostly middle to upper-middle-class Caucasian men, more often than not born in Canada, and employed in professional roles. Cultural familiarity meant they were generally aware of, and able to navigate, both federal and municipal laws to better evade arrest. Their monetary resources allowed them to pay a premium to access protected spaces where no meaningful enforcement of *PCEPA* occurs.

In a polling study (unpublished) of 95 participants from four STOP programs in 2018, Heinz found that 100% indicated on an anonymous questionnaire afterward that they wanted to discontinue buying sex. Their reasons included that the act was not filling the gap as they hoped, they were tired of secrets, and they feared exposure.

$ $ $ $

We are honoured to have a former STOP participant (arrested buyer) share how the program helped change his life. Please read "My Tangled Web—A John's Story" in Part Six, Guest Contributors.

Image credit: Unknown.

PART THREE:

CONFRONTING INDIFFERENCE

WHAT ARE THE COMPONENTS of a healthy society? What does it mean when society allows some members to be bought and exploited? How do we build healthy, equal, and respectful relationships? What kind of world do we want to create and leave for our children?

What does equality mean? How do women achieve equality? How have women been portrayed around the world over time? How does society respond to people who challenge standard morality? Why are there double standards?

Why have women been stigmatized in roles created for them by men? Is there ever a legitimate role for buying sex?

Can life be more than what we have learned to accept? Does evolution continue to teach and what can we learn?

Once you know the truth, you cannot "unknow" it. We ask readers to consider the implications of sexual exploitation worldwide and commit to freedom and equality in their community. We would rather build a world that does not need to heal from its trauma.

> Each time a woman stands up for herself, without knowing it possibly, without claiming it, she stands up for all women (Maya Angelou, *Caged Bird Songs*, 2014).

> Every woman who speaks up is a victory but we need to find a way to make each victory matter to the women who still have no voice (Melinda Gates, 2019, p. 219).

An experiential woman commented in 2005 that King's presentation (to a Senate sub-committee) inspired hope. The woman, who felt trapped in the sex industry, hadn't considered the possibility of social norms changing over time. "But," she added, "twenty years ago no one would ever have believed smoking would be banned in bars, and yet that has come to pass. Change is possible."

$ $ $ $

Readers are also invited to reflect on Juanita's poem "Familial Exploitation—LOYALTY or LOVE?" found in Part Five, Experiential Voices. It tells the sad story of a young girl groomed in her own home.

Maria's story "For My Sisters" also appears in Experiential Voices. Maria shares the trauma she experienced while providing "licensed services" as a student struggling financially.

CHAPTER 9:
GASLIGHTING OF SOCIETY

WHAT IS GASLIGHTING? What is psychopathy? What happens when the thinking of a whole society is controlled? How do we separate propaganda from truth?

What is the essence of our humanity? What are the values we want to embody and teach the next generation? What rights and responsibilities come with our unique status as human beings? Are we not intended to protect and nurture each other to develop our full potential?

Commercial sexual exploitation is part of a long patriarchal tradition of making the female body available for men's pleasure. That some women and children sell their bodies for survival or economic gain is not a judgment against them but an indictment of society and their buyers. It is terribly wrong that impoverished and traumatized women have been and still are stigmatized because of their exploitation.

> When a person can't find a deep sense of meaning, they distract themselves with pleasure (Viktor Frankl).

> Human empathy leading to collective actions saves lives and frees prisoners.... Unlike any other creature on this planet, human beings can learn and understand without having experience. They can think themselves into other people's places.... Many prefer not to exercise their imaginations at all. They choose

to remain comfortably within the bounds of their own experience.... They can close their minds and hearts to any suffering that does not touch them personally. They can refuse to know.... What is more, those who choose not to empathize enable real monsters; for without ever committing an act of outright evil ourselves, we collude with it through our own apathy (J. K. Rowling, Ted Talk, June 5, 2008).

$ $ $ $

Of the estimated 40 million trafficking victims in the world, half are girls and women sold or captured into sexual slavery. We know that every Canadian community has its share. Where are they? Why are they not visible? Some cites have created bylaws to establish illegal brothels for "harm reduction," or so they say. While the limited number of so-called practitioners who accept licensing may benefit from being identified, at the same time, they help buyers remain anonymous and avoid arrest.

Our hearts ache for those who feel they have no other options to meet their expenses, whether feeding their families, debt, or drug needs. It would be much simpler if those choosing to buy and those truly choosing to sell could find each other, and no one else was involved. Unfortunately, the demand for purchased sex far exceeds the availability of autonomous providers, so there will always be a push to expand the market.

So why do we care? Why do we challenge the prevalent myth of empowerment? It is because we believe all women deserve options that do not include sexual servitude and too many are caught in exploitation they did not choose.

There are incredible injustices in the world and any number of causes one could champion. Of course, the environment is important, education and public health are important, mental health is important, a strong economy is important, a secure social net is important, a democratic government is important, and a fair and equitable justice system is important. The common link is human rights. Different people have different priorities, and there are more than enough causes to be shared.

The essential issue is that we live in a world bigger than ourselves, and we are called to make it a better place. By whom are we called? What do we accept as the essence of our human nature? Our instincts are, of course, survival and procreation. Community, creativity, and exploration are also values intrinsic to human nature. Self-centred objectification and commodification appear as a distortion of social evolution.

Gaslighting generally refers to one's reality being obscured. It is a persuasive and widespread form of thought manipulation whereby observers are deliberately and systematically fed misleading information that causes them to question what they know. People experiencing gaslighting may often feel confused. *That doesn't feel quite right. Am I possibly being deceived?* Our preferred default is to assume people are telling the truth. We may question our perception of reality, or even our memories, as we try to balance new information with our intuitive sense of what is reasonable and true. Yet most of us also want to be team players and believe in the common good, so we may cautiously question our own skepticism.

People who gaslight others manipulate reality to their advantage for reasons of power and control. Gas-lighters promoting sexual exploitation may accuse abolitionists of distorted perception (judgmental, fear-mongering), ridicule their attempts to shift observations (moral panic, Dorothy do-gooders), or manipulate support systems to portray victims as less than deserving (oversimplification, bleeding hearts). This can lead those who challenge the status quo to be seen as obstructive rather than proactive.

There is ample evidence that countless sex sellers are coerced, pimped, or trafficked and suffer extensive mental and physical harm due to their involvement. Yet those who support abolition are met with a gaslighting contingent who claim that selling sex can be "empowering." This vocal minority accuses abolitionists of being unsupportive and "anti-feminist." More frighteningly, gas-lighters have garnered political support by suggesting that sellers are primarily and unfairly victimized by "stigma" rather than by buyers, and that stigma can be reversed by decriminalizing buyers.

Gaslight manipulations have grown more complex and potent, making it increasingly difficult for unsuspecting citizens to see the ugly truth behind the facades of "harm reduction" and "empowerment." In the case of commercial sexual exploitation, there are hordes of pimps, traffickers, brothel owners, and pornographers who want to profit from the hidden population of sex buyers. The vocal minority are understandably defensive about their income and anxious about survival.

As the status quo is challenged, those with vested interests rally to strengthen their narrative. The pro "sex work" people want society to believe women willingly participate in degrading and dehumanizing activities for financial gain. Of course, we want safety and respect for all women in all situations. However, this is not achieved, contrary to what the gas-lighters argue, by validating objectification and commodification. Trafficked women worldwide deserve better, as do the men whose life experiences are truncated, by a lack of meaningful relationships, to vacuous sexuality.

In summary, gaslighting is a manipulative tactic used to create an alternative belief system, often through minimalization or denunciation, which causes self-doubt. The antidote is becoming more aware. We respectfully submit that unquestioning citizens are being manipulated by political forces that benefit from the proliferation of commercial sexual exploitation. That would be pimps, profiteers, brothel owners, pornographers, many anonymous consumers, some self-identified "workers," and politicians who want to be seen as "liberal" or "feminist," as if monied objectification was suitable employment. We must be careful that we are not so "open-minded" that there is no room for insight to take hold.

As early as 1949, the United Nations defined prostitution as incompatible with human rights. However, Amnesty International often presents the argument of decriminalization vs. criminalization without considering the Nordic/Equality Model. Those with a vested interest attempt to justify oppressive practices against those with few options. What possible vested interest could Amnesty International have? According to Nordic Model Now! (March 28, 2017), Amnesty International's first draft was written by a pimp who encouraged his friends to ensure its adoption.

$ $ $ $

In the *Archives of Sexual Behavior* (Feb. 5, 2019), Rachel Moran and Melissa Farley present a detailed and well-referenced analysis of their position that prostitution is an exploitive practice rooted in sex, race, and class inequality. They state unequivocally that "prostitution exists *because of* the male demand for it, and racial and economic inequalities render women vulnerable to it."

Regarding the link between trafficking and prostitution, Moran and Farley agree that not all trafficking is prostitution, nor is all prostitution trafficking. However, trafficking for sexual purposes is "coerced/non-chosen/involuntary/pimped prostitution." They note when prostitution is normalized, trafficking increases. In thousands of their own interviews, prostitution was described as "paid rape, voluntary slavery, signing a contract to be raped (in legal prostitution), the choice that is not a choice, and domestic violence taken to the extreme."

Moran and Farley recognize that social vulnerabilities funnel women into prostitution, and poverty is associated with higher rates of sexually transmitted infections (STIs) and greater violence. Even in a legal context, prostitution places women at high risk for HIV when buyers and pimps coerce them into not using condoms. The authors also ask why harm *elimination* is not considered an option: "When social stigma is the only harm addressed, it appears that the goal is to obscure the more severe harms and focus on the less severe, so that prostitution can be promoted as labour."

The harm reduction approach, where "prostitution is assumed to be unpleasant but inevitable," has led to legal changes in some countries. While decriminalization of the person being sold is a positive step, decriminalization of pimps and traffickers is not. Violence from sex buyers, pimp control, and social stigma do not decrease when profiteers have fewer restrictions.

Moran and Farley cite studies concerning legalization in Amsterdam, which indicate it was impossible to protect women from organized crime. In Germany, 95% of the women in prostitution (legalized in 2002) were under the control of others, and many impoverished women were moved from surrounding countries to German cities. Prostitution was decriminalized in New Zealand in 2003. A report five years later found that violence and sexual abuse continued. Exit support was no longer considered necessary because "sex work" was considered a reasonable employment option.

Abuse in prostitution is denied primarily because the money transaction is not recognized as coercive, even though buyers may fully know the sex involved is unwanted. Moran and Farley (2019) emphasize, "Prostituted sex is coerced sex by its nature. The cash *is* the coercive force." Non-compliant sex in every other situation is considered abusive. Capitulation is not to be confused with consent.

Furthermore, as Moran and Farley explain, "in the sexual abuse of prostitution, the tolerance of unwanted sex for material gain is absolutely received as evidence of culpability, and women in prostitution are routinely shamed and shunned for it." They recommend that choice-based exit services should be a priority for feminist abolitionists and pro-industry advocates. The harm elimination/abolitionist model represents a significant shift that holds sex buyers and pimps accountable for harms perpetrated. At the same time, it decriminalizes and offers exit services to those being sold. Suggested benefits of buyer decriminalization have proven to be a myth.

Nordic Model Now! (June 5, 2021) provides a brief history on their website of the "sex work is work" movement. They suggest the sex industry "image problem" began in 1977 when a Swedish project revealed the tragic reality of what men do to women. They state, "Around the same time, feminists in the United States and elsewhere, such as Kathleen Barry and Andrea Dworkin, were making a powerful analysis of pornography and prostitution as key elements in the systematic subordination of women."

Various protest groups sprung up and introduced the euphemism "sex work" as normal and positive. World Congresses were held in 1985 and 1986 and adopted a manifesto demanding the decriminalization of prostitution and pimping. The prevention of HIV/AIDS was promoted by the distribution of condoms to women "at whose door the responsibility for preventing the spread of the disease to punters and their wives and partners is firmly laid" (Nordic Model Now! June 5, 2021).

In the early 2000s, the idea of unions became popular. However, only a small minority of women were formally employed, even in countries where prostitution was legal. Further research suggested that the groups were more interested in changing the image than the industry. Part of the "sex work" discourse focused on attacking feminists, which blocked analytical thinking. Another thread was that "sex workers" were not victims but strong women whose choices must be respected. In summary, Nordic Model Now! (June 5, 2021) reflects:

> In popular culture, it has become something of a taboo to describe someone as a victim of systemic oppression because, by definition, that draws attention to that systemic oppression and implies the possibility of a different system—one in which there is some form of social justice, for example.

$ $ $ $

Moran (June 7, 2021) refers to the trend of viewing "sex work" as acceptable labour as a "tsunami of ignorance." In "Sex Work Ideology as Cult-like Thought Reform," Heinz (2021) challenges the sanitization of sexual exploitation. Heinz argues that many of the strategies used by cult leaders to gain devout followers are similar to those promoted within a commoditized culture of hyper-sexualization.

The first dynamic is that authority lies with the mantra, while accountability lies with the recruited. Within "sex work," buyer anonymity tends to be fiercely protected, regardless of the legislative framework, whereas the sellers are considered willing participants.

The second dynamic is that cults dictate thoughts and feelings while discouraging or punishing doubt. Ideological "sex work" language is loaded with words such as "empowerment," "self-employed," "girl-boss," "fees for service," "flexible hours," and "customers" to reflect the positivity of a narrative glorifying depersonalized sex. The "sex is work" ideology leaves no room for nuance or critical thinking and includes economic and other rationalizations to compensate for dissension within the status quo. Heinz contends that using money to bypass consent is compensated sexual abuse. Genuine sexual consent cannot be purchased (Heinz, 2021).

In addition, cults create an exalted status for themselves, as does "sex work," by insisting sellers are empowered rather than victimized. Any criticism is construed as "us vs. them" and interpreted as anti-choice. "Many people, therefore, feel bullied or shamed into supporting an industry they don't actually agree with to be seen as an ally to the women within it" (Heinz, 2021, p. 53).

Just as cult members may be traumatized through abuse and thought control, so are sellers who believe the commercial sex myth that they can remain unscathed after multiple methodical violations. As Heinz (2021) reflects:

> I have been out of the sex trade for over eight years now but continue to battle dissociation and strong recurring waves of suicidal ideation. Nearly every exited woman I know tells me how she, too, struggles with trauma, anger, depression, anxiety, and numbness (p. 55).

Women deserve to live healthy and happy lives, free from brainwashing and delusions.

One would think an obvious resolution to the debate about the reality of sex selling is to listen to those who have exited or survived. Those with lived experience can speak retrospectively, free of rose-coloured glasses. They generally portray a more meticulous and realistic analysis of what they endured, whereas active "sex workers" tend to be defiant and defensive.

The City of Edmonton reported (2015) that licensing body rub parlours, in contradiction to 2014 federal legislation which made buying sex illegal, was considered regulation of non-accredited massage. This was innocuously defined as "physical external manipulation of the soft tissues of the human body ... in a manner that appeals to or is designed to appeal to erotic or sexual appetites or inclinations." One wonders how much lawyers are paid to come up with such euphemisms, how they live with themselves, and why the mayor and council allow such duplicity. How many ways are there to say "blow job"?

"Consensual workers" make up a small percentage of sex sellers in Canada and probably worldwide. A vocal minority seems determined to be recognized as having the right to objectify and monetize their own bodies as part of the "sex is work" ideology. These so-called gains are unfortunately achieved in a polarized fashion that nullifies and denies the reality of the majority. Moreover, the coerced, pimped, and trafficked are often denied the services "licensing" claims to provide.

Another common gaslighting argument is that buyers must be decriminalized to protect the human rights of "sex workers." Nothing could be further from the truth. Of course, we support that all sellers have access to justice, health care, education, financial support, alternative job training, social services, and information. A full range of services could be offered to sellers without requiring that they be licensed.

Sex sellers in Canada have sadly been stigmatized by social attitudes. Stigma may prevent full participation in society, just as it does for the mentally ill, the disabled, racial minorities, the addicted, and the socially inadequate. However, legalizing the depravity of buyers is hardly the answer. Human rights, in theory, already protect the vulnerable. At the same time, we are responsible for recognizing and implementing those rights. Readers need to remain vigilant against the propaganda of "choice" and "empowerment" permeating much of society. We proclaim and maintain our truth that honouring the dignity of all women excludes availability for sale.

Debra Haak (May 6, 2021), an assistant professor of law at Queen's University, notes that studies tend to reveal a bias depending on the questions asked. For example, responses from women who perceive their activities as "work" may vary considerably from those who have exited the industry, especially those who were trafficked. Studying only one population can result in a snowball sampling bias and distorted data. Policy makers and judges seeking more "empirical" evidence would be well served to ask different questions to discover what they don't know. More research is required from other areas outside of a harm reduction lens. Research must include survivors of commercial sexual exploitation and trafficking if one wishes to understand the full adverse effects of prostitution.

Many women have worked hard for freedom from oppression. In these "liberal" times, it often seems that government colludes with crime and traffickers. It is essential to recognize that men cause more than 90% of violence, and one in three women has been abused by men (Walker & Pugh-Roberts, 2021).

For every step forward, there seems to be one back. The authors were shocked and offended in 2021 when a local organization mandated with public education on human trafficking included a video suggesting that sex trafficking investigations could be misguided, morally suspect, and provoked by "do-gooders." We have chosen not to identify the agency in hopes that permanent rectifications will be made. Despite the common compartmentalization that "victims of sex trafficking are not to be conflated with sex workers," we believe this is not the appropriate focus of human trafficking education.

We acknowledge the right of service agencies to engage in debate. However, that does not change our position that the commercial sex industry is innately dangerous, exploitive to women, and contributes to sex trafficking. We believe it is a serious disservice to the public when organizations mandated to educate about human trafficking overlook concerns about the underlying demand and support "sex work" ideology that expands the market.

Every police department that does not enforce *PCEPA* and every politician who supports "decriminalization" of the sex trade indirectly supports the entitlement of buyers. Men who pay for sex behave as if women and girls are disposable; capitalist corporations that normalize exploitation, rape, and torture through pornography are among the new traffickers.

$ $ $ $

Even from a labour analysis, sex is seen as unacceptable work in many ways. Meagan Tyler, an Australian researcher, author, and lecturer, explores the overlap of sex as work and as possible exploitation. Labour literature identifies four interdependent components of "decent" work: dignity, equality, a fair income, and safe working conditions. These are tied to acceptable forms of labour and are generally deficient in "sex work."

Tyler (2020) identifies 12 dimensions of unacceptability pertaining to "sex work." These are listed below with related commentary:

1. Forced labour: "The sex industry is one of key destinations for the trafficking of girls and women worldwide.... Any clear distinction between 'forced' prostitution and 'free' prostitution is largely an illusion" (pp. 7–8).
2. Health and safety: "There is significant literature detailing both the physical and psychological risks and impacts that people experience in prostitution/sex work" (p. 8).
3. Income: Although seen as a way out of poverty for some, the notion of high income is not the reality for the majority of sellers.
4. Security: Security refers to contracts, benefits and employment protection, promotion prospects, and opportunities for development or training. "Sex workers," even when legal, are generally considered independent contractors rather than employees.
5. Working time: Normal employment benefits include paid annual vacation, rest times, predictable schedules, and protected night work, etc. When "sex workers" operate as

independent contractors, it is assumed they have personal control over their hours worked.

6. Representation and voice mechanism: Where organizations do exist, "there is an ever-present confusion between industry lobbying groups and workers' rights groups.... There is also a significant lack of voice or representation for those who have exited the sex industry and identify as survivors" (p. 9).

7. Child labour: Juvenile entry is routinely documented despite legal prohibitions to the point "it remains difficult to separate out the industry, as a whole, from reliance on coerced labour and child labour" (p. 9).

8. Social protection: Stigma still exists, with providers targeted rather than consumers.

9. Equality, human rights, and dignity: The more profound question is whether "sex work" compromises a human's dignity and worth. Broader questions are why the industry is based on economic, racial, and gender-based inequities.

10. Legal protection: There are significant barriers to protecting sellers, sometimes related to stigma or the lack of meaningful contracts.

11. Family and community life: Lack of a standardized employment relationship means protections are lacking.

12. Work organization: Control over work processes and excessive workload do not apply to private contractors.

In conclusion, if "sex work" exists as a form of unacceptable labour, the case for abolition takes on increased importance because "the existence of unacceptable work is, *itself*, a threat or barrier to the achievement of better working conditions for all" (p. 12, emphasis in original).

As discussed throughout this book, the Equality Model intends to address collective harm by shrinking the market. This innovative policy of reducing violence against women as a class is more comprehensive than attempting to reduce harm to individuals by the regulation of buyers. Phasing out "unacceptable work" would mean the government is responsible for providing sellers with transition support and retraining. "The potential to understand prostitution/sex work as an unacceptable form of work deserves further investigation" (Tyler, 2020, p. 15).

Although some women in Canada identify as being empowered by "sex work," their insistence that they do not "conflate" with human trafficking is not shared by most of the world. OSCE, the Organization for Security and Co-operation in Europe, representing 57 states, including Canada, in North America, Europe, and Asia, exposes the links between trafficking and commercial sex. A 2021 paper, "Discouraging the Demand that Fosters Trafficking for the Purpose of Sexual Exploitation," outlines why measures must be taken:

The first point is that THB [Trafficking in Human Beings] is fed by demand. Sexual exploitation is recognized as both financially lucrative and common, motivated by traffickers making money from men paying for sex from victims. "This means that sex purchasers are the creators of demand that is met by traffickers; while money is paid **to** traffickers, it is paid **by** users of trafficking victims" (OSCE, 2021, p. 10, emphasis in original).

The second point is that addressing demand also counters the many layers of sexual and physical violence faced by trafficking victims, harm which is "highly gendered, overwhelmingly created by men and disproportionately, though not exclusively suffered by women and girls who account for 92% of identified victims of trafficking for sexual exploitation" (OSCE, 2021, p. 10). The conclusion of the report bears repeating: The THB [Trafficking in Human Beings] business model is overwhelmingly based on men paying for sexual services that are frequently provided by victims.

Valiant Richey, OSCE Special Representative, in his foreword to the above-referenced "Discouraging the Demand" paper (2021) addresses the question of who really pays:

> With the global market for the goods and services from trafficking victims generating an estimated $150 billion each year, the question must be asked: Who is paying for these goods and services?

> The answer, as uncomfortable as it may be, is society at large. We, the citizens, residents, businesses, and governments of OSCE participating States, are the consumers who, knowingly or unknowingly, fuel THB within the OSCE region. Our collective purchases of goods and services produced by or extracted from trafficked individuals create the market force that encourages traffickers to exploit women and girls, men, and boys....
>
> It is only by addressing the root causes of trafficking that we can make sustainable progress toward ending it (p. 5).

Society at large is paying for the trafficking market. Only by addressing the root causes can we make sustainable progress to ending trafficking.

Liberal "sex-positive" feminism regurgitates men's rights activist (MRA) rhetoric. Both ideologies assume that a subset of women needs to be available for sexual access. We must create safe places for exited women and survivors of commercial sexual exploitation to tell their stories of the trauma they have suffered. One would hope the work of leading researchers and experts from many countries who collaborated on this project, and survivors' firsthand accounts of their lived experiences, would carry more weight than the vocal minority and the buyers who pay them.

$ $ $ $

Four women, who survived commercial sexual exploitation and successfully exited, share their stories in Part Five, Experiential Voices, as part of their commitment to public education and prevention.

Jenn's story is "Where Do I Belong?" She exposes the factors that led to her being trafficked internationally as a teenager.

Katie (not her real name) presents "Rescued." She speaks of the trauma of "voluntary" entry and the challenges of a successful exit.

Tanya's story "Out of the Shadows" tells of her being groomed as a young teen and enduring many years of horror before being able to escape.

Wendy shares part of her unpublished manuscript "When I Close My Eyes..." She was forced into prostitution by a man she considered her boyfriend.

CHAPTER 10:
PUBLIC HEALTH, SOCIAL JUSTICE, & ACADEMIC CRISES

WHAT IS THE IMPACT of sexual exploitation on the collective health of society? How do we deal with pornography? Poverty? Trauma? Addictions? What does it mean to have a healthy society? What does it mean to be a man or woman with healthy sexuality?

What really happens in "body rub" centres? Is "safety" an oxymoron in the context of sexual exploitation? How can we extend concern beyond those who agree to be licensed? Who protects the addicted, the marginalized, the trafficked, and those with no voice?

What does it mean to live in a just society? What does social and economic equality look like? Is social justice more than legislation? What about enforcement? Is justice different from enforcement? How does our legislative and political system express our social consciousness?

How do we move closer to justice? Has any municipal jurisdiction seriously considered the registration of sex buyers to enhance safety for sex sellers?

Robert Jensen raises similar questions in *The End of Patriarchy: Radical Feminism for Men* (2017):

> Is it possible to imagine any society achieving a
> meaningful level of any kind of justice if people from

one sex/gender class can be routinely bought and sold for sexual services by people of another sex/gender class? If one class of people were defined as 'available to be bought and sold for sexual services', is there any way that class of people would not be assigned subordinate status to the dominant class that does the buying? Is justice possible when the most intimate spaces of the bodies of people in one group can be purchased routinely by people in another group? (p. 97)

We believe that large numbers of women have experienced some form of male violence. Placing the human body and sex in the realm of the market reinforces the objectification of all women. Human beings are meant to belong, not to be purchased. As part of a social community, our health and well-being depend on positive supportive connections in all aspects of our physical, rational, emotional, and spiritual being.

Being forced to repeat sexual acts several times a day without physical desire is sexual violence. Commercial sexual exploitation exploits multiple forms of inequality: the domination of men over women, the rich over the poor, and majority groups over minorities. Trauma can have a collective impact through generations. Justice is about restoring loving awareness and respectful action.

Many people do not want the truth. They only want to be comfortable.

> The interplay of depravity between a prostitute and her client takes on a dizzying array of forms and an infinite number of nuances. These work in combination with each other in a busy spirit of production, and they never produce anything but depravity in a new and different form. Depravity here is self-propagating (Rachel Moran, 2013, p. 75).

> When we tolerate what we know to be wrong, when we close our eyes and ears to the corrupt because we are too busy and too frightened, when we fail to speak up and speak out, we strike a blow against freedom, decency, and justice (Robert Kennedy).

$ $ $ $

Health and safety protection is virtually absent in commercial sexual exploitation. In any other occupation (for example, dentistry) where there is a risk of exposure to body fluids, service providers are required to wear masks, gloves, goggles, and protective clothing. When it is not possible to make work safe in an open society, industries are closed. Standards require employers to rethink working practices to eliminate unreasonable risk.

Health challenges in commercial sex encompass a range of mental and physical concerns. "What's Wrong with Prostitution?" (Nordic Model Now! July 4, 2017b) lists three main health consequences for sellers: (1) dissociation, often including numbing with drugs; (2) post-traumatic stress disorder; and (3) physical injuries, such as chronic abdominal pain due to inflammation, premature aging due to persistent stress, and injuries caused by overuse of sexual organs and orifices or deliberately inflicted by punters. These include vaginal and anal trauma, sexually transmitted infections, and HIV/AIDS. Intersection with addictions is common, as many sellers use substances to cope with their chronic violations.

Implementing a public health approach to sexual behaviour would include identifying and preventing vulnerabilities that can lead to exploitation. These include poverty, addictions, a history of trauma, and social conditioning from media that breeds hyper-sexualization. We need to shift from public nonchalance to questioning the entitlement of buyers to commercialized sex and pornography.

Dines (May 6, 2021) speaks of the danger of girls growing up in a pornography culture. They learn to self-objectify, judging themselves on how they appear to others, and begin to value their worth as dependent on men's approval. Wanting to be seen as attractive and desirable sex objects can lead to increased anxiety, depression, and body-loathing. This sort of culture, unfortunately, provides preconditions for grooming by molesters.

Similarly, the consumption of pornography can impact men's health significantly. Pornography users are often their own worst enemies. They may lower their capacity for intimacy, be more likely to use coercive tactics, engage more frequently in risky sexual behaviour, commit sexual harassment and rape, experience anxiety and depression, become habitual/addicted substance users, and experience erectile dysfunction. Long-term negative side effects may result from short-term stimulation and release. Awareness of such potential harms may persuade some consumers to change their behaviour.

Pornography warps human sexuality (Jensen, 2017) when distorted encounters are presented as consensual. Objectification, hierarchy, submission, obedience, compliance, and systemic pervasive violence become normative. Most men use pornography as a masturbation facilitator, serving as sex education for many young men. Jensen identifies two claims that he initially resisted but came to accept as a pattern that helped him understand the world in which he lives:

1. Patriarchy is the appropriate term to describe the majority of human societies for the past several thousand years, including contemporary U.S. society.
2. Radical feminism is the most coherent critique of patriarchy and should be at the heart of comprehensive radical analyses needed to challenge the domination/subordination dynamic that defines the contemporary world (p. 35).

Jensen suggests that authentic feminism seeks to connect rather than alienate people. Contrast his thoughts about intimacy (May 7, 2021) with the brutal portrayals of pornographic gagging, choking, spitting, and ejaculating (May 6, 2021). Jensen describes sexual intimacy as joining light between partners. Our ongoing quest is to touch and be touched, to be fully alive. Our inability to love is the central hindrance to connection. This inability drives some men to seek escape in a fantasy world of domination and control.

By providing a glimpse of the experiential contrasts between stereotypic pornography and intimacy based on connection, Jensen (May 7, 2021) suggests intimacy as an alternative to sexual exploitation. If we believe in the joy and tenderness of shared intimacy, this can become the cultural and social norm in which young people are educated. Radical feminism advocates dignity, solidarity, and equality as values that support mutual caring and affection.

$ $ $ $

Brené Brown, a well-known researcher of vulnerability, courage, shame, and empathy, argues that dehumanization begins with language. That is, dehumanization is a process through which human beings are seen and represented as enemies and then demonized, rendering them unworthy of humane treatment. Once we see people as "other," conflict is binarized into categories of "good" and "evil," which become increasingly rigid. Most people agree fundamental human rights should not be violated. However, dehumanization creates categories that justify the exclusion of one group over another. We are all vulnerable to the insidious practice of dehumanizing; therefore, we are all responsible for recognizing and stopping it. As Brown (May 17, 2018) states, "If we believe there is good, or at least potential good, in everyone we meet, we need to honor their humanity. When we desecrate their divinity, we desecrate our own, and we betray our humanity."

Language is frequently manipulated to minimize assaults on women and children. Violence within family constellations is called "intimate partner violence," although men reportedly exhibit more physical aggression. Ritualized rape is renamed "sex work" when the terms "choice" and "payment" are introduced. Pimps and society at large use sanitized terms such as "adult entertainment," "escort," and "erotic massage." For instance, Edmonton has "body rub" facilities, just as Detroit has "health spas," to minimize the visibility of commercial sexual exploitation. As long as euphemisms are allowed, the brutality of sexual exploitation remains hidden and ideologically underground. People hear what is presented.

Sanitizing and mainstreaming sexual servitude is an alarming trend. Rather than uniting against commodification and the commercialization of sexual access, society remains largely unaware of the underlying harm and probability of exploitation. The notion of "sex work" appears to permeate culture as an alleged avenue for female empowerment and autonomy for sellers. In fact, it provides a cover for the entitlement and proliferation of buyers.

A registered massage therapist, Christy Kasur (2021) from Edmonton makes the point that legitimate medical and therapeutic massage services must be separated from euphemisms for sex:

> Massage therapy has historically been subjected to harmful, deeply embedded stereotypes that sexualize this health profession. As a result, massage therapists are sexually harassed, propositioned, and sometimes sexually assaulted by clients who assume that any massage has some possibility of access to the massage therapist's body.... It is important that municipalities recognize that their bylaws associating massage therapy and body rub establishments are perpetuating harmful stereotypes.... Municipalities licence body rub establishments out of safety concerns for sex workers. However, making a decision for the safety of one industry (the sex industry) at the cost of another (the massage industry) compromises the safety of massage therapists and has made it an important public issue.... Using appropriate definitions for body rub businesses and clearly advertising that they are bawdy houses or brothels would help clear up any confusion for the public (*The Edmonton Journal*, April 6, 2021, A7).

The more significant issue is that no one, not "even" sex sellers, should be subject to harassment or assault. Having disrespect from buyers "accidentally" carry over to another profession underscores the toxic atmosphere sex sellers face as part of their daily reality. It suggests that misbehaviour on the part of buyers is anticipated and tolerated within the sex industry.

We also acknowledge the frequent failure of social service systems to provide adequate support for those in economic need (Fein quoting Farley, 2021). In countries such as Germany, where many women are trafficked, they often are left without a social service net or basic health coverage. Ingeborg Kraus (June 6, 2021) notes the hypocrisy of serving only those women who "want" to exit. Some trafficked women have been conditioned to have no trust and to see themselves only as a product.

Consciousness raising includes speaking truth to power and refusing to collaborate by using words like "sex work" and "empowerment." We owe it to our next generation to mobilize words like "sisterhood" and "liberation" (Dines, May 7, 2021). Not much has changed in the last few decades. Many years ago, King with respected scholar and researcher Christopher Bagley noted, "While a society based on complete respect and mutuality is recognized as an ideal, this is, nevertheless, the model of health towards which political change must focus" (1990, p. 238).

It seems a mystery why some social causes generate a tremendous outpouring of public support while others remain unnoticed. Nevertheless, certain factors have been identified (King, March 10, *Winter: Moon Shadow* at MissingCara.ca):

(1) the presence of the media and the availability of images after a disaster,
(2) the concentration of victims of a disaster in terms of time and place,
(3) the lack of "otherness" in the victims (i.e., if it could have happened to us), and
(4) the extent to which victims are viewed as "blameless" for the tragedy they suffer.

In other words, media interpretations can shape public response. Victims clumped together tend to be more evocative than individual victims over time. For example, a serial killer is generally considered more terrifying and newsworthy than a subset of the population who kill only once. People are more inclined to be compassionate if they believe a disaster could have happened to them, such as an act of nature instead of intentional malice. Compassion is often mitigated by supposed culpability.

The mentally ill, addicted, and homeless are often considered less worthy because of a perception that they may be responsible for their own circumstances. Through such assumptions, we distance ourselves from the risk of such afflictions. Similarly, commercial sex is often considered a "victimless crime" by those who believe sellers participate by choice. The vocal minority claiming "empowerment" also skews the constrained and traumatic reality experienced by the majority.

$ $ $ $

Personal reflection, Kathy:

Unfortunately, it is easier to write about theories than to provide daily support to a real person suffering from repeated crises of addiction and homelessness. I am continually reminded of the words of Bill Sampson, a torture victim from a Saudi prison. When asked what had been most difficult, he replied, "What was most difficult was having to watch the pain and suffering of someone you love and having no way to stop it." (King, March 12, Winter: Moon Shadow at MissingCara.ca) The experience of helplessness is common among many social advocates.

$ $ $ $

The sale of sexual "services" is a major public safety issue (Walker & Pugh-Roberts, 2021). "Sex work" is not a viable career option. If it were, rape would become the theft of a service rather than a personal assault. In a political society, legislation defines our beliefs and directs our behaviour. Whatever society allows to happen to the least of us can be done to the rest of us.

Carole Pateman is a feminist and political theorist from England known for her criticism of liberal democracy. In *Sexual Contract* (1988), she discusses how patriarchy is affirmed through methods of contractual submission within the Western tradition. For example, marriage affords sexual access to a woman's body and the labour she provides as a wife. Prostitution likewise affirms the right of males to sex. When women's bodies are sold as commodities in a capitalist market, the terms of the original contract cannot be forgotten; the law of male sex-right is publicly affirmed. Pateman (1988) argues that we must be vigilant to the underlying oppression of women sanctioned by any social contracts.

Because buyer anonymity is fiercely protected within the sex industry, it is difficult to hold buyers accountable, regardless of the legislative framework in their respective communities or country. Even in countries like Canada that have adopted Equality Model style legislation, the "sex work" ideology assures predatory men that their "discretion" is prioritized. As a result, licensing cities (such as Edmonton) do not attempt to identify sex buyers, which could help with supposed "harm reduction." Instead, sellers are required to be identified and "licensed." This is especially alarming since sex buyers are responsible for a great deal of harm, and protecting their anonymity allows their brutality to flourish unchecked.

Violence is inherent in the sex industry, and no other industry is so dependent upon a regular stockpile of victims of trauma and abuse. To truly address trafficking and commercial sexual exploitation, it's critical to address the systemic factors that make girls and women vulnerable. These include poverty, gender inequity, racism, child sexual abuse, and the lack of educational and employment opportunities for women and girls globally. Rachel Lloyd is a survivor of Germany's sex industry and author of *Girls Like Us: Fighting for a World Where Girls Are Not for Sale* (2012). She emphasizes that sanctioning an industry that preys upon some of our society's most marginalized and disenfranchised individuals is not the answer.

While the harshness of our systems denies many people adequate economic services, the average sex buyer does not ask who is most in need. Better social nets need to be established for marginalized citizens so they have real options for shelter and security. We must honour the truth of women's experiences (Farley, 2021).

A constitutional challenge of the *Protection of Communities and Exploited Persons Act, 2014* was launched in March 2021 by the Canadian Alliance for Sex Work Law Reform. Whether Canada is required to allow a commercial market for sex is at stake (Haak,

April 15 & May 7, 2021). In choosing *PCEPA* in 2014, the govern-ment decided the commercial market could not be separated into voluntary and involuntary, noting that no policy approach could render prostitution safe. It also reasoned that a legal commercial market was inconsistent with gender equality. The Supreme Court has specifically held that generating business revenue is not a pro-tected right under Section 7 (life, liberty, and security of the person) of the *Charter of Rights and Freedoms*.

Valiant Richey (2021) makes the point that beyond common arguments about a high level of financial abuse, multiple levels of harm, and a highly gendered crime that disproportionately affects women and girls, international law requires Canada to be proactive in preventing sexual exploitation. The Palermo *Protocol*, passed by the United Nations in 2000, and ratified by Canada in 2002, requires that all countries work to discourage human trafficking. Canada is failing its international agreement. Many countries recognize that commercial sexual exploitation is a major factor in expanding the market that human traffickers rush to fill. It is regrettable how Canada has made no genuine attempt to reduce consumer demand, despite its Equality Model legislation.

$ $ $ $

Another disturbing phenomenon is that "sex work" ideology seems to have permeated the hallowed halls of learning. Political correct-ness and groupthink have created an informal censorship discourag-ing further discussion. Abolitionist theory is dismissed as polarizing and contentious.

When it was announced that the University of Leicester in England had published a *Student Sex Work Toolkit* (December 2020), protests began to rally across the Internet. Some claimed the toolkit was a guide to accessing the sex trade and was inap-propriate for an institution of higher education; the university stated it was committed to inclusive learning free from harassment and discrimination. The toolkit explained that consensual acts were legal and non-consensual were not. Students were warned to be aware of stigma and judgment. They were coached regarding the legalities of various concessions within the sex industry.

However, as critics pointed out, there were no warnings about the dangers of grooming or pimping and no resources for those who might want to exit the sex trade. There was no information about potential physical and psychological harm, nor any discussion of gender-based violence contributing to ongoing inequality between the sexes. The *Toolkit* appeared to encourage financially stressed students to consider a dangerous path.

> Call me old-fashioned, but I was sold the notion that going to university was one of the ways a woman could get as far away as possible from ever needing to sell sexual services (Grellbunt, Dec. 20, 2020, posted on a Mumsnet thread).

Nordic Model Now! developed an alternative *Supporting Students Impacted by the Sex Industry … A Handbook for Universities* (released Nov. 17, 2021) to provide students worldwide with a more realistic view of what "sex work" might involve. Heinz was asked to present introductory remarks at the launch. The following are some of the highlights from her speech. She began by sharing a Twitter post from an exited seller:

> I entered prostitution because my dreams of becoming an educated, self-reliant woman were so strong I was willing to do anything. I wish I had known what I thought was an "empowering" way to make fast cash would, in actuality, be what would almost destroy me so many times [@romamarie_] (Nov. 12, 2021).

Heinz continued:

> This tweet … perfectly sums up the plight of so many young women, including the woman I was at the age of 22. Desperate to get the opportunity for an education, for a stable career, and to subsequently be able to live independently, be self-reliant, [and] self-sustaining. To break free of the constraints of

patriarchy and sex-based inequality that are characteristic of women's lives all over the world.

Her tweet also highlights the naivety and ignorance
that so many young people have, not only surrounding the sex industry but also just in general given
their age and limited experiences. External forces
(such as the hyper-sexualization that is strongly
prevalent in pop culture and the media) can be
extremely influential on young impressionable minds.

What messages are we sending to the world about
equality and consent? What messages do we WANT
to be sending?

Increasingly, society is presenting sexual exploitation
as "sex work." Exploitation is repackaged as empowering, liberating, and progressive. This infectious
social narrative comes with an aggressive insistence
for no one to question men being granted unfettered
sexual access to marginalized young people. We
are to somehow readily accept that young women
truly desire to be groped and penetrated by 10
strange men or more every weekend in order to pay
tuition fees.

What is happening, in reality, is nothing short of
compensated sexual abuse. It is unwanted sexual
touching, sexual intrusion, and sexual invasion of
the body [...]

Can there not be but one space remaining within
society, one arena, that recognizes, hones, and
champions women's intellect? A place that equally
welcomes our participation within the working mind
of society, the place where decisions are made,
where the needle gets moved [...]

Universities are capable of doing more to address the
epidemic of sexual exploitation and sexual violence,
and they should be doing more.

Here in Canada, 71% of post-secondary students
reported experiencing unwanted sexual behaviour on

campus last year. That is the majority of students. Seven out of ten.

Given the magnitude of the problem on campuses everywhere, why any institution of higher learning would put out a Toolkit that approves the exact same behaviour because money was introduced is dumbfounding.

But that's what women receive. We receive lip service and band-aid fixes when it comes to tackling the influence of patriarchy upon our lives and our well-being. It is much easier for individuals, and now institutions, to stick to the palatable narrative of "sex work," the labour lens, and to rely upon Choice Feminism as their defence for maintaining the status quo.

If we broadened the conversation and brought forth all of the raw, inhumane, depraved moments, we would be forced to finally acknowledge and address the real root of the problem: male violence against women [...]

Women need and deserve exposure to radical and socialist feminist schools of thought to come to their own conclusions surrounding commercialized sex. Without access to diverse intellectual positions and open communication with others, women are left isolated with nothing but neoliberal "sex work" ideology to draw from. This hinders their ability to make fully informed choices in their lives.

I lecture regularly at colleges and universities here in my city.... After every presentation, there is always a handful of students who approach me and tell me they appreciate being informed of sex trade abolition. It is a position they all say they felt scared to explore until that point because they care about supporting those in the industry, and thought abolition was contrary to that goal.

Therein lies one of the issues. Believing that all women deserve to be treated respectfully and caring about those in the sex industry are not mutually exclusive. We care about those suffering from addiction and hope they can find a more rewarding and healthy life. We care about abused women and children without endorsing their situations. We care about victims of conflict, regardless of their position, without endorsing violence. We care about the poor and the under-employed without endorsing the conditions of society that allow for menial employment.

More importantly, to suggest that women can be "empowered" through sexual servitude implies that financial resources are still controlled by the male bastion and can be accessed from a deferential position. It is time for women to claim the ability and right to control their financial security as equal partners in a social economy. Surely women are worthy and capable of earning their own money without having to rely on selling their bodies.

On March 25, 2022, Nordic Model Now! announced that the Economic and Social Research Council (ESRC) of the UK was no longer funding the controversial "student sex work toolkit" or training. This is an example of a timely protest having an effective impact.

$ $ $ $

The discrimination and challenges faced by one Canadian university student who dared to question the status quo are presented by Anna Slatz. Her "Class Conflict" is found in Part Six, Guest Contributors.

CHAPTER 11:
COMMUNITY & FAMILY INITIATIVES

IF WE ALL BELIEVE in human rights and support women's autonomy over their bodies, can we work together?

Why do some minority groups react with such hostility to main-stream advocacy of abolition? Is there a way to accommodate those who choose to be monetized within the larger context of protecting women from objectification?

It is time to focus on societal and economic inequities that create buyer vs. seller scenarios. Connection requires commitment. Connectedness is key to transformation. It is vitally important to discern the facts of survivor trauma from fictions of "empowerment" that detract from the insidious depravity of sexual exploitation.

> Ending criminal penalties for sex workers is long overdue, but it's crucial to guard against exploita-tion as well.... Too often, however, the issue is framed as black and white.... This binary outlook fails to recognize a third, more thoughtful approach to the issue.... The true progressive solution is to work toward eliminating this harm and reducing the number of people involved in the industry by offer-ing them services, housing, and other exit strategies (Yasmin Vafa and Tina Frundt, 2021).

$ $ $ $

Everything old is new again. In 1984, the *Edmonton Journal* featured a four-part series on what was then called "juvenile prostitution." It was estimated that at least 50 children were selling sex on the streets of Edmonton and in shopping centres around the city. There were stories of older girls trying to discourage youngsters from getting into the "business," well-dressed men in expensive cars cruising neighbourhoods, pimps trolling for vulnerable girls in malls, the difficulty of prosecution, and limited funding for interventions. Alarmingly, in 1992, the Edmonton Police Vice Unit identified as many as 250 children being exploited (personal communication with Kate Quinn).

The provincial government responded with the *Protection of Children Involved in Prostitution* legislation in 1999, appropriately renamed *Protection of Sexually Exploited Children Act* in 2007. Social agencies responded by opening Safe Houses and Outreach Programs for exploited youth.

The City of Edmonton designated several one-way streets to slow the circulation of john traffic in targeted residential areas. In 1994, bylaws were introduced to regulate "adult entertainment," with the intent of harm reduction. The objective was to ensure that men could access "services" in facilities where minors and trafficked persons were not officially involved. While creating a dual system of "regulated" and "underground" may have made sense at the time, the city's insistence on maintaining such duality was questionable after the federal government introduced legislation in 2014 to criminalize consumer demand.

Although city bylaws set the tone for separating voluntary from involuntary sellers, there was no further attempt to provide services for the non-licensed adult populations other than through charitable organizations. That incongruity continues to the present, as the "we are not victimized" voices obscure the larger reality and absolve municipal jurisdictions of further responsibility.

CEASE, the Centre to End All Sexual Exploitation, dates back to the launch of Edmonton's first john school in 1996. Operating with a skeleton staff under the guidance of Executive Director Kate Quinn and a dedicated board, this small agency became the voice of hope for a disadvantaged and often misunderstood population. Over and above their signature program, now known as STOP: Sex Trade Offender Program, the CEASE organization has served as a social catalyst, expanding the city's capacity to respond to issues related to sexual exploitation. CEASE developed a three-pronged focus: heal the harm, build for the future, and inspire positive social change.

Some of the awareness and intervention programs developed by CEASE include:

An annual Memorial Service, held every August since 2000, is patterned after a Calgary memorial held for Karen Lewis, a 17-year-old victim found there discarded in a dumpster in 1994. The private (not open to the media) memorial is an opportunity for the community to grieve and honour loved ones who have lost their lives through sexual exploitation.

COARSE: Creating Options Aimed at Reducing Sexual Exploitation began in 2002 as a court diversion program aimed at women for whom sexual exploitation is a root cause of their conflict with the law. Women who want to make positive changes receive support to work on personal plans.

I CAN, an empowerment workshop, was developed in 2003 and continued to 2021 for women serving sentences at the local correctional centre. This workshop helped women break the cycle of addictions, homelessness, and exploitation by exploring options and opening doors to community resources.

A signature fundraising event, Men of Honour, was developed in 2006 to recognize and celebrate the contributions of men who support women's full integration and equality in all aspects of society. Since that time, over 100 men have been honoured.

Public awareness was recognized as key to changing attitudes. In 2000, a public awareness campaign questioned, *"When You Buy Sex ... Who Really Pays?"* with bus ads and billboards in several community locations. In 2006, a police initiative, "Report a John," was developed to target sex consumers. Community partners installed signs in impacted neighbourhoods that read, "This community does not tolerate sexual exploitation."

A Roomful of Missing Women, a provocative art exhibit created by British Columbia artist Betty Kovacic to honour the missing and murdered women of Vancouver, came to Edmonton as part of The Works Art and Design Festival in the summer of 2008.

CEASE has been an active member of Edmonton's Sexual Exploitation Working Group, a collaboration of diverse organizations that offer public awareness and tools for change. The first Sexual Exploitation Week of Awareness was held in 2009, with several educational events each year.

Building Blocks for Women and Families was developed in 2010 to help mothers with children in their care establish financial and social stability through coaching, peer support, and poverty relief. Participants generally experience challenges such as childhood trauma, physical illness, or unstable housing.

Project STAR: Support-Transition-Action-Recovery provides court support to sexually exploited persons who have been victims of crime, validating that many sellers are abused or raped over and above their expected transactions. Advocates help individuals know their rights, prepare for criminal proceedings, and access services.

Y-Step: Youth Stop Trafficking and Exploitation Program provided peer-based mentoring for at-risk youth and presentations to school groups. Empower-U is a financial literacy and matched savings program delivered in partnership with several community agencies. Below the Belt supported sexually exploited males and evolved into the CHEW Project: Community Health Empowerment & Wellness.

In 2021 CEASE received funding for a new Safety Coordinator position to help vulnerable women find resources and stability. The position is part of a larger federally-funded framework, including the Alberta Law Enforcement Response Team (ALERT) and REACH Edmonton, to combat human trafficking in Alberta.

CEASE is an excellent example of what can be accomplished by a small not-for-profit agency with a strong vision. CEASE has adapted to many challenges over the years, remaining faithful to its founding strategy of responding to the needs of women active in and exited from the commercial sex industries. With minimal core support, the organization depends on creative funding from project to project and the generosity of donors and volunteers.

$ $ $ $

Political causes are generally not considered charitable work. However, working for human rights is a legitimate philanthropic activity, and there is no more fundamental right than controlling one's own body. Sexual exploitation is a growing concern around the world. As advocates for abolition, we hope Edmonton will be a model of healing and prevention.

The following examples illustrate some of the many initiatives created by individuals and organizations across Canada:

1921: One hundred years ago, Soroptimist International was founded as a global volunteer network. It now numbers about 72,000 club members in over 100 countries, advocating for human rights and gender equality. They have branches in many Canadian cities and are active in assisting survivors of sexual exploitation and the agencies who support them.

1989: RESET (formerly Servants Anonymous) began in Calgary for women wanting to leave the sex trade. The agency has grown to offer many programs to facilitate and support safe exits from sexual exploitation.

2000: An international conference, "Answers to Action: Healing Sexual Exploitation and Prostitution," was held in Edmonton, the first global conference of its kind.

2001: The RCMP established Project KARE to investigate "high-risk" missing persons in Alberta.

2004: The Sisters in Spirit campaign was launched by the Native Women's Association of Canada to increase awareness of the many missing and murdered women across our country.

2007: ACT Alberta, the Action Coalition on Human Trafficking, was established in response to a growing concern about human trafficking in the community. Their vision was an Alberta free of human trafficking, and their mission was to increase knowledge and awareness.

2009: Trisha Baptie, community organizer and activist in Vancouver, started EVE: formerly Exploited Voices now Educating, a group of commercial sexual exploitation (CSE) survivors who consider prostitution a form of violence against women.

2010: Defend Dignity began as an initiative of the Christian and Missionary Alliance in Canada (about 440 local churches) to end sexual exploitation in Canada through awareness, advocacy, and support for survivors and active sellers. "Legalization will only continue to suffocate the voices of our most vulnerable women" (E.D. Glendyne Gerrard).

2010: Glendene Grant founded MATH: Mothers Against Trafficking Humans following the disappearance of her daughter, Jessie Foster, at age 21 after she was groomed and taken from Calgary to Las Vegas.

2011: Jacqui Linder, a psychologist trained in trauma therapy, established Chrysalis Network, a free hotline staffed by volunteers for victims of human trafficking.

2012: Daughters Day in Edmonton was initiated by the Canadians for a Civil Society to recognize the achievements of women.

2014: As previously discussed, the *Protection of Communities and Exploited Persons Act* was passed. Many thought this federal legislation would herald significant change, but it has been only sporadically enforced across Canada.

2015: Rachel Moran, the author of *Paid For: My Journey Through Prostitution*, was a guest speaker in Edmonton, hosted by REACH Edmonton Council for Safe Communities. REACH graciously donated a copy of Rachel's book to the first 40 attendees.

2016: After reading Rachel's book, Kathy King was so impressed that she purchased an additional 50 books over the next year and donated them to various community and political leaders, hoping that some might grasp the paradigm shift Moran so eloquently outlines.

2016: Diane Redsky, an Indigenous community leader from Winnipeg, was honoured with the Governor General's Award for strengthening Indigenous families and women's rights. She was later part of a group in 2021–2022 that challenged the Winnipeg City Council to change licensing bylaws for escort agencies and body rub parlours.

2017: Canadian country music artist Paul Brandt championed the #NotInMyCity campaign to raise awareness of human trafficking and to build alliances to create transformational change at the grassroots, practice, policy, and legislative levels. The campaign is guided by five strategic directions (notinmycity.ca, 2017):

(1) building community awareness and action,
(2) advancing leading practice,
(3) empowering individuals with lived experience,
(4) addressing the unique needs of vulnerable groups,
(5) supporting high-risk youth.

While addressing the demand and working toward abolition are not mentioned specifically, advancing leading practice is. This book, while supporting all of the above, also encourages direct action toward ending demand as a critical component of leading practice.

2018: Timea Nagy of Canada addressed the new Global Taskforce on Human Trafficking at the United Nations about her experience of being trafficked to Canada from Hungary.

2020: On the Edmonton Police Service website, "Buying Sex? Rethink Your Choice" was posted for information under Community Policing—Family Protection—Sex Trade Industry. It reminds potential buyers that paying for sex is illegal and can affect their ability to travel outside of Canada. A summary of the legalities and offences is also available.

2020: An online Global Summit, Coalition to End Sexual Exploitation: 10 Days, 100 Speakers, 10,000 Abolitionists, was held July 18–28 in Washington, D.C., hosted by the United States National Center on Sexual Exploitation. We, the abolitionists, seem to navigate a narrow path between those who still stigmatize and criminalize sellers, those who institutionalize and sanction exploitation, and the vocal minority who claim empowerment.

2021: The Canadian Sexual Exploitation Summit: Disrupt Demand was held online May 6–7. This was hosted by Defend Dignity.

2021, June 28: Enbridge Inc., a diversified energy company head-quartered in Calgary and operating across North America with a workforce of more than 1,200 people, made the following statement:

> Enbridge and our contractors have zero tolerance for illegal and exploitative actions. That is why we are joining with our contractors and unions to denounce the illegal and exploitive actions of those who partici-pate in sex trafficking. [...]

> We remain steadfast, united in our commitment to compliance with all anti-trafficking and anti-exploita-tion laws and our zero tolerance for those who seek to deprive others of the fundamental freedoms and human rights. [...]

> We recognize that human trafficking is an ongoing issue in our community and in society as a whole, and we encourage everyone to join us in our com-mitment to working together with law enforcement and government agencies to bring awareness to the victims of these crimes and end this illegal and exploitative behaviour.

2021, Oct. 28: The Joy Smith Foundation launched a National Human Trafficking Education Centre to serve all of Canada, aiding survivors, their families, and service providers. The foundation also provides educational intervention programs for students, teachers, and community organizations. This is in keeping with their stated position that education is the best defence against trafficking.

Interestingly, during the launch, amid an hour-and-a-half of well-deserved accolades and testimonies to the importance of education, awareness, and prevention, there was only one brief mention of sex buyers, and that came from Megan Walker. Another guest ironically noted, "Problems we can't see are the easiest to ignore." Perhaps it took Joy Smith to bring an awareness of human trafficking as a criminal reality in Canada. However, it seems the time has come to turn awareness into action by focusing on the demand perpetuating trafficking.

2021, Nov. 22: The Canadian Conference of Catholic Bishops released a pastoral letter affirming the inherently exploitative and abusive nature of purchasing sex and insisting the practice be criminalized. Their position was based on several foundational principles: (1) the life and dignity of the human person, (2) the rights and responsibilities of the human person, (3) the dignity of work and rights of workers, and (4) options for the poor and the vulnerable.

Casandra Diamond (2019) was one of several survivor voices featured:

> To the people of Canada: For nine long, horrible years, I was trafficked in the sex industry. I was not more than "girl number four," valued only for my outward appearance and ability to please customers. I regularly saw 12-14 men per night. I was punched, slapped, bitten, and worse, all in the name of my so-called "job." My customers wanted the porn-star experience, things that they wouldn't do with someone they loved or respected. My story is not an uncommon one … I can only say that to judge me, you truly need to have lived some of my experiences or have some of my vulnerabilities. But what you do need to know is that this abuse is occurring right in your communities, and you're likely not even aware.

2021, Nov. 22: In a presentation to the Edmonton Rotary Club, Paul Brandt spoke of the importance of hope, the clear connection of homelessness to human trafficking, and the importance of raising consciousness to disrupt human trafficking. He emphasized that sex trafficking can happen to anyone, that 97% of victims are women and girls, 75% were exploited as children, and over 50% of victims in Canada were Indigenous.

Brandt used the pandemic as an example of what can happen when the public and leaders come together to disrupt a threat. Rules change, people change the way they are living, and we see results. "Where is our disconnect?" he challenged. "Do we believe we are immune from human trafficking? Who gets to decide between good and evil?" Paul suggests we are all faced with the choice "to do something right," and he implores everyone to be engaged in effecting change for the betterment of society. Actions that support human rights and freedom benefit society and create ripples of hope.

2021: Diane Sowden, a former Coquitlam school trustee, was invested with the Order of Canada. She was recognized for her leadership in raising awareness of and preventing the sexual exploitation and human trafficking of children and youth. Diane founded the Children of the Street Society in 1995, which continues to host prevention workshops for parents and community organizations.

2022: The Blood Tribe Police Service for Kainai First Nation in southern Alberta, home to 13,000 band members, established Project Kokomi-Kisomm Aakii (Moon Woman) to investigate human trafficking cases while raising awareness of front-line officers. There is evidence of girls and women trafficked from the reserve through Alberta and to British Columbia.

There are undoubtedly many more initiatives that could be mentioned. This small sampling is intended simply to provide an example of the power of individual and community involvement.

$ $ $ $

Examples of initiatives worldwide also illustrate the breadth and scope of what can be accomplished:

CAP (Coalition for the Abolition of Prostitution) International is a coalition of 35 grassroots and survivor-led organizations in 27 countries. They provide direct assistance to victims of sexual exploitation and advocate for the adoption of abolitionist legislation in their respective countries. CAP International believes that prostitution and human trafficking cannot be separated and that fighting the exploitation must also include strategies to protect those being sold.

The 2020 CAP International *Activity Report* outlines four strategies:

(1) "The Last Girl First Campaign" attempts to identify and mobilize the most vulnerable groups in order to give them a voice.

(2) "Human Rights-Based Approach" recognizes prostitution as a violation of human rights.

(3) "Access to Decent Work" aims for work that respects and promotes dignity, health, safety, and well-being.

(4) "Parliamentarians for the Abolition of Prostitution" mobilizes countries to exchange best practices on the adoption of policies.

Dawn Hawkins in November 2021 was appointed CEO of the National Center on Sexual Exploitation (NCOSE) in Washington, D.C. after serving as executive director since 2011. She identifies three main objectives (Nov. 8, 2021) in her vision of a culture that embraces its responsibility to give each human being the opportunity to live life to their fullest potential:

(1) Destabilize the Pornography Industry and Make Pornography Intolerable in Society: "Responsibility must shift from individual accountability alone to holding the forces and influences that generate and distribute the material liable."

(2) Stop Sex Buying to End Sex Trafficking and All Exploitation: "Sex trafficking exists because the male demand for people to buy for sexual use outstrips the supply of those available for purchase."

(3) Protect Children Online: "As adults, we must do better and take a stand for these vulnerable children."

$$\$ \ \$ \ \$ \ \$$

Ending the demand, as discussed, includes conscious value clarification, early education for all youth so that they can recognize and reject sexual exploitation, providing support for families, economic stability for vulnerable populations, increased public education, exit opportunities for those being sold, alternative measures for buyer/offenders, prosecution of pimps and traffickers, and infusion of all activities with a sense of respectful connection.

While rallying a common vision and cause, discussion skirts around the question of what alternatives to human trafficking we seek. Do we want to end the entitlement of buyers or do we simply want to ensure that all sellers are informed and willing? It is relatively easy to agree that no one should be trafficked into sexual exploitation against their will. That still leaves the bigger question unanswered. Harm reduction is not enough. We need to eradicate the beliefs and behaviours that cause harm.

What can the average citizen do? A recent article (Robson, 2019) suggested that a successful nonviolent campaign requires 3.5% of the population to be actively involved. In fact, "those engaging a threshold of 3.5% of the population have never failed to bring about change."

That is our challenge. The population of Canada is just over 38 million. Earlier discussion suggests Canada is home to at least 2 million sexual consumers. That means they have already surpassed the threshold of critical mass of influence, as evidenced by their infiltration into social media and political thinking. The irony is that sexual consumers are not even working for their own self-interests, having convinced the vocal minority to advocate on their behalf. If JUST, the Standing Committee on Justice and Human Rights (2022), is any indication, it seems the vocal minority have endeared themselves to the NDP, Liberal, and Green parties within Canada. Any support of "sex work" by default endorses the sexual entitlement of buyers.

That means we need more than 2 million people to join the abolition movement and promote dignity, respect, equality, and the end of sexual purchase. The issue is more important than simply not being a consumer. It is critical to be a vocal part of the solution, to stand up and be counted rather than acquiesce to theoretical inevitability. We believe we have the numbers. We need the previously "neutral" or undecided to join our ranks to ensure effective change. Advocacy can include a range of activities from educating others, supporting end-demand movements, and volunteering, to working on legislation and improved service delivery for trafficked victims and exited sellers.

Community initiatives inspire and support legal changes. As Perrin (2011) explains, laws are important for at least two primary reasons. First, they express the values of a society. Secondly, they can instruct behaviour to produce positive changes over time.

> Government alone cannot solve the problem. The solution lies in a community response—and the realization that we all share in the responsibility to end trafficking and restore Canada as a safe and prosperous society for all of its citizens and newcomers (Perrin, 2011, p. 218).

The history of legislation in Canada is discussed in the following chapter.

CHAPTER 12:
HISTORICAL & POLITICAL PERSPECTIVES

HAS TRAUMA SEEPED THROUGH generations of history? How have women been treated around the world? Why are sellers rather than buyers traditionally stigmatized in the provision of sexual performances? Has the new PCEPA legislation changed that? How has the history of legislation evolved in Canada?

Can we move beyond judgment to understanding? Is it possible that good hearts sometimes choose poor methods? Is there a way to come together to support women without being separated by ideological judgments?

What do we, as citizens of Canada, want our legacy to be? Do we want a Canada that protects the dignity of women and girls or a Canada "opened" to commodification and sexual licence?

What is the legislative response in Canada to human trafficking? Is it enough? How do we convince Canadians that the existing PCEPA legislation is progressive? Why is it being ignored? Why are we reluctant to address the existing and growing demand for commercial sex? Is the sheer number of buyers intimidating? Is it because someone we know would be implicated?

What about social complicity? What can we say about jurisdictions that provide protection to offenders through bylaw creation?

Who are the people who have made a difference? What are they doing? Why is there political resistance? Do we believe that because a few women claim to be empowered by providing sex on demand, we can ignore the plight of the majority? Why is so much documented trauma ignored in favour of individuals claiming the right to "work"?

Historically, men's pursuit of unreciprocated sexual release has projected itself unto indebted, enslaved, and exploited women. Women rightly want to shed the shame and stigma that was never theirs to bear. However, it does not help to reduce predatory behaviour to an economic model. Women who choose payment are not spared harm by the self-centred indulgence of men. At what point do we say, "Enough is enough"?

> As women, we must stand up for ourselves. We must stand up for each other. We must stand up for justice for all (Michelle Obama).

> As we have learned during the pandemic, leaders must have the courage of their convictions, but unfounded convictions can have terrible consequences. The law is not always clear. Wisdom and confidence require humility, openness, listening to different points of view, and commitment to rational thought-provoking dialogue to arrive at truth and the real story in our complex world. We are all called to be leaders in our own way (former Chief Justice Beverley McLachlin, Leadership address, March 9, 2021).

$$\$ \ \$ \ \$ \ \$$$

Traditionally, history has displayed a tendency to criminalize and stigmatize sex sellers without consideration of their circumstances. Past and current events indicate that economically disadvantaged children are often groomed or trafficked for sale and that women and others with limited survival options become caught in the sex industry.

The laws of both France and England shaped norms and legislation before Canada became a country in 1867. Research into early 19th century Canadian legislation suggests citizens were as divided then as now about whether to treat prostitution as inevitable or coercive. Three distinct approaches of regulation, prohibition, and rehabilitation were all marked with racial and gender discrimination. Diseased women were confined to hospital as a public health measure although treatment of sexually transmitted disease was ineffective. Prohibition statues were enforced primarily against sellers, and women tended to receive longer incarcerations in the name of rehabilitation (Constance Backhouse, 1985).

Following confederation, laws began to form and dealt principally with pimping, procuring, operating brothels, and soliciting. Women under age 21 were protected from "defilement." Adult prostitution was not a criminal offence, and control was administered indirectly through vagrancy and bawdy house laws. The first *Criminal Code* in 1892 made it an offence to procure women "for unlawful carnal connection." However, such activity was largely tolerated in the Prairie Provinces. Brothels existed in most developing cities of Western Canada, with action by authorities limited, for the most part, to dealing with "public nuisance" or criminal complaints.

James H. Gray's down-to-earth account, *Red Lights on the Prairies* (1971, 1986, 1995), describes the brothels and "boozeries" that accompanied the development of the railway across the prairies in the late 19th and early 20th centuries. This was a time when immigrants were primarily young single men whose sexual dalliances seemed to be tolerated in the growing communities. As Gray explains, "In Edmonton, as elsewhere, the Mounties generally left the girls alone as long as the houses were operated with reasonable decorum," and it seemed "the police and the madams mutually accepted a system of fines in lieu of licence fees" (p. 114).

There were, of course, concerns of minors being recruited, unsuspecting women being tricked into losing their virtue, and tension between politicians and police as to how the brothels were best to be accommodated. During one period of lax enforcement, "word went out that Edmonton was back in business," and predictably, "as the town opened up, the underworld scum quickly moved in to take advantage" (Gray, 1995, p. 130). The pattern seems to continue; as tolerance for paid sex increases, traffickers rush to fill the male demand for expanded "services."

Around 1890, religious groups and early feminists began campaigning against brothels, condemning them as "social evil" and the "white slave trade." Threats of their brothels being raided resulted in women moving from established addresses to the streets (Gray, 1995). Changing demographics and government control of liquor were two main factors that shaped life in Western Canada after the first World War (1914–1918). As the population became more settled, with fewer single men, public opinion shifted to censure women providing sexual access. Prosecution and punishment of so-called deviant women became the status quo for many decades.

In 1927, five women from Alberta gathered to petition the Supreme Court of Canada to be recognized as "persons" in Canadian law. How disheartening that nearly a century later, in seeming contradiction to personhood, other women are lobbying to be commodified "without stigma."

In 1972, the vagrancy definition was replaced by Section 195.1 of the *Criminal Code*, which stated, "every person who solicits any person in a public place for the purpose of prostitution is guilty of an offence." Such a focus on sellers allowed police to "bust" desperate and emaciated women in the name of justice.

Street activity was considered a "plague." The Fraser Committee on Pornography and Prostitution (1983–85) considered three options: criminalize, decriminalize, or regulate. Recommendations from the Fraser Committee had elements of all three strategies. Prostitution was described as a social problem that required legal and social reform. For the first time, underlying economic and social issues were addressed.

The "common prostitute" provision of 1972 *Criminal Code* (section 164.1) was replaced in December 1985 with Bill C-49 (section 195.1) which criminalized communication "in a public place for the purposes of prostitution." The significance of this new law was that it was gender-neutral and act-specific, which meant, for the first time, male purchasers could be charged. The Edmonton Police Services, in what was considered "fair" at the time, attempted to target equal numbers of sellers and buyers.

With the C-49 Review (1987–90) came the recommendation that justice, health and welfare, and employment agencies develop holistic programs for those wishing to leave street solicitation. Bill C-15 (1988) made it an offence to to pay to rape a minor and increased the maximum penalty to 14 years for anyone convicted of living off the avails of a minor.

In response to social pressures, the City of Edmonton, in 1994, chose to license "body rub" facilities, escort agencies, strip clubs, and peep shows. This was done to reduce the involvement of minors and organized crime. Other cities followed suit. Most failed to realize that "licensed services" merely created an additional layer to the existing scenario. Unlicensed activity continued to thrive within the more relaxed attitudes of acceptability. It is also probable that some organized criminal operations simply found ways to comply with regulations to appear legitimate.

Licensing cannot ensure that a corresponding unlicensed subset will not exist, one probably frequented by consumers less motivated to play nice. We cannot be blind to the fact that unlicensed activity is rampant; a broad spectrum of "independents" includes the self-governing, the desperate, the addicted, and the trafficked, all competing for consumer dollars. It is crucial to find a way to extend the recommended "harm reduction" services, such as peer education, condoms, STI testing, and health and safety information, to this more hidden population of sellers.

Sweden became the first country in the world to pass a law that prohibits the purchase of sex, the *Violence Against Women Act* (*Kvinnofrid*) which came into force on Jan. 1, 1999. This was an attempt to address the root cause of prostitution and trafficking, namely the men who felt it their right to purchase sex. The legislation was considered ground-breaking at the time. Buying sex was officially acknowledged as part of the continuum of male violence, and the legislation was an attempt to move the country to full gender equality. The government also pledged assistance to women via shelters, counselling, education, and job training.

In 2002, Canada signed the United Nations Palermo *Protocol to Prevent, Suppress, and Punish Trafficking in Persons, Especially Women and Children, 2000*, signalling its agreement with global initiatives against human trafficking. However, the country did not have any of its own legislation until 2002 with the *Immigrant and Refugee Protection Act*. Finally, in 2005, the *Criminal Code* was amended to include the offence of human trafficking. As Perrin (2011) comments, that is just the beginning:

> Canada needs more than a human trafficking offence on paper. It needs Crown prosecutors who are willing to pursue these charges with vigour where evidence exists, judges who fully appreciate the enormous damage that offenders exert on their victims and a public that recognizes the pervasiveness of the crime, coupled with an insistence that offenders receive appropriate punishment (p. 131).

$ $ $ $

After years of court challenges and appeals, the Supreme Court of Canada, in its *Canada (AG) v Bedford* (2013) decision, ruled the laws related to "sex work" were unconstitutional. While prostitution itself was not criminalized, keeping a bawdy house (section 210), living off the avails (section 212), and communicating (section 213) were named offences. The Supreme Court ruled that these restrictions imposed dangerous and unsafe "working" conditions and gave the government one year to draft new legislation.

Innovative new legislation was created in the form of Bill C-36, which harmonized with the human trafficking legislation. The *Protection of Communities and Exploited Persons Act, 2014* was introduced in June, approved by Senate on Nov. 4, and came into effect on Dec. 6, 2014, the National Day of Remembrance and Action on Violence Against Women. Unlike previous legislation, this law recognizes the social harm of commodification. It seeks to reduce the demand for sexual services by targeting those who buy sex. A visionary response to exploitation was achieved. Finally, Canada had the legislative capability to criminalize the men who buy sex, as well as the pimps and human traffickers who supply the market.

The preamble to Bill C-36, the *Protection of Communities and Exploited Persons Act, 2014*, states:

> Whereas the Parliament of Canada has grave concerns about the exploitation that is inherent in prostitution and the risks of violence posed to those who engage in it;

> Whereas the Parliament of Canada recognizes the social harm caused by the objectification of the human body and the commodification of sexual activity;

> Whereas it is important to protect human dignity and the equality of all Canadians by discouraging prostitution, which has a disproportionate impact on women and children;

> Whereas it is important to denounce and prohibit the purchase of sexual services because it creates a demand for prostitution;

> Whereas it is important to continue to denounce and prohibit the procurement of persons for the purpose of prostitution and the development of economic interests in the exploitation of the prostitution of others as well as the commercialization of prostitution....

Across Canada, many saw this as ground-breaking, others as antagonistic. Some columnists reiterated tired rhetoric about the world's "oldest profession" and "personal choice," as if the women involved were free and equal players throughout history.

A notable exception was Kevin Hampson, whose column appeared in the *Edmonton Sun* on June 18, 2014. He pointed out:

> Legalized prostitution also leads to higher rates of human trafficking, according to a study of 150

countries by three economists. Again, this shouldn't be surprising; of course, human traffickers are going to set up shop in places where there's an unfettered consumer demand for female meat....

Our disapproval of cannibalism, slavery, and prostitution had nothing to do with consent or lack of it. We disapprove of these things because they turn people into objects, denying their inherent value as human beings. Permitting them would be socially destructive.... (p. 15).

Unfortunately, the federal government changed shortly after Bill C-36 was declared. The new Liberals minimized the *PCEPA* legislation as partisan, and it remained an empty promise, never rolled out or universally enforced across Canada. The City of Edmonton barely shrugged at the dramatic shift of focus and chose to maintain its status quo of licensed "body rubs" and "adult entertainment".

$ $ $ $

Advocates supporting the Nordic/Equality Model, on which the Canadian legislation is based, emphasize the impact of racialized, gendered, and economic oppression. The following considerations underscore commercial sexual exploitation as part of the continuum of violence against women.

(1) Human rights: Millions of women and children worldwide are trafficked yearly into sexual servitude. The extent and horror of this tragic reality are trivialized by the vocal minority who claim that it does not "conflate with their right to sell sexual services."

(2) Social justice and economic equality: Systemic drivers must be recognized. Until marginalized and disadvantaged women are given equal opportunities for education, employment, and social support, they remain vulnerable to predators.

(3) Best practices: Education, awareness, expanded exit strategies, and preventative initiatives are required. Focus on purchasers must be part of reducing demand.

(4) Pornography as a public health crisis: The growing association of sexual stimulation with degradation and violence creates unrealistic expectations of relationships and perpetuates demand.

A countermovement to end the criminalization of buyers sadly exists. Women who claim the right to choose "sex work" do not want their customers penalized. A group called The Canadian Alliance for Sex Work Law Reform launched a constitutional challenge in April 2021, claiming the new legislation continues to put "sex workers" at risk because they are operating in a context of criminality. These discussions do not fully address what and who perpetuates the harm and the inherent dangers within the market.

Human trafficking and commercial sexual exploitation have captured the world's attention in the 21st century. The many women and children who were coerced and trafficked into the sex industry far outnumber the few sellers who claim to engage freely. If we as a society turn a blind eye to their plight, we indirectly sanction consumer demand. We need to develop protective legislation and meaningful interventions.

$$\$ \ \$ \ \$ \ \$$

As previously noted, Canada passed legislation in 1985 that degenderized "communication." It allowed buyers to be charged, although many municipalities introduced "licensing" to provide immunity for a select population of purchasers. Highlights of the last 25-plus years are recognized, with changes in government noted for reference.

(June 2, 1997: The Liberal party won its second majority government under Jean Chrétien.)

1997: In one of its more questionable decisions, Human Resources Development Canada introduced the Exotic Dancer Visa Program to allow foreign women to work in Canada as "burlesque entertainers" and "buskers" in strip clubs after club owners allegedly reported a shortage of Canadian strippers. This allowed a surge in the trafficking of foreign "exotic dancers" from Eastern Europe, who were fast-tracked into Canada for "employment" in the sex industry. After an extensive investigation, hundreds of criminal charges were laid against club owners in 2000. The number of permits declined dramatically after 2004, and the bill was finally scrapped in 2007. The trauma of some girls and young women during that time is powerfully illustrated in the story of Timea Nagy, *Out of the Shadows: A Memoir* (2019).

1999: Sweden was the first country in the world to introduce legislation prohibiting the purchase of sex. This became known as the Nordic or Equality Model.

2000: The United Nations Palermo *Protocol* provided an international definition and philosophy just in case anyone wasn't clear. Human trafficking was defined as (1) the recruitment, transport, transfer, harbouring, or receipt of a person (2) by such means as the threat of use of force or other forms of coercion, abduction, fraud, or deception (3) for the purpose of sexual exploitation, forced labour, removal of organs, servitude, or slavery.

(Nov 27, 2000: The Liberal party won its third consecutive majority government under Jean Chrétien.)

2002: Canada endorsed the Palermo *Protocol to Prevent, Suppress and Punish Trafficking in Persons, Especially Women and Children* and added its first human trafficking prohibitions under the *Immigration and Refugee Protection Act*.

2003: The RCMP Project KARE task force was established in November to investigate the disappearance and deaths of 79 women from the Prairies and Territories. "Sex trade workers" (STWs as they were called at the time) were invited by Project KARE officers to provide their names, addresses, next of kin, and any identifying information to be kept on file to aid the investigation if or when more bodies were found. If deaths could not be prevented, identification might at least be facilitated.

(June 28, 2004: The Liberal party was re-elected to a minority government under Paul Martin.)

2005: On Nov. 25, Canada amended the *Criminal Code* (section 120) to include offences for Trafficking in Persons, in addition to 2002 Immigration legislation.

(Jan. 23, 2006: The Conservative party won a minority government under Stephen Harper.)

2006: Canada created temporary residence permits for international victims of trafficking.

2007: Motion M-153 was unanimously adopted by the House of Commons to combat human trafficking across international borders.

2008: Canada launched a Human Trafficking Hotline with Crime Stoppers.

2008: Canada's first human trafficking conviction was based on a guilty plea.

2008: Norway and Iceland adopted the Nordic Equality Model.

(Oct. 14, 2008: The Conservative party won a second minority under Stephen Harper.)

2009: In January, Joy Smith (Member of Parliament for Kildonan— St. Paul in Manitoba 2004–2015) introduced Bill C-268 to amend the *Criminal Code*, requiring a minimum five-year sentence for convicted child traffickers; the bill was adopted on Sept. 30.

2010, July: The United Nations General Assembly adopted The Global Plan of Action to Combat Trafficking in Persons.

(May 2, 2011: The Conservative party won a majority government under Stephen Harper.)

2012: Canada launched a National Action Plan to Combat Human Trafficking, including a special RCMP Enforcement team.

2013: Court challenges, claiming provisions of the *Criminal Code* violated the right to constitutional security for "sex workers," led to the *Canada (AG) v Bedford* decision.

As previously mentioned, in December 2013, the Supreme Court of Canada ruled that three provisions of the *Criminal Code* violated the *Charter of Rights and Freedoms* and were struck down. The three laws were s. 210, keeping a bawdy house; s. 212, living on the avails of prostitution; and s. 213, communicating in public. These were seen to violate the right to security of the person. The government was given one year to design new legislation and, appropriately, chose to curb demand by criminalizing buyers.

2014: In response to the heartbreaking story of Rehtaeh Parsons, the Conservative government passed the *Protecting Canadians from Online Crime Act* to stop the non-consensual distribution of intimate images and to empower courts to remove them from the Internet.

2014: In response to the *Canada (AG) v Bedford* decision, Justice Minister Peter MacKay, amended the *Criminal Code* to include Bill C-36. *PCEPA*, the *Protection of Communities and Exploited Persons Act, 2014*, specifically recognized objectification of the human body and commodification of sexual activity as social harm. Buying sex became a criminal offence. Sex sellers, for the most part, were granted immunity from prosecution, although some argue that is not the same as decriminalization. The hope was that these sanctions would reduce or eliminate the market.

Any legal response is ineffective without education and enforcement. Sadly, this legislation in Canada was largely ignored. Municipal compliance could have required notice to licensed facilities, a moratorium of new licences, phasing out of existing leases, and public education such as "don't be that guy" promotions. Billboards, editorials, and curriculums could have been developed to include consent and ethics. Registration of buyers could have been implemented.

2015: Ontario Premier Kathleen Wynn requested a constitutional review of *PCEPA*. Attorney General Madeleine Meilleur found that the new laws held "no clear unconstitutionality."

Nevertheless, many cities across Canada continued to circumvent federal legislation with bylaws licensing various sexual "services." Sellers who became licensed were named, registered, and subject to bureaucratic visibility stress (Heinz, 2020b). A parallel unlicensed market continues to thrive where the desperate and controlled are sold at reduced rates. Buyers operate largely undeterred, except where a few police forces conduct stings based on *PCEPA*.

(Oct. 19, 2015: The Liberal party, which had campaigned against *PCEPA*, won a majority government under Justin Trudeau.)

2015: Northern Ireland adopted the Nordic Equality Model.

2016: France adopted the Equality Model, the fifth European country to do so.

2017: The Republic of Ireland adopted the Equality Model.

2017, July: #NotInMyCity, chaired by Paul Brandt, began as a campaign geared toward raising awareness of human trafficking.

2018: Conservative Member of Parliament Arnold Viersen launched the All-Party Parliamentary Group to End Modern Slavery and Human Trafficking to unite parliamentarians across political lines.

Viersen gained a sort of infamy in February of 2020 by asking a female NDP colleague if she had considered "sex work" for herself after she spoke on behalf of the "sex work is work" voices and against the criminalization of buyers. Viersen was hoping to make a point about the nature of the activities under discussion. Interestingly, the media blew up at him for questioning what she was advocating.

The Member, Laurel Collins, somehow concluded that Viersen's question denigrated all women. In contrast, her support of the sex trade (albeit for others) was supposedly a way of keeping them safe. As Viersen said at the time, "I think this makes the point. I do not think that any woman in this country ever chooses this as a job. This is something they are trafficked into. This is something we have to work hard to end in Canada. Prostitution in Canada is inherently dangerous" (Maloney, Huffingpost.ca, Feb. 4, 2021).

2019: The National Strategy to Combat Human Trafficking 2019–2024 was released on Sept. 4 and echoed many politically correct themes.

The four pillars (4Ps) noted were prevention, protection of victims, offender prosecution, and building partnerships. However, "the Government of Canada also met with representatives of sex-worker organizations in Ottawa to hear their views on the importance of not conflating human trafficking with consensual adult sex work and the challenges faced with current approaches to law enforcement" (Appendix C). Subsequently, *PCEPA* legislation was conspicuous by its absence in the extensive report.

(Oct. 21, 2019: The Liberal party won a minority government under Justin Trudeau.)

2020: Ontario released a strategy to combat human trafficking.

2020: Israel adopted the Equality Model legislation.

2020: Feb. 20, Alberta launched a Task Force to Combat Human Trafficking and ambitiously announced a nine-point Action Plan with a report due in 2022, again without mention of the *PCEPA* legislation:

(1) Adopt the Palermo *Protocol to Prevent, Suppress, and Punish Trafficking in Persons, Especially Women and Children*;

(2) Create a provincial task force to bring together representatives to share information and coordinate action;

(3) Increase efforts to educate the public and report tips;

(4) Ensure appropriate training for judges, prosecutors, and first responders;

(5) Ensure the Ministry of Labour provides information to temporary foreign workers in Alberta about their rights;

(6) Work with community groups and other provinces to collect and better share data;

(7) Name and shame traffickers by publishing the names of businesses found to have knowingly facilitated human trafficking;

(8) Lobby the federal government to strengthen penalties against human traffickers;

(9) Introduce legislation to establish a restraining order process and to proclaim a Human Trafficking Awareness Day.

2021: Feb. 22 was adopted as National Human Trafficking Awareness Day by unanimous consent in the House of Commons. It was the first time a Human Trafficking Day of Awareness was recognized nationally in Canada.

2021: A constitutional challenge was filed March 30 against six key provisions of *PCEPA* (impeding traffic, public communication, purchasing, materially benefitting, recruiting, and advertising).

The danger is that a constitutional challenge may be argued on a sanitized "hypothetical" basis, with "expert" opinions given more weight than evidence from actual cases (Haak, May 7, 2021). When more attention is given to "rights" over infringement, empirical evidence fades into insignificance. We can only hope the judicial decision will be well reasoned and demonstrate a complete understanding of all circumstances.

2021: The town of Newmarket, Ontario, on June 22 passed new regulations for body rub parlours, essentially banning "storefront sex businesses." In what was reported as a "proud, proud day," Newmarket Town Council voted to support federal legislation and enforce desired community standards (Quigley, *Newmarket Today*).

(Sept. 20, 2021: The Liberal party won a second minority under Justin Trudeau, albeit with only 31% of the popular vote, a lower share than any other winning party in history.)

2022: Winnipeg City Executive Council, on Jan. 19, after an extensive seven-month study listening to all stakeholders, unanimously voted to repeal bylaws that licensed body rub parlours and escort agencies. This aligns with Manitoba's Sexual Exploitation Strategy and federal legislation.

2022: Following the vote of the Executive Council as above, the City of Winnipeg voted Jan. 27 to end business licensing of "body rub" parlours and escort agencies. Winnipeg was Canada's first major urban municipality to take this bold step. It is possible.

2022, June 20: The report, Five Years of Accomplishments for #NotInMyCity, was released, celebrating a significant shift in aware-ness, educational programs, and community cooperation.

$ $ $ $

Awareness and condemnation of sex trafficking is an important first step, but distinct hypocrisy prevails if we do not address the under-lying issue of consumer demand. It is not difficult to agree that sex trafficking exists and that it is wrong. The unanswered question, however, is: What alternative do we seek? Do we believe that com-mercial sex should be eliminated? Or do we believe that sex buyers have the right to "serviced" by seemingly informed and seemingly consensual sellers?

A significant question is whether the law needs to be based on theory or practice. Although some argue that an agreed-upon sexual exchange between two parties of equal status could be non-exploitive, the introduction of payment is intrinsically coercive. Global evidence suggests that sellers and buyers rarely share similar social and economic statuses. Many sellers are entrapped against their will, and most are likely to experience considerable trauma as a result of their forced participation. One must look to the law to protect those already marginalized and vulnerable, trafficked or not.

In the spring of 2022, the Liberal government conducted their promised *PCEPA* review by the Standing Committee on Justice and Human Rights. Several days of hearings were held from February through April 2022, with 48 witnesses heard and 72 briefs received. Passionate arguments were presented from different perspectives, while several committee members made no attempt to conceal their pre-existing prejudices. Many advocated for retaining and strength-ening legislation that criminalizes the purchase of sexual "ser-vices" and provides exit options for sellers. Others, unfortunately, advocated decriminalization of buyers, claiming prostitution is not inherently exploitative.

Suzanne Jay, with Asian Women for Equality (awcep.org/abolition-of-prostitution), provided a brief summary (March 4, 2022) that the issue is not about the so-called "sex workers" but rather an insidious global network pandering to and expediating buyer demand:

> The sex industry is not a homogeneous group. There are the exploiters, and there are the exploited. The exploiters' side is composed of sex buyers, pimps, and the media platforms that support the sex buyers and pimps to connect with each other. These people are overwhelmingly men, and they have a vested parasitic interest in growing prostitution as an industry.

The sex industry is not about empowering women. It is evident, however, that many buyers, pimps, and profiteers are threatened by attempts to curtail commercial sex and have strategically recruited sellers to their cause.

The Standing Committee on Justice and Human Rights released its report on June 22, 2022, with 17 recommendations. We agree with #1, which calls for more extensive consultation. We disagree with #2, which states that the Act causes serious harm to those engaged in prostitution by making the activity more dangerous. Arguments supporting that premise are puzzling and suggest sellers find it more challenging to negotiate with consumers who know they are criminalized.

We note that the use of labour language throughout the report tends to obscure the vulnerability of many who may be duped or deceived by the subterfuge of acceptance. This also sways public perception towards a more benign interpretation.

Further recommendations include (#3) repealing the sections related to communicating and advertising, (#4) monitoring court cases, (#5) encouraging data sharing, (#6) strengthening other measures in the *Criminal Code*, (#7) strengthening the *Criminal Code* on exploitation and trafficking, and (#8) building trust between police and sex sellers. Studying how a more consistent application of *PCEPA* could be encouraged (#9) is particularly significant, as the "review" was mainly based on hypotheses.

Additional recommendations call for (#10) changes in the *Immigration and Refugee Protection 2001* regulations, (#11) addressing the exploitation of migrant sex workers, and (#12) ensuring the most vulnerable sex workers will not experience disproportionately negative impacts from any changes. This would mean adequate resources and social nets for those wanting to exit. The Government of Canada is called upon (#13) to fully implement Calls for Justice from the MMIWG National Inquiry.

The final four recommendations focus on the need for social programs. It is recommended that (#14) any changes be preceded by funding agreements for programs related to sex workers' health and safety, (#15) support programs that address root causes, (#16) funding be provided for non-judgmental and trauma-informed services for sex workers, and (#17) additional supports be made available for vulnerable youth and individuals wishing to leave the sex industry.

Interestingly, no buyers were consulted or appeared in the process of this review. Support for *PCEPA* was presented by individuals and agencies who spoke to the global harms caused by consumer demand and felt curtailing demand was necessary for the protection of society. Challenges to *PCEPA* were presented by disgruntled sellers who felt their livelihood was threatened by criminalizing buyers.

$ $ $ $

Sometimes, although infrequently, charges are successfully laid against pimps who disguise themselves as "friends." One such case happened in Alberta. Wendy, in Part Five, Experiential Voices, shares part of her Victim Impact Statement which she was allowed to present to the court after the men controlling her were found guilty of various offences.

Installation by Andrea Heinz: Displayed in several locations in Edmonton on Sept. 28, 2021.

PART FOUR:

MAINTAINING MOMENTUM

HOW DO WE SUSTAIN wellness and healing? What is freedom? How do we move from stigma to dignity and respect?

What can we, as Canadians, do to improve economic equality and opportunities for marginalized populations? How do we reconcile the lack of poverty relief with gendered violence? Do we really want to keep part of the population vulnerable?

Why does this sometimes feel like war? Are gentle goals a compromise? Don't we want everyone to win? How is that possible when there seems to be such polarity? How do we build a more inclusive and accepting society? Is it possible for all members to have secure and happy lives?

How do we meet the needs of children and youth who have been trafficked and exploited? What services do we provide? How do we support the strength and resilience of families? What about prevention? Is that enough?

Peace comes from security within ourselves and families, respectful and loving relationships, and meaningful connections at a spiritual level.

Commercial sexual exploitation is a major obstacle to a free, respectful, and egalitarian society because it creates physical and emotional harm to individuals, is based on objectified relationships, and is devoid of spiritual energy.

> [Human trafficking] ... is a huge battle that needs a global response, from individuals to industries to nations. It requires that we do everything from educating our children—boys and girls—on respectful relationships, self-confidence, peer support, and [becoming] trafficking savvy, so they are less vulnerable to being lured, all the way to eliminating the acceptance of sex as a commodity. We need to de-normalize using pornography, hosting bachelor

parties with strippers, and visiting strip clubs or "massage parlours" as male rites of passage or merely "boys being boys" and then go more deeply into why there is so much demand in our society for sex work. If there wasn't the demand, there wouldn't be the supply (Timea Nagy, *Out of the Shadows*, 2019, pp. 333–334).

$ $ $ $

Our final section deals with collective actions moving forward in a positive direction. The Missing and Murdered Indigenous Women and Girls Inquiry report released in June 2019 calls upon Canada to recognize the sacredness of Indigenous women by making amends for a dark colonial period during which they were devalued and dehumanized.

We consider the challenges of distorted masculinity that are part of our patriarchal heritage and applaud men working to change themselves. Men and women must work as allies in forging a new path.

As the voices of many exited women and survivors proclaim, an essential shift is required to free all human beings from objectification and commodification. Marginalized citizens of the world deserve a life where they are not sold, and we, as a society, must ensure that sexual exploitation is never a last resort for survival.

Finally, we review the best practices for ending sexual exploitation and human trafficking. As we build a more equitable and loving society, we must be aware of the many possible dimensions of development, prevention, education, legislation, enforcement, exiting, rehabilitation, resilience, spirituality, and global advocacy.

CHAPTER 13:

MMIWG, CANADA'S SHAME & CANADA'S CHALLENGE

WHAT DID the MMIWG Inquiry reveal? Why were grave injustices done to our Indigenous people? How do we free ourselves from a colonial mindset and become inclusive?

What does it mean to be a sacred being?

How do we honour the missing and murdered while building for the future?

The Medicine Wheel, a symbol of peaceful interaction and connection among all living beings on Earth, lends itself to limitless interpretations and teachings. In Medicine Wheel tradition, time and space are circular; Sacred and Life are one. All power comes from the Creator at the centre of the unbroken circle. As days and seasons mark changes in time, there is an endless connection to the past, present, and future. Four directions reach to embrace all people of Mother Earth, supported and united by healing energy. Dimensions of body, mind, heart, and spirit balance the journey of Creation and the seasons of life (Kathy King, *Seasons of Life* at MissingCara.ca).

I am a strong Maliseet woman. I am content. If there ever comes a time where I disappear... where I go for groceries and do not return... where I go to run other errands and do not return... please know I did not voluntarily leave my family. I am not out partying. I did not go and commit suicide somewhere. If I ever DO NOT return home... know that someone took me against my will or worse. Do not make excuses as to WHY I might not have returned home, because it is a lie. Look for me. Please.

Being an Indigenous woman in Canada, there is a target on my back. I feel it, I really do! Too many of our women are disappearing (Erin Brooks, Nov 22, 2018, Facebook.com/emb.19830524).

$ $ $ $

In Indigenous wellness, wholeness embodies physical, mental, emotional, and spiritual dimensions. It is important to know and remember how Indigenous women lived and were honoured in their traditional roles and communities. The high numbers of incidences of sexual exploitation among Indigenous women is an example of a broken tradition.

Non-Indigenous citizens must respect the sensitivity of our Indigenous neighbours who have lost loved ones. Often, missing and murdered family members are judged, stigmatized, and blamed for their helplessness. Multiple factors contribute to vulnerability, as we have discussed. Racism, colonialism, systemic segregation, gender discrimination, and economic inequality are all factors.

Although citizens today are not responsible for historical decisions, we must acknowledge that so-called assimilation efforts were attempts to destroy the Indigenous nation. Reconciliation requires that we consciously attempt to restore equality through personal and government action. The structures of colonial violence, racism, marginalization, White cultural dominance (Eurocentrism), and institutional status quo continue to exist.

The alienation of First Nations people in Canada dates back to colonialization. The first wave of treaties occurred from 1871 to 1877, involving what is now southern Manitoba and extending north and west. In 1876, the *Indian Act* defined who was "Indian" and declared them legal wards of the Canadian Government. Residential schools were established to assimilate Indigenous children into the dominant culture by destroying their connection to family roots.

Children as young as four years old were required to attend these boarding schools. Indian agents or the Northwest Mounted Police (precursors of the RCMP) were instructed to forcibly remove children from families who would not comply. The schools were operated by churches; about half were Catholic, and the rest were from various Protestant denominations. Children were stripped of their traditional clothing, given uniforms and new names, and subjected to unfamiliar regimented schedules. They were forbidden to speak their own language and were often subject to horrendous punishments and abuse. Eleven such schools were established in Canada by 1880. Over 130 residential schools operated between 1831 and 1996, with 80 at their peak around 1930. An estimated 150,000 children attended across Canada, and an estimated 6,000 children died.

As colonization, capitalism, and patriarchy spread across Canada, First Nations women were also subject to controlling and compromising situations. There are historical reports of women enslaved, kept in brothels, and relegated to "country wife" status before the arrival of European women (Annemarie Tocher, 2012).

At this writing (2022), many unmarked graves are being discovered around former school sites across the country. Whether or how accurately the deaths were recorded is unknown. Documentation and translation would have been complicated due to the children having been given residential names different from their birth names. Oral history suggests many families were never informed about what happened to their children. The unmarked graves are a reminder of the genocide committed against Indigenous children and the dishonouring of Indigenous people that continued.

$ $ $ $

A Women's Memorial March was held on Feb. 14, 1991, in Vancouver to commemorate the more than 50 missing women in that city. Early investigations into their disappearances stalled, in part, because no bodies were found. Reports were finally taken more seriously after a joint RCMP-Vancouver police probe in 2001. Robert Pickton, then age 52, was charged in 2002 with six counts of first-degree murder, while 20 more charges were later stayed, and one was quashed. Of the only six charges that proceeded to trial, Pickton was found guilty of second-degree murder in December 2007.

Warren Goulding explored the surprising lack of media attention concerning another serial killer in Saskatchewan and his three young victims. They had been missing for two years before their bodies were found in 1994. Goulding's book (2001), *Just Another Indian: A Serial Killer and Canada's Indifference*, speculates that the accused maintained relative obscurity because the women he killed were Indigenous, notwithstanding that he had served 10 years for a 1981 murder and was a suspect in three others.

Goulding's (2001) investigation uncovered a more disturbing reality:

> The search turned up nearly five hundred women, reported missing in the previous three years, who matched the general criteria of age and background of the Saskatoon victims. Officials later disputed that number, but the number itself was almost irrelevant. Whether it was one hundred or five hundred, it was clear that something like an epidemic was raging virtually unchecked in western Canada (Goulding p. 33).

As distressing as it is to think that bodies could be raped, mutilated, and left exposed to the elements, social indifference is even more frightening. We may rationalize that people who murder make up a disturbed or malicious minority. However, the lack of outrage, that so many missing and murdered women could disappear over the years, is incomprehensible.

It is an indictment of our victim-blaming mentality that a whole population of vulnerable women can be exploited and discarded without public outcry. Thankfully, several initiatives have evolved to help create awareness of the challenges facing Indigenous women.

$ $ $ $

Sisters in Spirit was launched by the Native Women's Association of Canada (NWAC) in March 2004 to raise public awareness about the high rates of violence against Aboriginal women (as they were named at the time). Sisters in Spirit coined the term "racialized sexualized violence," recognizing women were targeted because of their ethnicity and gender. In Canada, racialized sexualized violence is associated with cultural isolation, the legacy of the residential school system, and societal indifference. Sisters in Spirit vigils, organized by NWAC, are still held annually on Oct. 4.

The first Memorial March for the Missing and Murdered Women of Edmonton, patterned after the Vancouver event, was organized by community activist Danielle Boudreau and took place on Feb. 14, 2006. Memorials continue to this day in many cities under various formats.

The first Stolen Sisters Awareness Walk in Alberta was created in Edmonton in May 2007 by April Eve Wiberg. The walk recognizes missing, murdered, and exploited women and girls targeted as visibly Indigenous.

NWAC's March 2010 report, *What Their Stories Tell Us: Sisters in Spirit Research Findings,* was one of the first attempts to document information about Indigenous women's deaths and disappearances and identify the impact of colonization. The study looked at a database of 582 Indigenous women and girls across Canada known to be missing or murdered at the time. Most cases identified were from the western provinces, with more than a quarter (28%) from British Columbia. Most of the collected data is confidential, except for 14 individuals whose life stories were shared.

The limited number of cases reflected only 30 years of history. Further limitations were that missing women may not have been reported due to a mistrust of authorities or simply not recorded due to deficient policing practices of the time. There was also no assumption of an investigation even if a report was noted.

The conclusion of the NWAC 2010 study guided the MMIWG Inquiry:

> Aboriginal women continue to be the most at-risk group in Canada for issues related to violence and continue to experience complex issues linked to intergenerational impacts of colonization and residential schools. Ending violence against Aboriginal women and girls lies with both men and women, with both Aboriginal and non-Aboriginal communities, as well as with all levels of government. It ends with recognition, responsibility, and cooperation. Violence against women ends with restoring the sacred position of Aboriginal women as teachers, healers, and givers of life.

In October 2010, the five-year project ended, and a second phase, "Evidence to Action," was funded. In 2013, the RCMP began developing their own database based on NWAC, the research of Maryanne Pearce (2013), and Statistics Canada.

From their internal confidential (nameless to the public) data, a 2014 RCMP report, *Missing and Murdered Aboriginal Women: A National Operational Overview*, counted 1,181 victims (including 164 missing) over the previous 33 years (1980–2012). It reported that the rate of missing and murdered women was four times higher among the identified Indigenous population. However, this population represented only 4.3% of Canada. This means the social impact of 1,017 homicide victims over 30 years within the Indigenous community would be the equivalent of over 23,000 murdered women across Canada and over 27,000 women if we include the 164 reported missing [calculation based on the number of victims divided by .043]. One wonders if that would be enough for the general population to take notice. Similarly, one wonders if society would have paid more attention if over 1,100 accountants, lawyers, or teachers had gone missing. It is generally believed that many cases of missing women were not investigated or even recorded due to alleged police bias.

$ $ $ $

The REDress Project began in 2012 by Jamie Black as installation art, an aesthetic response to the national issue of murdered and missing Indigenous women. Black, a Métis artist based in Winnipeg, sought to create increased awareness of social and political events with her work. She explained:

> Through the installation, I hope to draw attention to the gendered and racialized nature of violent crimes against Aboriginal women and to evoke a presence through the marking of absence.... The colour red is a very important sacred colour, the only colour spirits can see. Red is a "calling back of the spirits" of these women and allowing them a chance to be among us and have their voices heard through their family members and community (*CTV News*, 2014).

Black's original intention was to collect 600 red dresses to be installed in public places as a visual reminder of the women who are no longer with us. The first year of the REDress Project was remarkable. Exhibitions were installed at the University of Winnipeg, Manitoba Legislature, the University of Ottawa, Thompson Rivers University, the University of Manitoba, and the University of Alberta.

In 2014, a permanent exhibition, "From Sorrow to Strength," was installed at the Canadian Museum of Human Rights in Winnipeg. The site of the museum is considered sacred ground by First Nations people, who came to trade there long before the Europeans. The exhibition features an image of dozens of red dresses in a forest of mostly birch trees.

The Museum of Human Rights is close to the Red River, in which the body of 15-year-old Tina Fontaine was found in 2014. Fontaine, a reportedly "troubled" child in and out of youth shelters, had been reported missing on Aug. 9. On Aug. 17, her body was found wrapped in a plastic bag and recovered from the river. Her story symbolized failures in the child welfare system and the lack of protection for vulnerable girls. A 53-year-old man was charged with second-degree murder and later acquitted in February 2018.

Rinelle Harper, also aged 15, lived to tell the story of her attack. Her family had moved to Winnipeg from northern Manitoba in 2014 for better educational opportunities. That November, Harper was celebrating the completion of high school midterms when she became separated from her friends. She was attacked by two young men, sexually assaulted, beaten, and thrown into the freezing Assiniboine River. She was miraculously rescued, survived, and became an advocate for missing and murdered women.

October 4, the National Day of Vigils, is one of the days when the public is invited to display red dresses as a show of support for missing and murdered women. Hundreds of Sisters in Spirit vigils and rallies have been held in communities across Canada since 2010. May 5, 2018, was first declared in the United States as the National Day of Awareness for Missing and Murdered Indigenous Women and Girls and is also known as "Red Dress Day" in Canada. Many memorial exhibitions have been created.

In Edmonton, the Redress Photography Project was created in 2015 by local photographer Mufty Mathewson. She assembled over 30 individuals to photograph red dresses in various locations. Subsequent exhibits were displayed in many locations around Alberta for several years, with Mathewson often invited to share her story.

$ $ $ $

On Dec. 8, 2015, the Government of Canada announced an independent inquiry would be launched to address the missing and murdered Indigenous women and girls. It was to be a two-phase approach; phase one was a consultation on the design by the Government of Canada, led by Crown-Indigenous Relations Canada. More than 2,000 survivors, family members, loved ones, and service providers participated in 17 pre-inquiry meetings across Canada. The official launch began on Sept. 1, 2016.

Earlier in 2016, then Minister of Indigenous and Northern Affairs, Carolyn Bennett, stated to the *Globe and Mail* (Feb. 17) that the numbers of MMIWG were "way bigger" than 1,200. The names, however, are still confidential, so families have no way of confirming if or how their loved ones are included and counted.

Gladys Radek, co-founder of Walk4Justice, claimed to have collected more than 4,000 names by 2011, of whom between 2,500 and 3,000 were Indigenous. All vulnerable women must be considered to determine the additional risk of racial heritage, addictions, mental illness, exploitation, and homelessness. If an ethnic bias exists among those who share such vulnerabilities, further implications for both cause and prevention must be considered.

Maryanne Pearce completed the first comprehensive and fully public list of missing and murdered women as part of her doctoral dissertation in law, *An Awkward Silence: Missing and Murdered Vulnerable Women and the Canadian Justice System* (2013). Pearce spent seven years cross-referencing newspaper articles, police websites, court documents, and other public sources.

$ $ $ $

Personal reflections, Kathy:

The National Inquiry into Missing and Murdered Women and Girls came to Edmonton Nov. 6–9, 2017. The Inquiry was to be about truth gathering, and to be meaningful and safe. Despite poor publicity, the opening ceremonies were open to the public. I attended the fire ceremony, offered a prayer bundle to the flames, met Chief Commissioner Marion Buller, and listened to speeches thanking Creator for the sacred gathering and the opportunity for healing. Stories heard by the Inquiry were to be considered powerful and important. It was acknowledged that the MMIWG were a Canadian problem.

Attendees learned there were two rooms for public testimony. The names of those chosen to be discussed were not made public before the meetings started. Therefore, it was only by chance which stories observers heard or did not hear. Family members chosen to testify were required to swear an oath of truth. They were guided through their stories by questions from legal counsel provided by the Inquiry. It was unclear how or why some families were chosen to give public testimony, and others were not.

My first witnessing was testimony regarding the disappearance of Amber Tuccaro. Her family expressed serious concerns that, even in 2010, the investigation of her disappearance by local police left much to be desired. A formal complaint was met with no apology but a reassurance that "policy had changed." One would hope. Recommendations included more outreach to family members, more health resources, and better ways for the Inquiry to contact community members.

Members of the Inquiry offered eagle feathers, gathered from Haida Gwaii, to families who testified. The feathers were to lift their spirits and give them strength in return for their sacred gift of testimony. Families shared stories in which they mentioned their frustrations with reporting and doing their own search through walks, posters, Facebook, and media. They expressed discouragement when police reported investigations were "exhausted" and feelings of anger, fear, and power imbalance.

Although my daughter's story had not been chosen for public testimony, I was invited to present it privately to a statement gatherer. I graciously accepted, supported by three friends. However, as a precaution, I also printed and gifted four copies of Cara's story with my recommendations to Chief Commissioner Marion Buller.

Also, I was humbled and honoured to support a beautiful and brave survivor who chose to testify anonymously at that time. She had been lured into exploitation as a homeless teen, controlled by various organized crime groups, and eventually ended up in the United States with many American politicians and high rollers among her "customers." She created exotic pedigrees for herself while exploited as an escort because, as an Indigenous woman, she was less valued and more at risk for abuse and murder. Even though several years had passed since her liberation, she feared her life could still be in danger if she was identified.

The anonymous survivor revealed later that her turning point came one evening when she was expected to go on a "call" while deathly ill. She was trafficked from a New York City penthouse brothel managed by the Mafia and was marketed as Latino, Italian, and Japanese, with hairstyles to match each persona. Although she was considered one of the "top girls," she knew at that moment the honeymoon was over and she was merely a product in the eyes of her traffickers. She also knew her option was to die in New York City, a "jane doe," because no one would even come forward to identify her body. A friend from home, although a drug dealer, showed compassion with a one-way ticket, and she was eventually able to plot her departure. Exhausted, scared, and under the influence, she finally stumbled back into Canada and was able to slowly rebuild.

She told her story to help the Inquiry understand the elements of cross-border trafficking and organized crime in the disappearance of Indigenous women and girls. At all levels, racism is the underbelly of society.

$ \quad $ $ \quad $ $ \quad $ $

An interim report of the Inquiry, *Our Women and Girls are Sacred*, was published on Nov. 1, 2017, and raised many questions to explore. These included: How do we define violence? What is trauma? What is colonialism/colonization? What is an Indigenous nation? Who do we mean by "LGBTQ2S people"? What was the "Sixties Scoop"?

The report notes (p. 49) that "recent changes to Canadian prostitution laws may have negative impacts on more vulnerable Indigenous women." The context for such a remark is not clear. It seems to allude to skepticism about the *Protection of Communities and Exploited Persons Act, 2014* which is surprising given the disproportionately high incidence of exploitation among Indigenous women. The implication that some vulnerable Indigenous women might benefit from sexual exploitation is extremely alarming and emphasizes the need for social and economic reform.

The 728-page report, *Reclaiming Power and Place,* released on June 13, 2019, is thoughtful and thorough. King spent 11 months composing and posting chapter summaries paired with reflections on her blog on the MissingCara.ca website (June–July & November 2019, March–April 2020).

The introductory principles of the report include:

- Canada needs to challenge institutions that violate basic human rights.
- We need a new decolonized social order.
- Healing centres are needed. The Inquiry marks the beginning, not the end, of the process of healing.
- We need to protect rather than protest. Our women and girls are sacred.
- We need to serve the wholeness in each other and in life.

Sacredness has a multi-faceted meaning of Creator-gifting, Creator-centred thinking, using gifts for the good of humanity, sharing and bringing new life into the community, encompassing the balance of male/female, and following the teachings of kindness, respect, truth, honesty, humility, love, and wisdom.

The report speaks of genocide as the systemic destruction of Indigenous people as a nation and of the sacredness of their women and girls. The Canadian statistics cited indicate that Indigenous women and girls in Canada are more likely to be murdered or missing than other women in Canada. Between 2001 and 2015, the homicide rate for Indigenous women was "nearly six times higher" than for non-Indigenous women (p. 7). The report outlined several ways in which the Indigenous people were targeted:

- Political—the disintegration of existing territorial agreements
- Social—the imposition of a new restrictive justice system
- Cultural—language and customs were forbidden
- Economic—the destruction of their financial base
- Biological—new diseases
- Physical—mass killings
- Moral—attempts to create debasement and unworthiness.

Connection to the land and each other is noted in the report as the source of emotional and spiritual grounding for Indigenous people. When we are connected, we carry one another's pain. We inherit the sense of what happened to our ancestors as well as the wisdom, strength, and courage that helped them survive. Individual healing is grounded in social healing because (1) individual suffering is due to historical trauma caused by colonization, and (2) communities must join in healing activities to create healthy homes. Creator has chosen women to be the portal between the spiritual and physical realm. They are the only force on earth powerful enough to navigate unborn spirits onto this planet.

$ $ $ $

The Stolen Sisters & Brothers Action Movement is a grassroots advocacy movement taking action and raising awareness of the human rights crisis of Missing, Murdered, and Exploited Indigenous People (MMEIP). Their Facebook page (Sept. 21, 2022) states:

> The SSBAM is a 100% Grassroots Movement for Social Justice (grassroots = NO FUNDING).
>
> The Epidemic of Missing, Murdered, and Exploited Indigenous Women, Girls, Gender Diverse, Men, and Boys is a national tragedy and growing human rights crisis (GENOCIDE). Since contact, hundreds of thousands (if not more) of Indigenous people have been murdered, exploited, or have gone missing without a trace. These individuals deserve justice, and their families deserve answers.
>
> Are we not entitled to the same basic human rights as our fellow citizens?
>
> The SSBAM is not funded by government or business. Our mission is to raise awareness (not money), support families and survivors, and help stop/prevent the Canadian Genocide of Indigenous people.
>
> For the past 14+ years, with the support of our community and its citizens, the Stolen Sisters & Brothers

Awareness Walks have been possible. Thank you to all who have stood with us in Love, Justice, and Solidarity.

Formerly named the Stolen Sisters Awareness Movement, the Stolen Sisters Awareness Walk was created in May 2007 and was the first awareness walk in the province of Alberta, Canada, raising provincial, national, and international awareness specifically of the violence and the disproportionate number of missing, murdered, and exploited Métis, Inuit, Non-status, and First Nations Women and Girls.

TAKE ACTION TOGETHER. NO MORE STOLEN SISTERS & BROTHERS.

April Eve Wiberg has been living the spirit of the MMIWG Inquiry for many years. She is an Edmonton activist, human rights advocate, and volunteer who often works behind the scenes. Her traditional name is Medicine Spirit Dancer, and she is from Mikisew Cree First Nation, about 1,000 kilometres north of Edmonton. She was honoured with the Aboriginal Commission on Human Rights Social Justice Award in 2012 and Daughter of the Year Award in 2013 by the Canadians for a Civil Society. Wiberg also received a Rotary Integrity Award in 2017 and was named an Edmonton Woman of Vision by Global TV in June of that year. Another honour was the Esquao Award in 2018 from the Institute for the Advancement of Aboriginal Women, which celebrates exceptional Aboriginal women.

Wiberg provided the following statement as host of Daughters Day on July 3, 2020:

The epidemic of violence affects all races on this continent and beyond. We, as Indigenous survivors of violence, know from our own personal experiences what it is like to be specifically targeted for racialized and sexualized exploitation. There is no shortage of predators and they come in all forms. This is a day-to-day struggle and a systemic issue in all facets of our society that has been allowed to go on for centuries. We as Indigenous people are facing a human rights crisis in regard to our personal safety and security. The time for talk and words on paper is over, the time for action is now!

$ $ $ $

April Eve's story "My Voice is My Power" is found in Part Five, Experiential Voices. She shares the horror of having been groomed in Canada and trafficked to the United States, illustrating a common phenomenon of exploitation being the vehicle, prostitution the destination.

CHAPTER 14:
MASCULINITY REVISITED

WHAT DOES IT MEAN to be a man in today's world? Is there any experience in life more profound than connecting with another human being? What enables men to have healthy and meaningful relationships? Is there power in teamwork, reciprocity, and partnership?

What is a healthy man? If we are interconnected sacred beings, how do we honour the gift of our sexuality? How are we connected to our world? Do our relationships reflect love, respect, and mutual growth?

> There is a big difference between a loud voice and a strong voice. The loud voice of a man who has no inner life and is a stranger to his own grief is never a voice for justice; it's a voice for self-interest, dominance, or vengeance. Strong male voices for freedom and dignity come from men like Gandhi, King, and Mandela who mastered their pain, gave up on vengeance, and preached forgiveness (Melinda Gates, 2019, p. 257).

> Human beings can learn from suffering. Working through our trauma can teach wisdom.... Trauma is what happens inside of us because of bad things that happen. It is a disconnection from ourself that happens when it is too painful to be emotionally connected (Gabor Maté, 2021).

In a world where many women are abused by men, objectified by men, exploited by men, and killed by men, it is important to focus on the good and honourable men among us and to know there are men who support the struggle for dignity, respect, and equality. Justice in North America has been primarily a White male construct, so we need men as allies in shifting legislation and enforcement to better protect women. We need men who are comfortable enough with themselves to cherish respectful relationships rather than domination and pornified objectification.

Hate, violence, and exploitation are signs of a culture in trouble. We need to ratify respect, equality, and dignity for all people world-wide. Healthy relationships are not either/or; all have the potential of becoming more respectful and joyful. Like physical fitness, healthy connections require intentional vigilance and attention for optimal vitality.

$ $ $ $

The following list of men have come to our attention as noteworthy in supporting the cause of equality. We hope that possibly up to 80% of the male population are not sexual consumers, and we know that many men spontaneously demonstrate respectful relationships without pretention. Our list is intended to be illustrative of qualities we hope will continue.

Jackson Katz, an international educator from Los Angeles, was an early advocate in challenging gender violence. In 1993, he co-founded Mentors in Violence Prevention, insisting violence is a men's issue because men commit most acts of abuse. His goal was to shift the paradigm to prevention by changing norms in male culture and challenging men to intervene with other men when they see them acting in sexist or abusive ways. His premise is that violence against women needs to target those doing the violence.

Thankfully, Katz continues to be active as an internationally acclaimed speaker. Men of the world are called to honourable behaviour, which includes treating all others with dignity and respect. Male allies are essential to ensure that men's and women's interests are aligned. Unhealthy men are toxic to women.

Tomas Perez of Oregon began his anti-trafficking fight in 2010 and soon noticed men were the primary force behind the demand that drove sexual exploitation. He developed the EPIK Project as an attempt to engage men effectively, and his all-volunteer effort has grown to an international endeavor. He believes genuine empathy involves the capacity to see the world and to use "man strength" for the benefit of others rather than wielding power sustained by an appetite for justice. Evil is relentless and insatiable. Rather than distinguishing consumer/predators from protectors, Perez calls on all men to work with women to create a safe world (2021).

Ashton Kutcher slowed his acting career to focus on child sex trafficking. In response to the spread of CSAM on the internet, Kutcher, with actress Demi Moore, co-founded a human rights organization, DNA Foundation, in 2009. This was renamed Thorn: Digital Defenders of Children in 2012. Their goal was to develop new technology to help identify child victims sold online. Thorn's work is guided by three principles: (1) accelerate victim identification, (2) equip companies to implement child safety procedures, and (3) empower youth by increasing awareness to resist online threats.

Simon Häggström, a Swedish author and police officer, has specialized since 2009 in crimes related to prostitution and human trafficking. He shares some of his experiences in *Shadow's Law: The True Story of a Swedish Detective Inspector Fighting Prostitution* (2016) and is a well-known lecturer on the subject. Häggström summarizes the impact of the originally controversial 1999 Swedish legislation in his preface:

> We have been successful in reducing prostitution and trafficking and in changing how people think about prostitution and what it really is. The legislation on purchase of sexual services has been a vital part of that work. From being legal up until 1999, buying sex in Sweden is now, 17 years later, one of the most shameful crimes you can get arrested for. Studies show that about 70% of the Swedish population are

supportive of the legislation and there is a definite political unity regarding the legislation (p. 11).

Robert Jensen has critiqued pornography and masculinity. His powerful book, *The End of Patriarchy: Radical Feminism for Men* (2017), challenges readers to question institutional male violence that controls and dehumanizes women's sexuality. His stance is unequivocal:

> When men use women in pornography and prostitution—whether or not we say it out loud, whether or not we even think about the question—we are implicitly endorsing that idea: *That's what women are for, to get fucked* (emphasis in original).

> When men decide not to participate in the sexual-exploitation industries—either in selling or buying women's sexuality—we are stating that we believe women are fully human, deserving of dignity, and do not exist to satisfy men's sexual pleasure. When we make that choice, men are also stating that we believe we are fully human, too (p. 114).

Garrett Jonsson of Utah began his service as a public speaker and podcast developer in 2017 to share knowledge about the harmful effects of pornography. He was first exposed at age nine and used to watch a few times a week as he grew, convincing himself it was not that bad. He continued to say "this is the last time" but couldn't stop. When he turned 30, Jonsson finally faced the truth. He ran "30 in 30"—30 marathons in 30 days—wearing handcuffs to raise awareness of the addictive nature of pornography. He later biked coast-to-coast, dragging chains to demonstrate the heaviness of addiction and recovery. His website "Fight the New Drug" (ftnd.org) contains interactive information, a documentary, and over 1,000 articles.

Nicholas Kristof, an American journalist and former columnist with the *New York Times*, has already been mentioned. He travelled to more than 150 countries, focussing his work on human rights abuses and social injustices worldwide. Several books, including *Half the Sky: Turning Oppression into Opportunity for Women Worldwide* (2014), were coauthored with his wife, Sheryl WuDunn.

In December 2020, Kristof exposed pornographic content involving minors on the website *Pornhub* and its parent company, MindGeek, which led to further action from the Canadian government. He makes the point that sex positivity can exist without exploitation.

$ $ $ $

Personal reflection, Andrea:

Working in the field of sex trade abolition is not easy on the spirit. Advocates and activists regularly face verbal abuse and a never-ending onslaught of personal attacks from those pushing open markets for transactional sex. We are also constantly chasing limited dollars and resources. However, every so often the Universe provides us some support, I believe, in an effort to raise our hope and bolster our determination.

For me, that support came in the form of a message on Twitter in the summer of 2021. A man I refer to as "B" joined the social media platform as a former sex buyer, saying he was determined to share his insights and resources in order to make a difference in the lives of others. Through a series of direct messages, we spoke about how we'd both blindly supported the choice/empowerment narrative, and the guilt and remorse that come with having harmed women as a result.

"B" asked if I had any personal projects that required funding, or if I knew of any active, or recently exited, sex sellers in need of support. He had recently benefitted from a financial transaction and wished to share his one-time bonus. Over the course of five months, B's donations were distributed to more than one hundred sellers globally and numerous non-profit organizations working to end demand and address harm.

Some highlights of B's contributions include:
- *$60,000 toward a media project about commercial sex,*
- *$50,000 to launch a credit repair program for exploited women,*
- *$30,000 for a woman to seamlessly leave a violent situation,*

- *$25,000 for a visual art installment on women's vulnerability, and*
- *$20,000 toward editing and publishing costs of this book.*

In addition, "B" paid for post-secondary tuition fees, job train-ing costs, outstanding rent and utility bills, trauma counselling and drug/alcohol rehabilitation, clothing and school supplies for children of exploited women, prescription drug costs, and much more. Being given the opportunity to distribute many of these funds, I can say the experience was nothing short of monumental and life-changing, for both me and the recipients. To witness true transformative change is inspiring and uplifting!

It is very easy to become cynical when it seems the world in which we live is one of hyper-individualism and gross indifference to others. Whatever resources we are able to offer, we should know they have the ability to provide immeasurable hope and relief to those on the receiving end. We can all give something, whether that is our time, our money, or simply our friendship and empathy. If we collectively mobilize to support exploited women, we will start to see the necessary changes that bring us closer to equality and prosperity for all.

$ $ $ $

Personal reflection, Kathy:

It is not only women who carry traumatic memories. I would like to honour a young man, age 17, who was helping his father harvest their crop one early September morning before heading off to his first day of university. He stopped for an obstacle in the field, which turned out to be the body of a young woman who had disappeared from the streets of Edmonton a month earlier. Thank you, Dave, for finding my daughter.

$ $ $ $

While the Canadian government seems committed to compensating injustices from previous decades, we anticipate future generations will need and receive an apology for attitudes and actions that are prevalent today. Perhaps an apology will be extended to women trapped in the sex trade who have long been marginalized and blamed for their own exploitation. Hopefully, that apology would include regret for the government's short-sighted preoccupation with the vocal minority, avoidance of the more significant issues of personal freedom, and lack of realistic exit opportunities.

In the meantime, we highlight Canadian men who are working as allies. We recognize and honour men within our community who take on traditional roles of providing for their families, protecting the vulnerable, helping others, and healing themselves. What could be more self-evident than the need to include them in strategies to reduce violence and exploitation?

The White Ribbon Campaign is a global movement of men and boys working to end violence against women and girls by transforming social norms to promote gender equality, healthy relationships, and a new vision of masculinity. White Ribbon began in Toronto in November 1991 in response to the 1989 Montreal massacre of 14 female students. Initiatives have since been organized in over 60 countries around the world. Members work through education, awareness-raising, outreach, technical assistance, capacity building, and partnerships.

In 2006, the Edmonton agency, now known as CEASE: Centre to End All Sexual Exploitation, created an innovative fundraising initiative known as the Men of Honour Awards. The intent was to affirm positive male role models and community leaders, a welcome reprieve from the world of johns, pimps, and drug dealers who plague the women served by CEASE. Over 100 men have been honoured to date, inspired by the definition formulated for the CEASE event:

> Men of Honour are those who act in meaningful ways
> to foster respect, encourage healthy relationships,
> and create positive opportunities for people.

> Men of Honour strengthen their families, communities, and workplaces. They respect the integrity, individuality, and humanity of vulnerable children and adults.
>
> Men of Honour may be well known, or they may be quiet workers or volunteers. Men of Honour are found in many families, ethnocultural communities, trades, professions, neighbourhoods, networks, and organizations.

Victor Malarek, a former journalist and host of CBC's *The Fifth Estate*, brought world attention to the horrors of human trafficking with *The Natashas: Inside the Global Sex Trade* (2003). He also dared to expose buyer demand with *The Johns: Sex for Sale and the Men Who Buy It* (2009).

Benjamin Perrin, a law professor at the University of British Columbia, is involved with human trafficking research and activism. He wrote *Invisible Chains: Canada's Underground World of Human Trafficking* (2010) and helped Joy Smith develop the National Action Plan to Combat Human Trafficking (2011) which challenges Canada to better address the issue.

The Moose Hide Campaign was inspired by Paul Lacerte and his daughter Raven in 2011. The campaign is an Indigenous-led grassroots movement of men and boys, intended to reach all Canadians. It is founded on the belief that men and boys need to step up and take action to end male violence against women and children, challenge behaviours that lead to violence, and develop a culture of healthy masculinity. All citizens are invited to wear a small square of moose hide as a sign of their commitment to end violence.

Peter MacKay, Conservative Member of Parliament from Nova Scotia 1997 to 2015, has many credits to his name. He is remembered here as the federal Minister of Justice, under Prime Minister Stephen Harper, who brought forward the *Protection of Communities and Exploited Persons Act (PCEPA)* in 2014.

Paul Boge is an author, speaker, filmmaker, and professional engineer. Among his books is *The True Story of Canadian Human Trafficking* (2018), for which he received the Joy Smith

Foundation Award in 2019 for Leading Canadian Author to Combat Human Trafficking. Joy Smith's work is featured in his book, as well as a chilling portrayal of the grooming of young victims for sexual exploitation.

Mike Cameron, an Edmonton writer and speaker, is a former businessman who turned his energy to advocating against gender-based violence following the murder of his girlfriend in 2015. He shares his philosophy in his book, *Becoming a Better Man: When "Something's Gotta Change," Maybe It's You!* (2019). He writes:

> As men, we're discouraged from showing our emotions. We're taught to suppress, deny, and try to ignore negative feelings under the guise of being strong. It seems like such an oversimplification to say the key is *allowing yourself to feel* (p. 252, emphasis in original).

Cameron's questions about why men murder also apply to why some men exploit or traffic women:

> Could [their] deaths have been prevented by a society that actually teaches, respects, and values virtues like empathy and compassion and kindness over domination, conquest, and victory? How did our societal propensity to encourage unhealthy masculinities contribute to this event? How do we stop men from perpetuating violence against women? How do we build a better restraining order? How do we improve the justice system? (p. 257).

Although justice system questions are valid, Cameron suggests we also need to address the root cause:

> How do we prevent men from getting to this point in their lives where they can commit these atrocities? One of the most important things we can do to achieve this long-term and for generations to come is to teach men to examine their tender sides, to explore and connect with their emotions without fear of vilification by their counterparts or, worse, their partners.

> We need more men who will speak up and embrace compassion, empathy, and kindness. We need men to show the world that a combination of these characteristics helps to embody what it means to be a "real man" (pp. 257–258).

Cameron, in a Facebook post Sept. 15, 2021, spoke about his business leadership journey. He was taught 25 years earlier that leadership meant competition, domination, and ultimately, conquest. Although that led to material "success," the cost was isolation, disconnection, and feelings of inadequacy. Over a decade ago, he shifted his framework to values, intentions, and milestones. His mission is to teach men the power of vulnerability while recognizing the ongoing cost of the patriarchy to themselves and their families:

> The reason I am so passionate about teaching men the art of emotionally connecting with self and others is simple.
>
> Emotionally connected men make better leaders.
>
> They make better partners.
>
> They make better fathers.
>
> They are secure in who they are and not afraid to elevate those around them.
>
> They create cultures of safety, transparency, and trust.
>
> They are champions of diversity, equity, and inclusion.
>
> They seek help when needed and value curiosity over judgment.
>
> The reason this is personal to me is because I also recognize that emotionally connected men do not kill people. They do not kill themselves. They do not seek to do harm in the world. Emotional disconnection is the number one threat facing humanity today. As leaders, we have an opportunity to change that.

Next Gen Men (nextgenmen.ca) is a group working to create a future where boys and men feel less pain and do less harm. Jake Sitka is the co-founder and executive director. In a Facebook conversation, Sitka (2021) recognizes that patriarchy is based on "father power." Men tend to unload on the women in their lives and let them do the emotional labour. It is a system in which we all exist. The consequences of distorted masculinity and suppressed emotionality include three-quarters of suicides being male. Eighty per cent of overdoses happen to men; men are the primary perpetrators of violence and are incarcerated at higher rates than women. Next Gen Men believe we need to move beyond masculine/feminine definitions to define and embrace positive traits as human qualities.

John Cassells of Ontario has been a youth minister for over 30 years and is a human trafficking specialist with SIM (Serving in Mission) Canada, a faith-based community that sends workers to over 70 countries. He was called upon to advise the Standing Committee on Justice for Bill C-36 in 2014 and provided input to Ontario's Strategy to End Human Trafficking in 2016. Cassells developed and is the director of a project named Lifeworthy, which supports victims of human trafficking and their families and provides training for Toronto-area churches and youth agencies. He is also the founding director of Men Ending Trafficking, which supports victims through recovery, and he developed a SafeGuard program to provide court support for witnesses. In addition to a Facebook page, educational clips are posted regularly on his website (johncassells.com).

Arnold Viersen has been mentioned several times in this book. Relatively new on the political scene, he was first elected as a Conservative Member of Parliament in the riding of Peace River— Westlock, Alberta, in 2015. Viersen is a champion for condemning all forms of human trafficking, listening to victims and survivors, raising awareness of the magnitude of modern-day slavery, and taking steps to combat human trafficking.

MP Viersen is credited with launching a national conversation on pornography. On International Women's Day, March 8, 2016, he introduced Motion M-47 which called for the examination of the public health effects of violent and degrading sexually explicit material. The motion was passed unanimously, marking the first time in 30 years Parliament had studied the issue of pornography in Canada. Subsequently, MP Viersen was appointed on Jan. 13, 2022, to the Subcommittee on International Human Rights. Regular updates are posted on his social media accounts.

Revolution Engine, an Edmonton-based rap-rock band, has incorporated social messaging in their music since 2009. Their song "Objectified" will be included in the docuseries *Labeled*.

Guerrilla Motion Pictures Inc. in Edmonton is a shining example of a company that cares about raising awareness on the issue of violence against women. When approached in 2019 to create a documentary about sexual exploitation, owners Justin Kueber and Sam Reid did not hesitate to take on the taboo topic, volunteering three years of their time to chronicle the stories and impact of exploited women and girls. The project, which struggled initially to secure funding, produced over 80 shoots and over 500 hours of recorded interviews and events. It is rare to see busy young professionals give an extensive amount of time without a guarantee of monetary compensation. The docuseries, *Labeled*, executive produced by Heinz, is set to be released in 2023.

Rob McDonald, teacher and coach from Cape Breton, reflects on the importance of male mentoring in his forthcoming book, *That's Just What Brothers Do*. He believes that men want to be authentic and respectful and need to give each other space for open conversations.

Many more men could be mentioned, those who treat the women and children in their lives with dignity and respect daily. Some are vocal about their values; others choose to live quiet lives of integrity and example. Others donate money to supportive agencies and, in a myriad of ways, move the needle on societal attitudes, policies, and practices.

We also acknowledge the over 3,000 men who have attended Edmonton's STOP: Sex Trade Offender Program since 1996. Most participants expressed gratitude for their unexpected opportunity to learn new perspectives and knowledge from the program. Their responsiveness reinforces our belief that most men want to do good and can do better with education and encouragement.

$ $ $ $

Hennes Doltze is a social worker and educator from Manitoba who works with men in combatting sexual exploitation and domestic violence. He shares some of his experiences and insights with "Engaging Men and Boys" in Part Six, Guest Contributors.

Tomas Perez's reflections and his work with EPIK, which has a branch in Alberta, are also shared in Guest Contributions.

CHAPTER 15:
SEARCH FOR SOLUTIONS

WHAT CAN WE DO to prevent the trafficking of human beings? How do we help those who have been trapped to escape? What services do they need? How do we help them address their trauma? How can we expand prevention and healing along with compassion, validation, love, and a willingness to listen?

Authenticity is the strength of the collective. Inaction is complicity. We must build a new world order of respect and caring for all citizens.

As we work to prevent violence and reduce harm, we must take a stand against the depravity that exists.

Some maladaptive behaviours may be transformed through education and treatment; in other instances, malice must be contained to protect society.

> A girl who is given love and support can start to break the self-image that keeps her down. As she gains self-confidence, she sees she can learn. As she learns, she sees her own gifts. As she develops her gifts, she sees her own power; she can defend her own rights. That is what happens when you offer girls love, not hate. You lift their gaze. They gain their voice (Melinda Gates, 2019, p. 114).

> What anyone really wants is a secure home, a job that pays enough, and a loving relationship. Healthy persons are the sum of all their relations. Individual

healing is grounded in social healing. Wellness is found in the continuous flow of honouring both your thoughts and feelings. The Indigenous view is that all humans are inherently good and put on Mother Earth to contribute to Creator's grand design. Traditional teachings include being thankful for everything we are given and creating strong relations to gain a strong sense of self-worth. Healthy land encourages a deep sense of spiritual connectedness. Our ancestors celebrate when we do the work to deal with the past (Priscilla McGilvery, 2021).

$ $ $ $

Harm reduction is often touted as a response to social problems where no solution is apparent. While there is merit in meeting sellers where they are, why would we settle for simply "lessening" their suffering? A more comprehensive response is required with interventions aimed at the prevention of sexual exploitation and elimination of consumer demand. Freedom from exploitation is a basic human right; sexual servitude cannot be sanitized with payment under "safer" conditions.

Prevention requires sensitivity to the fragility of vulnerable populations. A network of supports needs to be developed, such as economic security, shelters, healing resources, the inclusion of marginalized communities, and exit options. The stigma of selling sex needs to be addressed, not by legitimizing buyers' entitlement but by respecting the intrinsic humanity of those sold. Communities of allies need to be established to provide education and support for poor and vulnerable youth. Marginalized populations deserve to be empowered through mentoring and opportunity rather than being encouraged to accept money for sexual access to their bodies. Young people deserve to know that their fundamental human rights include personal integrity. They deserve access to resources within a community that respects their unique potential.

Sometimes advocacy is extending a hand; other times, it is helping create a new culture of accountability. Wherever there is injustice, there will inevitably be anger. For too long, sellers have been blamed for their own exploitation. It is time for society to address the "buyer mentality" of disconnection and misogyny that is a prerequisite to exploitation, pimping, trafficking, and objectification. We must also address the economic and social inequalities that allow the subordination of some citizens into sexual servitude and bondage.

An article calling for political response was published in the Fall 2016 issue of *The Advocate,* a magazine of the Alberta College of Social Workers. The writing was prompted after a pro "sex work" city councillor made a guest appearance at a Sexual Exploitation Awareness conference, presumably to show support. After hearing reservations about the city's bylaw approach, he commented that there seemed to be an elephant in the room. "Elephants in the Room" (King, 2016) calls for social workers across Canada to rally around the *PCEPA* legislation in place and to support a full range of best practices for dealing with commercial sexual exploitation. These include empowering women and communities, curbing demand, raising political awareness, training law enforcement, providing hotlines, peer support, exit strategies, and media campaigns as well as improving services for identified victims.

$ $ $ $

We honour voices who lend credibility and poignancy to the abolition movement, especially exited and survivor women. Sellers who look back on their experiences in the sex industry after exiting tend to have a more analytical and comprehensive interpretation than those actively involved.

In *The Pimping of Prostitution: Abolishing the Sex Work Myth* (2017), Julie Bindel identifies some early abolition movements in the United States. WHISPER (Women Hurt in Systems of Prostitution Engaged in Revolt) was founded in 1985 as a direct challenge to prostitution as free choice or labour. CATW, the Coalition Against Trafficking in Women, followed in 1988 with affiliations worldwide.

SAGE (Standing Against Global Exploitation) was founded in 1992 by Norma Hotaling as a resource, advocacy, and counselling centre for women. Hotaling (1951–2008) was a survivor of child sexual abuse, street prostitution, and heroin addiction before working to support other women. Breaking Free was founded in 1996 by Vednita Carter in Minnesota to serve a young African American population.

In *Trafficked: The Terrifying True Story of a British Girl Forced into the Sex Trade* (2012), Sophie Hayes shares her horror of being forced into the sex trade in Italy after visiting a man she thought was her friend.

Rachel Moran of Ireland provides an eloquent, provocative, and paradigm-shifting analysis in *Paid For: My Journey Through Prostitution* (2013) based on her experience selling sex for survival from age 14.

Prostitution Narratives: Stories of Survival in the Sex Trade (Norma & Tankard Reist, Eds. 2016) is an anthology of 19 women's accounts of sexual exploitation: Linda, Jade, Annabelle, Kat, Rhiannon, Tanja, Christie, Jan, Kendra, "Mademoiselle," Autumn, Donna, Christine, Simone, Jacqueline, Genevieve, Charlotte, Rebecca, and Suzzan.

Nordic Model Now! Supporting Students Impacted by the Sex Industry … A Handbook for Universities (Nov. 17, 2021) includes stories of 21 women and one man who want to alert others about the hazards of the sex trade. Some of the names were changed to protect their identities. Readers are encouraged to review their testimonies on sadly familiar themes:

> Abi (started webcamming, was stalked by a "client"),
>
> Alice (was homeless, few options available),
>
> Andrea (still struggling to heal nine years after exiting),
>
> Chelsea (stigma from men thinking it's OK to dehumanize her),
>
> Chrissy (false sense of control quickly faded),
>
> Christina (the way out proved much more difficult than the way in),

Courtney (while involved, had to reject life outside, drank to cope),

Dana (was told to lie about being a student, chronic depression),

Debbie (still struggles with dissociation years later),

Elle (felt dead inside, not really there),

Esther (never got over the fear of not being able to breathe),

Harriet (beaten, raped, threatened, choked, scared every second),

Huschke (legalization covers up the abuse that happens),

Jen (no emotional connection, women are there to serve),

Laura (strange variety of random men, smelly, ugly, old),

Megan (pimped by her boyfriend for months),

Ophelia (hardest was continually pretending to orgasm),

Peter (felt sick having to sell his body, wants to warn others),

Rae (experienced body brutality, thoroughly exhausted spirit),

Rebecca (not aware of the slow, insidious cumulative effects),

Sarah (men didn't want give and take, just to be the centre),

Tara (was homeless and drank to endure the violence).

Tanya Michelle from Alberta shares the anguish and sorrow of her life on the streets in Vancouver and Edmonton. Her book, *Out of the Shadows: A Memoir of a Childhood Lost, Modern-day Slavery, and a Life Reborn* (2018), outlines her remarkable recovery.

Timea Nagy was trafficked from Hungary to Toronto at age 20. She was able to escape and shares her story in *Out of the Shadows: A Memoir* (2019).

$$\$ \ \$ \ \$ \ \$$$

The work of some Canadian activists is outlined in more detail:

Katarina MacLeod (born 1972) is a survivor of childhood sexual abuse, domestic violence, addiction, kidnapping, and sex trafficking. She describes being in abusive relationships with men since the age of 12 and having abandonment issues through what she refers to as a "Daddy wound." This led her to be an easy target for a female pimp she met at a support group, who recruited her at age 21 with the promise of big money and a glamorous life. Although she was later able to get away from her exploiter, she continued to sell sex "independently" in massage parlours as well as escorting to hotels and private homes. Later, she was trafficked throughout Ontario by another pimp, totalling 15 years spent in prostitution.

Katarina was able to free herself from her exploitation and went on to found "Rising Angels," an organization that educates professionals and the public. The agency also provides supportive services and safe environments to women affected by commercial sexual exploitation, allowing them to experience physical, mental, social, and spiritual restoration in their lives.

In July 2014, Katarina approached Sun News Network to publish an essay in support of Bill C-36 wherein she stated:

> This is not a spiritual or religious issue. This is an issue of exploitation and violence against women. I want more for our daughters. I want women to be respected and valued. I want our men to know that it is not right to use and abuse someone for their own gratification.

Trisha Baptie (born 1973) is a Vancouver-based journalist, community organizer, and activist. She was forced into prostitution at the age of 13 and spent 15 years caught in the exploitation of the sex industry, mostly in Vancouver's Downtown Eastside area. At the age of 28, she was finally able to exit.

In 2007, Baptie became a citizen journalist to cover the murder trial of Robert Pickton. Many of his victims were known to her. She founded Honour Consulting in 2008, focusing on abolitionist theory and looking at issues related to the sex trade through the lens of women's equality and violence against women. In 2009, she co-founded EVE, formerly Exploited Voices now Educating, a non-profit organization of women who had survived commercial sexual exploitation. The group is dedicated to exposing the violence of the sex trade and seeking abolition through political action, advocacy, and public education. They challenge the idea of sex as "work" and believe the demand for paid violence against women is the product of systemic oppression.

Baptie believes we will not see justice for women until we shift the focus from those who sell to those who buy sex. She publicly encourages all citizens to identify their power and privilege and use it to change the world for those who do not have the same resources or opportunities. In 2009–2010, she was a community mobilizer in the "Buying Sex Is Not a Sport" awareness campaign in preparation for the 2010 Olympics in Vancouver. Baptie appeared in a documentary film, *Our Lives to Fight For,* in 2010, and her work was featured in the 2013 film, *Buying Sex*.

Baptie joined forces with fellow advocate Cherry Smiley to present a strong and non-apologetic statement in a special feature article for *Policy Options* (Feb. 12, 2020):

> Can prostitution be made safe? ... The short answer is no. Those who support the full decriminalization of prostitution as a way to make the industry safer fail to acknowledge the inherent violence of prostitution and to ignore the context in which it occurs. The only way to end the violence is to end prostitution.
>
> All women have the right to live free of male violence and the threat of male violence. This includes being free to say yes or no to sexual partners and to sexual acts without guilt, fear, or consequence.... When "sex

work" is tolerated or promoted, so is the message that it is entirely acceptable for men to demand particular sex from women.

It is disingenuous to suggest that Canada's prostitution laws are to blame for the deaths of women.... The blame lies with the men who murder women.... Legislation, however, is only one part of the solution to this global abandonment of mostly poor, Indigenous, and women of colour to "sex work." We must take a stand against men's entitlement to women's bodies, improve the material conditions of women's lives, and educate ourselves about the connections between prostitution and women's oppression.

Baptie also provided testimony (June 22, 2021) to the Indigenous and Northern Affairs Committee on its study of the sex trafficking of Indigenous peoples. Speaking as a non-Indigenous person, she asked:

What if we flipped the whole question and conversation and asked why we think men should be able to pay for sex? Where is the legally binding policy or human right that states that men paying for sex is a protected act? How does allowing any Canadian man to pay for sex help create a safer society for Indigenous women and girls—or anyone, for that matter?

We keep sex consensual by not commodifying it, and *PCEPA* helps us do this.

Natasha Falle (born 1973) is a former Canadian professor in the Police Foundations program at Humber and Sheridan Colleges in Toronto. She was forcibly prostituted from age 15 to 27 and has become a recognized international speaker exposing the sex trade. In 2001, Falle established Streetlight Support Services and, in 2007, co-founded Sex Trade 101, Canada's first survivor-led political activism coalition. Sex Trade 101 operates Covenant House in Toronto as a haven that provides 24-hour support and resources to sex-trafficked individuals.

Falle's team helped craft the government's appeal of the *Canada (AG) v Bedford* (2013) decision and the formulation of the 2014 Nordic Model style legislation. Her contributions include training over 4,000 police in several countries.

Bridget Perrier (born 1977) was pimped from age 12 in Ontario. She co-founded Sex Trade 101 and is a First Nation educator. She also spoke (June 22, 2021) to the Indigenous and Northern Affairs Committee on its Study of the Sex Trafficking of Indigenous Peoples:

> I was lured and debased into prostitution at the age of 12 from a child welfare-run group home. I remained enslaved for 10 years. I was sold to men who felt privileged to steal my innocence and invade my body. I was paraded like cattle in front of men who were able to purchase me, and the acts that I did were something no little girl should even have to endure here in Canada, the land of the free....
>
> I was traded in legal establishments, street corners, and strip clubs. I even had a few trips across the Great Lakes serving ship men at the age of 13. The scariest thing that happened to me was, at 14 years of age, being held captive for a period of 43 hours and raped and tortured repeatedly by a sexual predator who preyed on exploited girls.
>
> My exploiters made a lot of money and tried to break me, but I fought for my life.... After many years, I was able to exit and rebuild my life, and my education became a tool... We must look at who is doing this. It is the men....
>
> Sex Trade 101 believes that prostitution is not a choice, but it's a lack of choice that keeps women and girls enslaved.

Casandra Diamond (born 1977) is a Toronto-based survivor of sex slavery from age 17 and a leading advocate in the fight against human trafficking. In 2014, she founded BridgeNorth Women's Mentorship and Advocacy Service, a survivor-led charitable organization that seeks to end sexual exploitation in Canada. She was inspired to assist other women, as she realized many people did not even understand what was happening in their own society.

Diamond talks about the human cost of trafficking (2018):

> Trafficked persons experience very harsh living con-
> ditions. Traffickers often withhold the necessities of
> life, denying victims food and sleep and forcing them
> to work long hours. A trafficked person begins to feel
> as if society has turned against them, and they stop
> trying to be "normal"....
>
> Not everyone comes out intact, we're talking about
> having branding, tattoos, broken teeth and bones,
> being HIV positive. But the effects are not only physi-
> cal. Victims of human trafficking also have high rates
> of PTSD, dissociation, mental illness, and suicide.

She confirms that being a young female is the primary risk factor for human trafficking, with those who had suffered sexual abuse being more vulnerable. However, she warned there are many more girls from "mainstream society" in the sex industry due to the "hyper-sexualization of our culture and the ease of traffickers to groom victims with social media" (Diamond, 2018).

Diamond grew up in a family with mental health problems and was recruited by a "massage club" owner. Despite regular raids, no one ever offered her help, and that was her life for nearly nine years. She felt unloved and unwanted, which made her the perfect victim. She shared her story in a Ted Talk (2020): "The licensed brothel system provides a facade of acceptability, safety, and options, hidden in plain sight.... Everyone knows about the problem, but no one is taking the lead to solve it.... I was sex trafficked for years. Brothels are hidden in plain sight."

Diamond started BridgeNorth as part of the solution and lobbied for the Nordic Model legislation to address systemic problems. However, action is still missing in Canada. In her Ted Talk, Diamond advocates for (1) the abolition of sex trafficking, (2) improved exit opportunities for women, and (3) more public support. Politicians say they can only address what constituents bring to their attention, so we all have a responsibility to make our voices heard on behalf of women who are denied freedom.

Timea Nagy-Payne (born 1978) was 20 years old and living in poverty in Hungary when she came to Canada to work as a babysitter. After arriving in Toronto, she was held hostage, put to work in a strip club, and forced into the sex industry. She and others were fed once a day, tortured emotionally and physically, and raped frequently. Fortuitously, friends helped her escape after three months, and she later became a public speaker and social advocate.

In 2008, Nagy-Payne created Walk with Me Canada Victim Services to help combat human trafficking. She founded Timea's Cause in 2014, a social enterprise that educates, unites, and mobilizes communities on a grassroots level while employing victims of human trafficking. She has trained numerous agencies in Canada, the United States, and Europe and was invited to join a United Nations task force fighting human trafficking worldwide.

Out of the Shadows: A Memoir was released in May 2019. As Nagy-Payne explains, the human cost of trafficking is that it robs people of lives they could have lived.

> We cannot accept that there are millions of people currently trafficked and enslaved worldwide—more than at any other time in history, even when keeping slaves was legal—for none of us has true freedom or prosperity if it comes at the cost of others' freedom, labour, and even lives. It needs to end, because the collective freedom of our human family is at stake, especially that of the next generation. We can do it (pp. 335-336).

Alexandra Stevenson (born 1986) is a British Columbia-based survivor of commercial sexual exploitation. Her entry into the sex industry was facilitated by her misguided and naive belief that it would be empowering. It was not until 10 years after she exited that Alexandra came to understand the force and coercion she experienced constituted trafficking, rather than a series of her own bad decisions. This newfound understanding spurred Alexandra to co-found "Uprising," a US-based anti-trafficking non-profit, as well as

"The Laughing Survivor," her Canadian-based business from which she shares her story, educates, and advocates for the abolition of commercial sex.

In 2022, Stevenson spoke at the Federal Justice Committee's review of the *Protection of Communities and Exploited Persons Act*. She stated:

> It is impossible to ascertain that only willing bodies are working in the commercial sex industry. Some people are unable to identify their experience as exploitation. Some people are terrified of being deported, or repercussion from their boyfriends, bosses, or pimps. Some workers may have chosen their work, but they chose it because they were desperate or in survival mode, and a choice made in desperation is not a choice at all. As ideological as it might be to draw a line around consensual sex workers and suggest that *PCEPA* must be repealed to keep them safe, it is unrealistic. The decriminalization of sex work will result in collateral damage that looks like an entire population for whom a lifetime of complex trauma will be the cost of living in Canada.

Andrea Heinz (born 1983) joins this small but mighty force of experiential Canadian abolitionists. She has published several articles, as noted, and is Executive Producer of an eight-episode docu-series, *Labeled,* to be released in 2023. She also founded the Blue Sky Bursary at CEASE which provides funds to active and exited sellers who wish to pursue studies in policing, corrections, women's studies, governance, or law.

We acknowledge and express our gratitude to the many exited voices worldwide speaking their truth to support their sisters still suffering in silence. We hope to strengthen the voice and experience of solidarity.

In summary, what exited voices say, and global statistics confirm, is that most providers involved in commercial sex have limited or no agency. Coerced sellers, whether children, youth, or adult, deserve society's full and compassionate attention. Increased awareness of the reality of human trafficking cannot be an end in itself. We must look to the protection, not just of identified individuals, but of all impoverished or entrepreneurial youth who might be convinced that selling themselves is an acceptable option. Promotion of "sex work" is not an acceptable alternative to trafficking. Our society must be clear that all persons deserve freedom and equality in their sexual expression. Abolition of sex buying is important in creating a world of respect and dignity.

CHAPTER 16:
BEST PRACTICES & CALLS TO ACTION

WHAT CAN WE SAY to people who feel helpless and overwhelmed about the increase of human trafficking and sexual exploitation worldwide?

During the preceding chapters, there are four main messages we hope readers hear:

First is that empathy trumps ideology. Concern for those choosing or forced to sell sex is the meeting point of the various belief systems discussed. An underlying concern is that many sellers are socially marginalized, come from gender and racial minorities, and operate in a context of economic inequality. While ideologies may be polarized regarding proposed solutions, respect and improved services are paramount when responding to the sellers involved.

Second, harm reduction is not a sufficient response. Where harm is known to exist, society has an obligation to recognize and address root causes. The harms to individuals and communities from commercial sexual exploitation are well documented and must be addressed in a proactive manner. This is why we must focus on consumers.

Third, neutrality serves oppression. All citizens have a responsibility to become educated about the forces of coercion and the impact of gaslighting so we/they are not lulled into compliance with the status quo. The health of society depends on continued vigilance and discernment.

Fourth, a holistic model of integration and positivity is needed as an alternative to commodification and dehumanization. Although not previously articulated, we present the traditional Medicine Wheel teachings of body-heart-mind-spirit as a reminder to honour all aspects of individual, community, and global humanity.

> Prostitution and trafficking can only exist in an atmosphere of public, professional and academic indifference—it is a failure to educate people in law, psychology, public health, and criminal justice which makes the issue largely invisible and when it is seen, it's a normalization of an inevitable social evil (Melissa Farley, 2004).

> Having heard all of this you may choose to look the other way, but you can never again say that you did not know (William Wilberforce, Speech to Westminster Parliament Calling for the Abolition of Slavery May 12, 1789, quoted by Benjamin Perrin, 2011, p. 240).

$ $ $ $

Our first point is that all sex sellers deserve compassion. Our vision is a world of equality, dignity, prosperity, and joy, where sexual activity is mutually desired and pleasurable for all who choose to participate. We want young people to grow up with sexual integrity, confident of their right to be treated with respect and having the courtesy to treat others in the same fashion.

While we focus on demand, our passion is driven by concern for the millions of women, children, and marginalized individuals worldwide who are trafficked, enslaved, or coerced into commercial sexual exploitation. We agree that sellers, with all citizens, deserve services such as medical care, legal advice, financial relief, education, housing, and peer support. It is important that labelling not be used as an excuse to exclude those in need from receiving appropriate resources. Our intent is to shift attention to the underlying causes that allow buyer/seller inequities and to promote more respectful connections.

Our vision is that individuals, families, communities, and the world benefit from increasing respectful connections with each other. We share responsibility for ensuring greater economic equality and a secure social net for vulnerable populations so that poverty is not a motivation for desperate actions. Best practices include increased awareness and education as well as prevention, improved social networks, trauma-informed care, exit strategies, and advocacy. We need a community that understands and believes in full equality for women. We need commitment to the prevention of exploitation. We need comprehensive and enforceable legislation, plus we need the political will to implement those laws effectively.

$$\$ \ \$ \ \$ \ \$$$

Our second point is that harm reduction is not a sufficient response. We must be prepared to tackle the source of harm. We must not be so immune to the inevitability of sexual exploitation that we protect buyer rights while trying to not "conflate" a minority of sellers who identify as consensual. We cannot pretend the acquiescence to economic opportunity overrides the insidious harm caused by buyers.

We must not settle for encouraging parents and educators to warn children about the evils of grooming instead of targeting consumers and traffickers directly. Education is simply one tool of prevention. Timely information may help protect some youth, but unless we tackle the bigger issue of demand, we simply download exploitation to the person next in line who is more vulnerable and less aware. It is not reasonable to believe that exploitation can be prevented without legal sanctions and political will.

As outlined in Nordic Model Now! (Jan. 4, 2020) a systemic problem requires a systemic solution. Legislative changes will only be as successful as the political will to implement them. Real measures are needed to address poverty and inequality, which are both the cause and consequence of prostitution:

> We need to make it clear that we **refuse** to live in
> a world where men have their so-called right to buy
> sexual access to women and girls enshrined in law.
>
> We must make it clear that women **are** human beings
> and we will not rest until **our** full human rights are
> enshrined in law and implemented in policy (empha-
> sis in original).

Human trafficking is a global crime and demands a coordinated response. Countries around the world have addressed the problem in various ways with diverse results. "Some are complicit in the crime, while others punish and blame the victims. Many simply ignore it" (Perrin, 2011, p. 197). Many countries, however, are becoming more active, and we hope Canada will lead the way in reviewing, evaluating, and creating best practices in terms of human rights education, prevention and identification of abuses, prosecution of offenders, as well as exit options and support programs for all who seek a better life.

$ $ $ $

Our third point is that neutrality serves oppression. While many citizens may strive to find a "middle" ground in the midst of polarized controversy, we know that increased tolerance of commercial sex increases the demand, which fuels trafficking. Professed neutrality about the sex trade is extremely dangerous because any support of the "right to sell" implies endorsement of the "right to buy."

Nor is it enough to say we want to end human trafficking; we must look beyond that assertion to the alternatives offered. Many politicians and celebrities who smile and nod in support of anti-trafficking initiatives seem to believe decriminalization is an acceptable option. That implies society needs only to provide a steady supply of legally-aged sellers who declare they accept "sex work" as legitimate employment and believe any discomfort or violations are worth the compensation. Such hypocrisy, in the name of fighting trafficking, undermines respect for and the integrity of all women, while providing protection for buyers.

Rather, we promote the courage to move toward abolition and the elimination of commercial sex to ensure economic and social equality for all citizens. Sex trafficking is an inhumane system that promulgates violence by devaluing people and perpetrates both racial and gender injustice. It has been demonstrated, and quoted frequently in the preceding chapters, that decriminalization and tolerance of the purchase of sexual "services" creates a fertile breeding ground for trafficking, regardless of political platitudes.

Activism is optimism in practice; abolition is an affirmation of sexual equality. We are confident in our vision that an equitable and just future is possible. Abolition requires a qualitative change, a commitment to awareness, a negation of gaslighting, and a willingness to confront inherent buyer mentality and practices. We need to develop protectiveness toward the whole planet and its people. What happens in our hearts can change the world.

There have been many references throughout history to tragedies exaggerated by good people who do nothing, who choose not to be involved, or who pretend injustices are not their responsibility. One such atrocity was the unspeakable horror of the Holocaust. While not attempting to compare the targeted destruction of a defined ethnic group to global slavery of diversely marginalized, the words of one Holocaust survivor come to mind. Elie Wiesel was winner of the Nobel Peace Prize in 1986 for *Night,* his chilling account of the Holocaust. The following words are part of his acceptance speech, 40 years after his survival:

> We must take sides. Neutrality helps the oppressor, never the victim. Silence encourages the tormentor, never the tormented. Sometimes we must interfere... There is so much injustice and suffering crying out for our attention.
>
> Human rights are being violated on every continent. More people are oppressed than free. How can one not be sensitive to their plight? Human suffering concerns men and women everywhere.... Violence is not the answer. Terrorism is the most dangerous of answers.... There is so much to be done, there is

so much that can be done.... **Our lives no longer belong to us alone; they belong to all those who need us desperately** (emphasis added).

We believe in a world where no human being is sexually exploited, and where no system is allowed to profit from exploitation. The larger community needs to join the conversation and influence the process of change. This may take readers into activism through front-line work, fundraising, supporting victims, rehabilitating offenders, providing education, developing research, legislative changes, law enforcement, political action, and advocacy.

$ $ $ $

Our fourth point is that a healthy model of integration and harmony is needed to replace objectification. Unfortunately, pornography and commodification seem to be growing in certain segments of our culture. It is not too late for the positive voices of sacred connection to gain momentum. Indeed, the survival of humanity is at stake. We need a universal spirituality and a global voice. We need political will to shift attitudes, to ensure economic equality, and to hold buyers accountable for the harm they cause.

The traditional Medicine Wheel is one model that teaches balance through ongoing change. It describes the sacred circles of life and continuous interactions of people within their environment. Although interpretations vary with different cultures, there are generally four elements accepted as sacred:

> Physical Body—Individual: Birth is the time of new beginnings and nurturing. We grow into maturity with healthy food, shelter, and partnership with Mother Earth.
>
> Emotional Heart—Family: Emotional well-being in youth depends on a sense of belonging within an accepting family. We learn dignity and respect. We expand our hearts through love and laughter.
>
> Intellectual Mind—Community: As we grow into adulthood, we develop knowledge, unity, and equality in

a larger community. We express our understanding through teachings.

Essential Spirit—Global: We achieve wisdom, hope, congruence, and healing through our connection with Creator. Our sacred spirit is strengthened through reflection, creativity, and celebration.

The importance of prevention, protection, regulation, and recovery are discussed within each dimension.

BODY:

We come into this world as a physical body and require a safe and healthy environment in order to thrive. Children are naturally spontaneous, enthusiastic, and creative as they awaken to their unique potential. Prevention of exploitation means ensuring that basic needs are provided for all citizens. Unfortunately, greed, violence, and oppression provide obstacles that impede our natural drives. No child wants or deserves to be abused or exploited.

At the individual level, when prevention fails, we must focus on rescue and recovery. Many victims are vulnerable even before they are exploited, and their struggle for healing is complicated by their accumulated indignities. Offenders, including buyers, pimps, and traffickers, may be eligible for individual treatment programs. Those who cannot be deterred or rehabilitated must be contained for the greater protection of society.

HEART:

Over and above having their physical needs met, children deserve to be valued and to know they are cherished. Family is where we/ they first hope to experience love, acceptance, and belonging. Parents who were not adequately nurtured have difficulty caring for their children. They deserve support and encouragement rather than blame. Buyers also need to be treated with compassion so they can receive education, treatment, and support, allowing those who are able to reach their positive potential.

Options to exit commercial sexual exploitation need to be readily accessible, as many sellers do not recognize or admit their trauma except in retrospect. Sellers who are criminalized face unfair burdens and may face additional stigma in their recovery. Compassion and support need to be administered as opposed to punishment. Participant-centred thinking, multi-faceted trauma recovery, wrap-around services, culturally appropriate healing, and educational bursaries can be helpful to survivors. Others, who were already marginalized before their exploitation, may need additional long-term caring resources.

MIND:

Knowledge and justice are expressed through legislation and social programs, which exist for the protection of society over individual greed. It is abundantly clear that sex buyers contribute widespread damage to vulnerable populations, and for that reason alone, they must be curtailed. Interventions at the societal or community level include prevention, protection, education, awareness, legislation, enforcement, and rehabilitation if possible.

Safety includes the presence of connection as well as the absence of threat. Policy and programs need to focus on the majority who are silenced and trapped in the sex trade rather than a minority of self-proclaimed consensual participants. As researched best practices indicate, prevention includes focusing on offenders and reducing demand. Educating young men about the reality and harms of sexual exploitation is an important part of creating a shift in social understanding.

Education and awareness initiatives such as STOP (Sex Trade Offender Programs aka john schools) have been well received and shown to shift buyer behaviour. These could possibly be expanded to male populations outside of the judicial system. Promotion of healthy sexuality needs to include warnings about the danger of pornography addiction. Education initiatives need to be developed for the general public alongside age-appropriate school curriculum. Topics need to include human rights, respect, and consent, as well as critical analyses of systemic factors such as injustice, poverty, and grooming.

PCEPA, the *Protection of Communities and Exploited Persons Act, 2014* recognizes the social harm caused by objectification and commodification. This legislation marks the first time in Canada's history that the purchasing of sexual access was criminalized. It rightly shifts focus away from sellers, previously stigmatized and blamed for their own exploitation, and places accountability on buyers. Unfortunately, widespread enforcement of this legislation is still lacking, as are awareness campaigns and preventative services. Alternative measures programming could be expanded across Canada with provincial and municipal cooperation.

We need political will and enforcement as well as legislation to regulate social behaviour. We already have the political imperative of the Palermo *Protocol*, wherein Canada committed to join the United Nations in addressing demand. As well, we have a new mandate with the *MMIWG Report* to regard women as sacred and for all levels of government to acknowledge and condemn violence. We hope Canada will honour its commitment to both.

SPIRIT

Global change requires a spiritual connection and reverence for life. As Indigenous wisdom and many traditions teach, we live in an interdependent world. Compassion requires that we see ourselves in the other person and recognize that their experiences could happen to us or someone we love. Healing work includes universal caring as humanity continues to evolve. Global witnessing allows us to observe the collective trauma caused by social inaction. Trauma symptoms of numbness, apathy, and polarization across many populations can slow our ability to mobilize responsively.

It is important to understand how trauma impacts all aspects of our social development, from individuals to families, communities, and even ancestral history. Incarceration, mental illness, and addiction cause ripples of distress across systems, while the suffering of the vulnerable is often compounded by blame rather than compassion for their plight. Social complicity is the tendency to accept and adapt to the status quo, to withdraw into neutrality rather than to risk questioning.

Heinz echoes the challenge:

> We have to work collectively for what is good for women as a whole, and that is not reducing us to a mere purchasable commodity for men. We need to work toward genuine equality in the mainstream workforce, access to affordable healthcare, and leadership positions within government. We will not improve our social positioning by giving oral sex in a brothel (radicailin, 2020).

As Jody Wilson-Raybould (2021) discusses, speaking truth to power involves making decisions with a deep love for the well-being of all human beings and the planet we inhabit, as well as deep knowledge and expertise of the subject matter at issue. "When we do this, we act justly, and with wisdom. Good governance requires honesty, integrity, and independence." The dimension of love cannot be legislated, but it must infuse our legal decisions.

It is not simply a question of transferring shame from sellers to buyers, although legislative accountability is a good beginning. The "right to purchase" is a one-dimensional carnal expression devoid of emotional connection and social understanding, and it certainly lacks appreciation of spiritual sacredness. Addressing sexual exploitation as a physical, emotional, social, and spiritual deficiency on the part of consumers is necessary for sexual relationships to be transformed into respectful and reciprocal sacred activity.

Calls to action based on Medicine Wheel reflection incorporate prevention, awareness, legislation, and recovery. Opportunities for involvement are unlimited.

Body: Ensure safe and nurturing environments for all children.

Provide education about consent, respect, and equality.

Create political will to reduce poverty, sexism, and racism.

Provide exit opportunities, resources, and protection for exploited persons.

Heart: Be prepared to witness trauma and suffering.

Support agencies that support survivors.

Influence others. Create networks of concerned citizens.

Support an Equality Model that holds buyers accountable.

Mind: Be open to education. Strive to build a more just and inclusive community.

Work together in developing answers. Practice what to say.

Prepare to engage with media and politicians.

Anticipate resistance and gaslighting.

Spirit: Know and believe that we share a common humanity.

Expand and celebrate equality, respect, dignity, and joy.

Stand in solidarity with the less fortunate and speak for human rights.

Celebrate reverence for life as the primary essence of our spirit.

$ $ $ $

We end with two final voices. One is a female survivor of sexual exploitation from South Africa; the second is a warrior woman from Canada.

Survivor and human rights activist Mickey Meji lives and works in Cape Town, South Africa. She was quoted on Dec. 21, 2021, by the Coalition Against Trafficking in Women:

> We rise for our children and for a better future without sexual violence, paid or unpaid. We rise in the names of those we left behind on the streets and in graves. **We rise until our lawmakers and society see us, hear us, believe us, and do the right thing** (emphasis added).

Diane Redsky from Manitoba has worked on the issue of sexual exploitation and sex trafficking for over 20 years. She, with former Member of Parliament Joy Smith, spoke in favour of five motions to change bylaws in Winnipeg (Executive Policy Committee, Jan. 19, 2022 @ 44:15 min.) to remove the unintended harm of women and girls being sold.

Speaking on behalf of Indigenous women and girls, Redsky's message nevertheless has universal implications:

> This is also about education and awareness, support services for women and girls, addressing the demand, and addressing the root causes of poverty.... It is really important to understand the power dynamic in the sex industry, who has power and who benefits....
>
> There are countless survivors over the years who have shared with me, "if you were to ask me about being in the sex industry while I was in the sex industry, I would have defended it to the death because that is what I had to do to justify in my own mind the victimization I was experiencing." ... Girls are getting younger, there are more of them, and adult women are having to do more sex acts they don't want to do in order to get enough money to pay their rent or to buy food for their children. And it's becoming more violent....
>
> **Let us not make laws to benefit the few when we know it harms the most**.... This is an opportunity to harmonize laws with the provincial strategy and federal legislation.... We must challenge the demand for paid sex in Canada.... Women and girls are paying dearly through violence, and their life-long healing journey, and sadly too often with their lives.... **Please help us.... It is the right decision** (emphasis added).

Who really pays when the commercial sex industry is allowed to flourish unchecked? Those being sold pay with their health and happiness, families pay with heartbreak and helplessness, buyers and traffickers pay with shallow and compulsive lives, communities pay with danger and deception, and the world weeps with tears of shame and sorrow. We believe humanity deserves equality, freedom, respect, spiritual connections, and mutually joyful expressions of community.

Uncomfortable truths can be overwhelming. There may be cognitive and emotional distancing at play, a withdrawal for protection when faced with unpleasant reality, a drawing back from what is too painful to comprehend. This is the "freeze" response instead of "fight or flight." Yet it is only in daring to find space to face painful truths that we are able to shift the status quo. We must address consumer demand in order for freedom to triumph over human trafficking and sexual exploitation. Vulnerable people of the world deserve no less than our full support and compassion.

REFERENCES FOR
CHAPTERS 1-16

Backhouse, Constance B. (1985). Nineteenth-Century Canadian Prostitution Law: Reflection of a Discriminatory Society. *Social History*, Vol. XVIII, No. 36: pp. 387-423.

Bagley, Christopher & King, Kathleen (1990). *Child Sexual Abuse: The Search for Healing*. London and New York: Tavistock/Routledge.

Bagley, Christopher A.; Madrid, Susan; Simkhada, Padam; King, Kathleen; and Young, Loretta (2017). Adolescent girls offered alternatives to commercial sexual exploitation: A case study from the Philippines. *Dignity: A Journal on Sexual Exploitation and Violence*: Vol. 2: Iss. 2, Article 8.

Baptie, Trisha (June 22, 2021). Presentation to the Indigenous and Northern Affairs Committee on its study of the sex trafficking of Indigenous peoples. Government of Canada. https://ourcommons.ca/Committees/en/INAN/StudyActivity?studyActivityId=11274129

Baptie, Trisha (2008). Things you can do to help make a difference. Honour Consulting: https://honourconsulting.com

Baptie, Trisha & Smiley, Cherry (Feb. 12, 2020). Quebec City murder underscores need to abolish prostitution. Policy Options: IRPP. org. https://policyoptions.irpp.org/fr/magazines/february-2020/quebec-city-murder-underscores-need-to-abolish-prostitution/

Barnard, Elissa (Oct. 14, 2021). A Battle Against Torture: Shining a Light on Women's Truths. NS reviews: https://nsreviews.blog

Bedford v Canada, 2010 ONSC 4264 (CanLII). http://canlii.ca/t/2cr62

Bell, Nicole (Jan. 17, 2016). In Her Own Words: Nicole Bell, A Survivor's Story. Worcester, MA: *Worcester Sun*. https://worcester.ma/2016/01/in-her-own-words-nicole-bell-a-survivors-story/

Bindel, Julie (2017). *The Pimping of Prostitution: Abolishing the Sex Work Myth*. London, UK: Palgrave Macmillan.

Boge, Paul H. (2018). *The True Story of Canadian Human Trafficking*. Castle Quay Books.

Brandt, Paul (Nov. 22, 2021). Step Up to the Plate. Presentation to the Rotary Club of Edmonton.

Brown, Brené (May 17, 2018). Dehumanizing Always Starts with Language. https://brenebrown.com.

Cameron, Mike (2019). *Becoming a Better Man: When "Something's Gotta Change" Maybe It's You!* Self-published: https://mikecameron.ca

Canada (AG) v Bedford, 2013 SCC 72, [2013] 3 SCR 1101

Canadian Charter of Rights and Freedoms, Part 1 of the *Constitution Act*, 1982, being Schedule B to the *Canada Act* 1982 (UK), c11.

Canadian Conference of Catholic Bishops (Nov. 22, 2021). Pastoral Letter on Human Trafficking and Sexual Exploitation in Canada. https://cccb. ca/announcement/2021-pastoral-letter-on-human-trafficking-and-sexual-exploitation-in-canada/

Canadian Sexual Exploitation Summit (2021). Disrupt Demand. https:// sexualexploitationsummit.ca/home-2/

CAP (Coalition for the Abolition of Prostitution) International (2020) Activity Report. Paris, France. https://coordinationsud.org/wp-content/ uploads/4.-CAP-Internationals-Annual-Report-2020.pdf

CATW (Coalition Against Trafficking Women) Australia (Aug. 27, 2021). Global letter condemns Victorian Government's decriminalisation of the sex industry. https://catwa.org.au/wp-content/uploads/2021/08/ MEDIA-RELEASE-Global-letter-condemns-decriminalisation-pdf

CATW (Coalition Against Trafficking in Women) International (Aug. 27, 2021). Global Letter Condemning Proposed Legislation to Decriminalize the Sex Trade in Victoria, Australia. https://catwa.org.au/wp-content/ uploads/2021/08/MEDIA-RELEASE-Global-letter-condemns-decriminalisation.pdf

City of Edmonton (April 2015). Body Rub Centres Task Force. https:// edmonton.ca/residential_neighborhoods/community_safety/ body-rub-centres-task-force

Cline, Matt (June 21, 2021). Breaking the Porn Trap. In conversation with Mike David Cameron. https://facebook.com/mikedavidcameron

Cotter, Adam (June 23, 2020). Trafficking in persons in Canada, 2018. Statistics Canada. https://www150.statcan.gc.ca/n1/pub/85-002-x/2020001/article/00006-eng.htm

Criminal Code RSC (1985) c C-46. https://laws-lois.justice.gc.ca/eng/ acts/c-46/

Criminal Intelligence Service Canada (2008). Strategic Intelligence Brief: Organized Crime and Domestic Trafficking in Persons in Canada. Retreived from https://www.unicef.ca/sites/default/files/imce_uploads/DISCOVER/OUR%20WORK/CHILD%20SURVIVAL/sib_web_en.pdf

Dearnley, Ruth (June 27, 2013). Prevention, Prosecution, and Protection—Human Trafficking. *UN Chronicle.* https://un.org/en/chronicle/article/prevention-prosection-and-protection-human-trafficking

Diamond, Casandra (Fall 2018). Casandra Diamond's Fight to End Human Trafficking. *Perspective: A Publication of the Ontario College of Social Workers and Social Service Workers.* https://ocswssw.org/2018/10/03/casandra-diamonds-fight-to-end-human-trafficking/

Diamond, Casandra (Oct. 18, 2019). How I was Recruited into Sex Trafficking: Survivor Casandra Diamond reveals Canada's Dark Underbelly. https://thekit.ca/living/sex-trafficking-canada-casandra-diamond/

Diamond, Casandra (2020). I was sex trafficked for years. Brothels are hidden in plain sight. Ted Talk. https://ted.com/talks/casandra_diamond_i_was_sex_trafficked_for_years_brothels_are_hidden_in_plain_sight/

Dines, Gail (May 7, 2021). From Porn as Violence to Porn as Empowerment: What Happened to Feminism? Canadian Sexual Exploitation Summit: Disrupt Demand.

Dines, Gail (May 6, 2021). Growing Up in a Porn Culture: Harms and Solutions. Canadian Sexual Exploitation Summit: Disrupt Demand.

Dines, Gail (Oct. 26, 2021). Porn Industry: The Driving Force of Prostitution. Podcast organized by Resistenza Femminista. https://resistenzafemminista.it

Dines, Gail (2010). *Pornland: How Porn Has Hijacked Our Sexuality.* Boston: Beacon Press.

Exodus Cry (Sept. 30, 2021). *Raised on Porn.* [Documentary]: Magic Lantern Pictures.

Farley, Melissa (Oct. 2004). Bad for the Body, Bad for the Heart: Prostitution harms women even if legalized or decriminalized. *Violence Against Women.* Vol 10, No. 10, pp. 1087–1125. https://journals.sagepub.com/doi/10.1177/1077801204268607

Farley, Melissa (2003). Prostitution and the Invisibility of Harm. *Women & Therapy* 26 (3/4): 247–280 https://researchgate.net/publication/232850326_Prostitution_and_the_Invisibility_of_Harm

Farley, Melissa (2006). Prostitution, Trafficking, and Cultural amnesia: What we must *Not Know* in order to keep the business of sexual exploitation running smoothly. *Yale Journal of Law and Feminism.* Vol. 18: p. 132. https://openyls.law.yale.edu/handle/20.500.13051/6946

Farley, Melissa (March 29, 2021). The Life's Work of Dr. Melissa Farley, Prostitution Researcher. https://podcasts.apple.com/bb/podcast/lifes-work-dr-meliss-farley-prostitution-researcher/

Farmer, Ben (Nov. 3, 2021). Desperate Afghans selling daughters to avoid starvation. *National Post.* https://pressreader.com/canada/national-post-national-edition/20211103/281500754475382

Fein, Luba (March 29, 2021). The Life's Work of Dr. Melissa Farley, Prostitution Researcher. https://podcasts.apple.com/bb/podcast/lifes-work-dr-meliss-farley-prostitution-researcher/

Ferris, Wendy (2019). *When I Close My Eyes...* Unpublished memoir.

Fieldstadt, Elisha (Dec. 15, 2021). Billie Eilish reveals she watched porn at young age, calls is "a disgrace." NBC News. https://nbcnews.com/news/us-news/billie-eilish-reveals-watched-porn-young-age-calls-disgrace-rcna8863

Fleury, Theoren & McLellan Day, Kirstie (2009). *Playing with Fire.* Toronto: HarperCollins.

Fonseca, Esperanza (July 27, 2020). A Socialist, Feminist, and Transgender Analysis of "Sex Work." https://proletarianfeminist.medium.com/a-socialist-feminist-and-transgender-analysis-of-sex-work-b08aaf1ee4ab

Froutan, Aziz (Nov. 30, 2021). Concern is Not Enough: While human trafficking continues to tear lives apart, new research reveals Canadians are shockingly unaware of the realities or how to make a difference. The Canadian Centre to End Human Trafficking. https://canadiancentretoendhumantrafficking.ca/author/afroutan/page/2/

Gates, Melinda (2019). *The Moment of Lift: How Empowering Women Changes the World.* New York: Flatiron Books.

Gerassi, Lara B. & Nichols, Andrea (2017). Sex Trafficking and Commercial Sexual Exploitation: Prevention, advocacy, and trauma-informed practice. Springer Publishing Company: Connect. https://springerpub.com/sex-trafficking-and-commercial-sexual-exploitation-9780826149749.html

Global Slavery Index (2018) https://globalslaveryindex.org/2018/findings,country-studies/canada/

Goulding, Warren (2001). *Just Another Indian: A Serial Killer and Canada's Indifference.* Calgary: Fifth House Ltd.

Government of Canada (Sept. 4, 2019). National Strategy to Combat Human Trafficking 2019-2024. Public Safety Canada. https://www.publicsafety.gc.ca/cnt/rsrcs/pblctns/2019-ntnl-strtgy-hmnn-trffc/index-en.aspx

Gray, James H. (1971, 1986, 1995). *Red Lights on the Prairies*. Calgary: Fifth House Ltd.

Haak, Debra M. (April 15, 2021). Is Canada constitutionally required to allow a commercial market for sex? Opinion, *Ottawa Citizen*. https://ottawacitizen.com/opinion/haak-is-canada-constitutionally-required-to-allow-a-commercial-market-for-sex

Haak, Debra M. (May 6, 2021). The Limits of Evidence about Prostitution: Sex Work and Sex Trafficking in Canada (2014-2019). Canadian Sexual Exploitation Summit: Disrupt Demand.

Haak, Debra M. (May 7, 2021). The Case of the Reasonable Hypothetical Sex Worker: Update on Constitutional Challenges to New Criminal Commodification Offenses. Canadian Sexual Exploitation Summit: Disrupt Demand.

Häggström, Simon (2016). *Shadow's Law: The True Story of a Swedish Detective Inspector Fighting Prostitution*. Sweden: Bullet Point Publishing.

Hampson, Kevin (June 18, 2014). Let the prostitution bill debate begin. *The Edmonton Sun*.

Harvard Law and International Development Society (June 12, 2014). Does Legalized Prostitution Increase Human Trafficking? An analysis of 115 countries. Posted in LIDS LIVE. https://orgs.law.harvard.edu/lids/2014/06/12/does-legalized-prostitution-increase-human-trafficking/

Hawkins, Dawn (Nov. 8, 2021). NCOSE CEO Dawn Hawkins Shares Her Vision for a World Free from Sexual Exploitation. National Center on Sexual Exploitation. https://endsexualexploitation.org/articles/dawn-hawkins-vision-for-a-world-free-from-exploitation/

Hawthorn, Grace (July 31, 2019). The World is Built Around Men's Orgasms – Dear Men. https://grace-notes.blog/2019/07/31/dear-men/

Hayes, Sophie (2012). *Trafficked: The Terrifying True Story of a British Girl Forced into the Sex Trade*. London, UK: HarperCollins.

Heinz, Andrea (2020a). A Mule for the Patriarchy: Waking up to the harm of prostitution to wives and families. *Dignity: A Journal on Sexual Exploitation and Violence*: Vol. 5, Iss. 3, Article 5. https://digitalcommons.uri.edu/cgi/viewcontent.cgi?article=1234&context=dignity

Heinz, Andrea (2020b). On Exiting from Commercial Sexual Exploitation: Insights from sex trade experienced persons. *Dignity: A Journal on Sexual Exploitation and Violence*: Vol. 5, Iss. 1, Article 8. https://digitalcommons.uri.edu/cgi/viewcontent.cgi?article=1177&context=dignity

Heinz, Andrea (2021). "Sex Work" Ideology as Cult-like Thought Reform. *Radical Notion*: Iss. 3. https://theradicalnotion.org/tag/prostitution/

Hemphill, Chrissy (March 12, 2021). There's nothing harmless about sex buying. *Detroit News*. https://detroitnews.com/restricted/?return=https%3A%2F%2Fwww.detroitnews.com%2Fstory%2Fopinion%2F2021%2F03%2F11%2Fopinion-there-nothing-harmless-sex-buying%2F4646896001%2F

Ibrahim, Dyna (2019). Trafficking in Persons in Canada, 2019. Juristat Bulletin-Quick Fact: Statistics Canada. https://www150.statcan.gc.ca/n1/pub/85-005-x/2021001/article/00001-eng.htm

Immigration and Refugee Protection Act 2001 (Alta) (c. 27) (CAN). Retrieved from https://laws.justice.gc.ca/eng/acts/i-2.5/page-1.html

International Labour Office (2014). Profits and Poverty: The economics of forced labour. International Labour Office: Geneva. https://ilo.org/wcmsp5/groups/public/---ed_norm/---declaration/documents/publication/wcms_243391.pdf

International Labour Office (2017). Global Estimates of Modern Slavery: Forced Labour and Forced Marriage Executive Summary. International Labour Office: Geneva. https://ilo.org/wcmsp5/groups/public/@dgreports/@dcomm/documents/publication/wcms_575479.pdf

International Labour Organization (Sept. 19, 2017). Modern Slavery and Child Labour: 40 million in modern slavery and 152 million in child labour around the world. News: United Nations. https://ilo.org/global/about-the-ilo/newsroom/news/WCMS_574717/lang--en/index.htm

Jansen, Tamara (March 26, 2021). Gender-based Violence. Speaking to the Canadian parliamentary debate. https://facebook.com/tamarajansenofficial

Jay, Suzanne (May 6, 2021). Asian Women in Prostitution: The Intersection of Racism, Sexism, and Class. Canadian Sexual Exploitation Summit: Disrupt Demand.

Jensen, Robert (May 7, 2021). Pornographic Distortions: The Struggle for Intimacy in the 21st Century. Canadian Sexual Exploitation Summit: Disrupt Demand.

Jensen, Robert (May 6, 2021). Pornography and Prostitution: What's Patriarchy Got to Do with It and Why Should Men Care? Canadian Sexual Exploitation Summit: Disrupt Demand.

Jensen, Robert (2017). *The End of Patriarchy: Radical Feminism for Men*. Victoria, Australia: Spinifex.

Kasur, Christy (April 6, 2021). Draw Clear Lines Between Massage Therapy, Sex Work. Guest article, *The Edmonton Journal*, A7. https://edmontonjournal.com/opinion/columnists/opinion-time-to-draw-a-line-between-massage-therapy-and-body-rub-establishments

Kennedy, Sheldon & Grainger, James (2006). *Why I Didn't Say Anything*. University of Michigan: Insomniac Press.

King, Kathy (Fall 2020). Andrea Heinz: Levels of Exploitation. *The Advocate: Alberta College of Social Workers*. Vol 45: Iss. 3. https://issuu.com/acsw/docs/d04374_bird_acsw_advocate_fall_2020

King, Kathy (Fall 2016). Elephants in the Room. *The Advocate: Alberta College of Social Workers*. Vol 41: Iss. 3. https://acsw.ab.ca/document/2062/FIN_FallAdvocate2016.pdf

King, Kathy (Aug. 14, 2000). Family Reflection. Presentation to CEASE memorial.

King, Kathy (March 2, 2021). Presentation to Soroptimist International AGM, Edmonton, following receipt of the JOY Award.

King, Kathy (2018). *Seasons of Life*. Four-part series of reflections. https://missingcara.ca

Kraus, Ingeborg (Oct. 18, 2021). The Nordic Model of Prostitution: A change in perspective in protection of human dignity. Nordic Model Now! https://nordicmodelnow.org/2021/09/18/the-nordic-model-of-prostitution-a-change-in-perspective-in-protection-of-human-dignity/ Press release on European Day against Trafficking in Human Beings.

Kraus, Ingeborg (2020). "Shadow Women: Wives Betrayed by Sex Buyers." *Dignity: A Journal of Analysis of Exploitation and Violence*: Vol. 4: Iss. 4, Article 3. https://digitalcommons.uri.edu/dignity/vol5/iss3/9/

Kraus, Ingeborg (June 6, 2021). Trauma and Prostitution. Webinar. Nordic Model Now! https://nordicmodelnow.org/2021/07/08/trauma-and-prostitution/

Kristof, Nicholas (Dec. 4, 2020). The Children of Pornhub: Why does Canada allow this company to profit off videos of exploitation and assault? Opinion: *New York Times*. https://nytimes.com/2020/12/04/opinion/sunday/pornhub-rape-trafficking.html

Kristof, Nicholas & WuDunn, Sheryl (2010). *Half the Sky: Turning Oppression into Opportunity for Women Worldwide*. New York: Vintage Books.

Lee, Alice; Jay, Suzanne, and Farley, Melissa (March 25, 2021). Prostitution is a Racialized Hate Crime Against Women. https://thistlefarms.org/blogs/prostitution-is-a-racialized-hate-crime-against-women

Lloyd, Rachel (April 19, 2012). Legalizing Leads to More Trafficking. Room for Debate: *New York Times*. https://nytimes.com/roomfordebate/2012/04/19/is-legalized-prostitution-safer/legalizing-prostitution-leads-to-more-trafficking

Loyie, Florence (Oct. 19, 2009). Men who buy sex feeding brutal human trafficking trade, says author. *The Edmonton Journal*, A7.

LucianN (Nov. 7, 2021). Sex Work Should Never Be Considered a Career Choice. https://medium.com/fourth-wave/sex-work-should-never-be-considerd-a-career-choice-75ece2abd20c

Malarek, Victor (2010). *The Johns: Sex for Sale and the Men Who Buy It*. Toronto: Key Porter Books.

Malarek, Victor (2003). *The Natashas: Inside the New Global Sex Trade*. New York: Arcade Publishing.

Maloney, Ryan (Feb. 4, 2021). Tory MP Arnold Viersen Apologizes for Asking MP if She "Considered" Sex Work. https://huffingtonpost.ca

Marr, Stella (April 12, 2012). Nevada's Legal Brothels are Coercive Too. *New York Times: Room for Debate*. https://nytimes.com/roomfordebate/2012/04/19/is-legalized-prostitution-safer/nevadas-legal-brothels-are-coercive-too

Maté, Gabor (2009). *In the Realm of Hungry Ghosts: Close Encounters with Addiction*. Toronto: Vintage Canada.

Maté, Gabor (2021). The Wisdom of Trauma. [Documentary film] produced by Zaya & Maurizio Benazzo, Science and Nonduality (SAND). https://thewisdomoftrauma.com/?gclid=EAIaIQobChMI6NSQiPvH_AIVcSCtBh0HvAB0EAAYASAAEgILSfD_BwE

McGilvery, Priscilla (March 16, 2021). Indigenous Healing. Presentation to Walking in Wellness conference sponsored by Alberta Family Information Liaison Unit.

McLachlin, Beverly (March 9, 2021). The Challenge of Leadership Today. Presentation to the Rotary Club of Oakville Speaker Series.

Mianti, Mariangela (Oct. 11, 2017). Prostitution is Paid Rape, and Men Know It. Il Manifesto: Rome. https://global.ilmanifesto.it/prostitution-is-paid-rape-and-men-know-it/

Michelle, Tanya (2018). *Out of the Shadows: A Memoir of a Childhood Lost, Modern-day Slavery, and a Life Reborn*. Self-published.

Mickelwait, Laila (May 6, 2021). Big Porn Sites. Canadian Sexual Exploitation Summit: Disrupt Demand.

Missing and Murdered Indigenous Women and Girls (MMIWG) Inquiry (May, 2019). *Reclaiming Power and Place: The Final Report of the National Inquiry into Missing and Murdered Indigenous Women and Girls*. https://mmiwg-ffada.ca/final-report/

Moran, Rachel (June 7, 2021) In conversation. What Massachusetts needs to know about prostitution. Sponsored by the Emma Coalition. https://poua.org/poua-news/what-massachusetts-needs-to-know-about-prostitution

Moran, Rachel (2013). *Paid For: My Journey Through Prostitution*. New York–London: W. W. Norton & Company.

Moran, Rachel & Farley, Melissa (Feb. 5, 2019). Consent, Coercion, and Culpability: Is Prostitution Stigmatized Work or an Exploitive and Violent Practice Rooted in Sex, Race, and Class Inequality? *Archives of Sexual Behavior*: SpringerLink. https://link.springer.com/article/10.1007/s10508-018-1371-8

Mott, Rebeca (March 29, 2021). Rebecca Mott: A Journey. https://rmott62.wordpress.com

Mott, Rebecca (June 6, 2021). Trauma and Prostitution. Webinar. Nordic Model Now! https://nordicmodelnow.org/2022/06/04/trauma-and-prostitution-the-transcipt/

Nagy, Timea E. & Moroney, Shannon (2019). *Out of the Shadows: A Memoir*. Doubleday Canada: Penguin Random House.

National Strategy to Combat Human Trafficking 2019–2024 (2019). Public Safety Canada: Government of Canada. https://publicsafety.gc.ca/cnt/rsrcs/pblctns/2019-ntnl-strtgy-hmnn-trffc/index-en.aspx

Native Women's Association of Canada (March, 2010). What Their Stories Tell Us: Research finding from Sisters in Spirit initiative. https://nwac.ca/assets-knowledge-centre/2010_What_Their_Stories_Tell_Us_Research_Findings_SIS_Initiative-1.pdf

Niethammer, Carmen (Feb. 2, 2020). Cracking the $150 Billion Business of Human Trafficking. Diversity. https://www.forbes.com/sites/carmenniethammer/2020/02/02/cracking-the-150-billion-business-of-human-trafficking/?sh=5161f25f4142

Nordic Model Now! (June 5, 2021). A brief history of the 'Sex work is work' movement. https://nordicmodelnow.org/2021/06/05/a-brief-history-of-the-sex-work-is-work-movement/

Nordic Model Now! (March 28, 2017). Amnesty's Dangerous Wishful Thinking on Prostitution. https://nordicmodelnow.org/2017/03/28/amnestys-dangerous-wishful-thinking-on-prostitution/

Nordic Model Now! (Nov. 17, 2021). *Supporting Students Impacted by the Sex Industry... A Handbook for Universities*. https://nordicmodelnow.org/the-nordic-model-now-handbook-for-universities/

Nordic Model Now! (July 4, 2017a). Prostitution Policy and Law: What are the Options? https://nordicmodelnow.org/2017/07/04/prostitution-policy-and-law-what-are-the-options/

Nordic Model Now! (Jan. 4, 2020). Prostitution: What are the problems and how do we solve them? https://nordicmodelnow.org/2020/01/04/prostitution-what-are-the-problems-and-how-do-we-solve-them/

Nordic Model Now! (July 4, 2017b). What's Wrong with Prostitution? https://nordicmodelnow.org/2017/07/04/whats-wrong-with-prostitution/

Norma, Caroline & Tankard Reist, Melinda (Eds.). (2016). *Prostitution Narratives: Stories of Survival in the Sex Trade*. Victoria, Australia: Spinifex.

#NotInMyCity (2017). Our Focus: Five Strategic Directions. https://notinmycity.ca

#NotInMyCity (June 20, 2022). Five Years of Accomplishments for #NotInMyCity. https://notinmycity.ca

OSCE: Organization for the Security and Cooperation in Europe (June 10, 2021). Discouraging the Demand that Fosters Trafficking for the Purpose of Sexual Exploitation. Vienna, Austria. https://osce.org/cthb/489388

Pateman, Carole (1988). *The Sexual Contract*. Oxford, UK: Polity Press.

Pearce, Maryanne (2013). *An Awkward Silence: Missing and Murdered Vulnerable Women and the Canadian Justice System*. University of Ottawa.

Perez, Tomas (May 6, 2020). Telling a Better Manstory. Canadian Sexual Exploitation Summit: Disrupt Demand.

Perrier, Bridget (June 22, 2021). Presentation to the Indigenous and Northern Affairs Committee on its Study of the Sex Trafficking of Indigenous Peoples. Government of Canada. https://ourcommons.ca/Content/Committee/432/INAN/Evidence/EV11455914/INANEV44-E.PDF

Perrin, Benjamin (2011). *Invisible Chains: Canada's Underground World of Human Trafficking*. Toronto: Penguin Canada.

Post, Dianne (2011). Legalization of prostitution is a violation of human rights. *Nat'l Law. Guild Rev., 68, 65*. https://scholar.google.ca/scholar?q=Dianne+Post+legalization+of+prostitution+2011&hl=en&as_sdt=0&as_vis=1&oi=scholart

ProCon.org (June 1, 2011). Percentage of Men (by Country) Who Paid for Sex at Least Once: The Johns Chart.

Prostitution Reform Act 2003. (NZLR). Retrieved from https://www.legislation.govt.nz/act/public/2003/0028/latest/DLM197815.html

Protecting Canadians from Online Crime Act 2014 (c. 31). (CAN). Retrieved from https://laws-lois.justice.gc.ca/eng/annualstatutes/2014_31/fulltext.html

Protection of Children Involved in Prostitution (PChIP) Act 1999. (Alta.) (CAN). Retrieved from https://open.alberta.ca/publications/3054566#:~:text=The%20Protection%20of%20Children%20Involved%20in%20Prostitution%20(PChIP)%20Act%20was,sexual%20abuse%20and%20require%20protection

Protection of Communities and Exploited Persons Act 2014. (CAN). Retrieved from https://www.justice.gc.ca/eng/rp-pr/other-autre/c36fs_fi/

Protection of Sexually Exploited Children Act 2022. (Alta.) (CAN). Retrieved from https://open.alberta.ca/publications/p30p3#:~:text=Description,ceasing%20their%20involvement%20in%20prostitution

Quigley, Joseph (June 22, 2021). 'Proud, proud day for all of us': Newmarket bans 'storefront sex businesses.' *Newmarket Today*. https://newmarkettoday.ca/local-news/proud-proud-day-for-all-of-us-newmarket-bans-storefront-sex-businesses-3894216

Radicailin (2020). Interview with a former brothel madam. https://radicailin.com/interview-with-a-former-brothel-madam-andrea-heinz/

Rahm, Tanja (2016). Internalizing the Violence in *Prostitution Narratives: Stories of Survival in the Sex Trade*. Victoria, Australia: Spinifex.

Raman-Wilms, Menaka (May 4, 2021). Human trafficking in Canada at record high, data show, but likely still underreported. *Globe and Mail*: Ottawa. https://theglobeandmail.com/politics/article-human-trafficking-in-canada-at-record-high-data-show-but-likely-still/

Ramos, Norma (April 19, 2012) Legal Prostitution Can Never Be Safe. Room for Debate: *New York Times*. https://nytimes.com/roomfordebate/2012/04/19/is-legalized-prostitution-safer/legal-prostitution-can-never-be-safe

Renzetti, Elizabeth (July 24, 2021). Who protects wealthy sex predators? Just about everyone. Opinion, p. O2: *Globe and Mail*. https://theglobeandmail.com/opinion/article-who-protects-wealthy-sex-predators-just-about-everyone/

Reynolds, Christopher (March 15, 2021). More than 70 lawmakers call for criminal investigation of MindGeek. *Toronto Star*. https://theglobeandmail.com/opinion/article-who-protects-wealthy-sex-predators-just-about-everyone/

Richey, Valiant (May 6, 2021). Why We Must Address Demand to End Trafficking. Canadian Sexual Exploitation Summit: Disrupt Demand.

Robson, David (May 13, 2019). The 3.5% rule: How a small minority can change the world. In Depth Politics: BBC. https://bbc.com/future/article/20190513-it-only-takes-35-of-people-to-change-the-world

Rowling, J.K. (June 5, 2008). The Fringe Benefits of Failure. Ted Talk. https://ted.com/talks/jk_rowling_the_fringe_benefits_of_failure

Santos-Longhurst, Adrienne (Updated Feb. 12, 2019). Your Guide to Sexual Consent. Healthline Media: Red Ventures. https://healthline.com/health/guide-to-consent

Sarson, Jeanne & MacDonald, Linda (May 7, 2021). Non-State Torture and Sexualized Exploitation: Lynn's Story—Challenging Sellers' and Buyers' Impunity. Canadian Sexual Exploitation Summit: Disrupt Demand.

Sarson, Jeanne & MacDonald, Linda (2021). *Women Unsilenced: Our Refusal to Let Torturer-Traffickers Win*. Victoria, British Columbia: FriesenPress.

Sex Work Act 1994 (No. 102 of 1994) (Former title: Prostitution Control Act 1994). (Austl.). Retrieved from https://www.legislation.vic.gov.au/in-force/acts/sex-work-act-1994/097

Sitka, Jake (April 9, 2021). Patriarchy: What is it and why do men fear it? In conversation with Mike David Cameron. https://facebook.com/mikedavidcameron

Slater, Alexandria (March 15, 2021). The Irony of Choice Feminism. Empoword Journalism. https://empowordjournalism.com

Standing Committee on Justice and Human Rights (June 22, 2022). JUST Committee Report 4 – Preventing Harm in the Canadian Sex Industry: A Review of the *Protection of Communities and Exploited Persons Act.* https://ourcommons.ca/DocumentViewer/en/44-1/JUST/report-4/

Statistics Canada (May 6, 2021). Human trafficking at a record high in Canada. https://www150.statcan.gc.ca/n1/daily-quotidien/210504/dq210504d-eng.htm

Stubbs, Shannon & Viersen, Arnold (Jan. 5, 2021). The Moral Stain of Canada's Tech Sector. Opinion: *Toronto Sun.* https://muckrack.com/shannon-stubbs/articles

Tocher, Annemarie (April 2012). *Domestic Trafficking in Aboriginal Persons: The Legacy of Colonization and Sexual Exploitation. A Review of the Literature*. The HindSight Group. http://firstpeoplesgroup.com/mnsiurban/PDF/reports/Tocher_A-Legacy_of_Colonization_and_Sexual_Exploitation_(2012).pdf

Tyler, Meagan (Nov. 2020). All roads lead to abolition? Debates about prostitution and sex work through the lens of unacceptable work. *Labour & Industry: A journal of the social and economic relations of work*. Vol 31, 2021, Iss. 1. https://researchgate.net/ publication/346902797 All roads lead to abolition Debates about prostitution and sex work through the lens of unacceptable work

United Nations General Assembly (Nov. 15, 2000). *Protocol to Prevent, Suppress and Punish Trafficking in Persons Especially Women and Children, Supplementing the United Nations Convention against Transnational Organized Crime.* Retrieved from https://www.refworld. org.docid/4720706c0.html

United States of America, Department of State (June 2020). Trafficking in Persons Report, 20th Edition. https://state.gov/wp-content/ uploads/2020/06/2020-TIP-Report-Complete-062420-FINAL.pdf

United States of America, Department of State (July 2021). 2021 Trafficking in Persons Report. https://state.gov/ reports/2021-trafficking-in-persons-report/

V (formerly Eve Ensler) (June 14, 2021). Trauma in the Body of the World. In conversation with Gabor Maté. [Documentary movie]: *The Wisdom of Trauma.* https:// thewisdomoftrauma.com/?gclid=EAIaIQobChMI6NSQiPvH AIVcSCtBh0HvAB0EAAYASAAEgILSfD BwE

Vafa, Yasmin & Frundt, Tina (Feb. 10, 2021). Looking Beyond Binaries: The case for partial decriminalization of the sex trade. Commentary: *U.S. News.* https://usnews.com/news/health-news/articles/2021-02-10/ why-the-sex-trade-should-only-be-partially-decriminalized

Walker, Megan & Pugh-Roberts, Caroline (May 7, 2021). Women Forcing Change. Canadian Sexual Exploitation Summit: Disrupt Demand.

Wiberg, April Eve (July 3, 2020). Presentation to Daughters Day, Edmonton.

Wilson-Raybould, Jody (Sept. 2021). Plum Exclusive: Behind the Scenes with Author Jody Wilson-Raybould. Indigo Chapters.

"**"Legalizing prostitution is a gift to johns. It is an invitation to rape and will only exacerbate demand. It will not empower women, as the message that it will convey is 'It is okay to buy and sell the bodies of women.'"**

Victor Malarek

PART FIVE:
EXPERIENTIAL VOICES

1.

APRIL EVE'S STORY: MY VOICE IS MY POWER

April Eve first shared her story with the Alberta Human Trafficking Task Force on Jan. 7, 2021. Appreciation is expressed to Paula Worthington, Consultant Communications for #NotInMyCity, who helped April Eve with her script.

My Voice Is My Power

My story is one of struggle, exploitation, determination, and the pursuit of Truth. I use my story to support other survivors of sexual exploitation. I suffered in silence for many years, but now I know that my voice is my power.

I grew up in a difficult household with substance abuse and violence, and I was the victim of racial slurs and bullying in school. I grew up without my birth mother.

My own substance disorder started when I was still in diapers. I remember being so thirsty that I went from discarded beer bottle to beer bottle while my dad and

244

stepmom slept. I remember spitting out a cigarette butt after choosing the wrong bottle.

I started using alcohol and drugs as a youth to calm my anxiety. At 16, I took a one-way trip from rural Saskatchewan to live with my birth mother for the first time in Edmonton, hoping for a better life. Sadly, as a residential school survivor, my mother didn't have the tools to be able to parent me. I later became homeless and dropped out of high school.

I met an older man who introduced me to cocaine and the nightclub life, where I met new people who made me feel like I belonged. Through him, I met an older woman, an ex-bikini model. She would dress me up and tell me I was beautiful and encouraged me to enter bikini contests in nightclubs around the city. I was only 16, and she fully knew this.

As I got older, I struggled to get by and felt desperate. At a nightclub, I met a young woman who everyone seemingly looked up to. She told me she could take me to a place where I could make money by giving massages. The men asked for more than massages. I was terrified. I got moved around, eventually ending up in New York City, and I was trafficked in various locations for almost 10 years.

Although I am Indigenous, through my exploitation I was always "advertised" as an exotic. Because of my so-called exotic look, I could pass for Latin, Asian, and other races. Clients wanted to buy into a fantasy that doesn't really exist.

By the grace of the Creator, I was able to escape my traffickers and find my liberation. I know I am lucky to have survived; there were so many situations where I could have been murdered or gone missing. Today I have transformed those experiences of trauma to prepare me to be the advocate I am. You need a certain level of dissociation to walk into a hotel room with a complete stranger. I was always afraid, wondering if each day would be my last. I still carry a level of fear to this day, although I am learning to refocus my energy to expose the urgent crisis of human trafficking.

Using my voice and sharing what is so deeply personal is frightening, but I am tired of hiding. What happened to me was not my fault, nor was it the fault of my family. What happened to me is a larger issue in our society. We must break down the myths and educate ourselves and our communities about what sexual exploitation and trafficking are really about.

It is paramount that we dismantle the stigma and shame survivors experience by supporting others like me, providing them opportunities to share their stories if they so choose in culturally safe, non-judgmental, and caring spaces. I know there are other April Eves out there, and I will do everything in my power to protect those who need it most.

2.

COCO'S STORY: TRIUMPH OVER TRAGEDY

Coco (not her real name) shares the tragic impact of intergenerational trauma and familial exploitation on her life. Although she spoke publicly for many years, she did not want her identity revealed in video or print to protect other family members. This story was first presented in *Autumn: Survivor Stories*, Sept. 26 at MissingCara.ca (2018). The names of Coco's family have also been changed.

Triumph Over Tragedy

The tragedy of Coco's life stemmed from several generations of trauma, with many tragic details lost to history. She describes her parents as a "hot mess." Her mother was a First Nations woman who lived with her grandparents as a youngster between residential schools and hospitals; her father was raised by his Black grandmother.

The history of residential schools includes generations of children forcibly removed from their parents, punished for expressing their own language and culture, dressed in unfamiliar clothes, and forced to conform to strange new routines. As well as enduring these indignities, many children were singled out for acts of sexual abuse from their caregivers. Coco's mother, "Deedee," was removed from her grandparents with placements in several different foster homes and institutions and became a ward of the government at age 13.

Deedee met Dayton, three years her senior, when she was 16 years old, and they had three children together. Coco was the second child, born when her mother was just 18. Deedee and Dayton's relationship was short-lived, and their children were frequently in government care, as Deedee herself had been, returning intermittently to various family members.

Coco's understanding is that her mother lived in oblivion and drank through all three pregnancies. Deedee had endured years of physical and sexual abuse where she learned "don't talk, don't trust, and don't feel." Everything that had been done to her, she acted out on Coco—beatings, face slapping, name calling, hair pulling, and even turning a blind eye when visiting men molested her. Pretending to sleep was a protection Deedee learned in residential school, when the girls who were awake at night were the ones taken out of their beds to be raped.

Coco's father, Dayton, also learned to survive in a harsh environment. Born in British Columbia to a White woman, he was reportedly abandoned in hospital until claimed by his Black grandmother. "Nelly" was part of a movement of Black Americans who'd left Oklahoma in the early 1900s to escape racism. Whatever had been done to her, she too probably acted out on the children in her care. Young Dayton became Nelly's personal servant, constantly reminded that he was indebted to her for having been rescued.

Dayton grew up with alcohol and drugs, as Grandma Nelly ran a bootlegging operation in north Edmonton. Such establishments, with adjunct brothels, were part of the anecdotal folklore of Western Canada before, during, and even after Prohibition (1916–1923). Coco often spent time, between foster homes, with her father Dayton and his Grandma Nelly. There she used to watch girls come in the front door to meet men and leave by the back door with a supply of drugs.

Dayton's alcohol use led him to experience massive blackouts. He used to wake Coco when he was drinking, call her names, beat her, and the next morning be friendly and loving, with no recollection of what he had done the night before.

Coco was a hungry eight-year-old when a man offered her $20 to lift her shirt. She did as she was asked because she wanted to feed herself and her brothers. She remembers going to the corner store that day and eating "like a king." The man returned regularly, and his requests became more intrusive as the weeks went by. Coco consoled herself with knowing that, on those days, she would be able to eat and not be hungry.

Later, Coco was groomed by a neighbour who addressed her physical and emotional needs by offering gifts, compliments, safety, meals, and "love." Such positive attention would be comforting to any young girl hungry for belonging, but "grooming" is simply another name for manipulation. After gaining Coco's trust, her new "friend" sold her to a pedophile, a man who handcuffed her to a bed, injected her with drugs, and raped her for hours. The tragedy was that no one told, and no one seemed to care. Coco ended up being the man's sex slave for two years when she was only nine to eleven years old. She thought she would be free when the man was shot on his front yard, but she was addicted to speed after frequent forced injections.

"You're sitting on a gold mine, baby. You'll never be hungry."

Coco remembers Grandma Nelly telling her she would never have to worry about money because she was a girl. All she had to do was open her legs. Dayton in turn positioned Coco to procure income by arranging for her to have sex with strangers eight to ten times a day while he watched from inside the closet. Dayton and Coco would shoot up together between visitors. Coco accepted their association as love because it was the only father bond she knew at the time. They remained allied when Dayton later provided childcare for Coco while she "worked" the street.

Coco's mother, Deedee, had attempted suicide on many occasions. After separating from Dayton, she continued to be involved with abusive men, unable to protect herself or her daughter. Coco recalls rescuing Deedee many times after she cut her wrists or overdosed with pills. Coco was age 24 with her own baby girl when she received the last phone call from her mother and found her body in bed, the phone still clutched in her hand.

Coco estimates that she endured over 50,000 sexual violations during 27 devastating years of drug abuse and exploitation. She survived many broken condoms, seven attempted murders, two babies kicked out of her stomach, and needles in every vein of her body. She thought she was living the life she was born to live, didn't know how to quit, and did not believe she was worthy of anything different.

Amazingly, Coco was slowly able to turn her life around. Although plagued with chronic health concerns from years of abuse and addiction, she is finally able to celebrate a new life with healthy children. "There's no shame to my game anymore," she proclaims. "I broke the cycle of abuse, and I want to save young people from having to go through what I went through."

Coco credits many supportive people with teaching her new skills and helping her channel the inner strength she didn't know she had. She was a regular speaker with Edmonton's STOP: Sex Trade Offender Program and passionately volunteered to educate youth about the dangers of grooming and exploitation.

3.

JENN'S STORY: WHERE DO I BELONG?

Jenn speaks of feeling alienated at home and trying to find her way as a young teen, illustrating how easily vulnerability can become victimization. Trafficked as a minor from Edmonton to Vancouver and transported internationally when she was merely 18 in the early 1990s, Jenn miraculously returned to Canada and rebuilt her life as a responsible single parent, professional employee, and home-owner. Her story was first shared with Udunma Ikoro from Nigeria in her book, *The Intentional Woman* (2021), which features women who overcame various obstacles. Jenn continues to give back to other women who want to leave the sex trade.

Where Do I Belong?

I was born in Ottawa, Ontario, on a frosty November morning in 1975. I flew into this world two months pre-maturely, weighing a tiny three pounds. I was kept in the hospital for an extra month to fatten me up to five pounds before I was allowed to go home. My mother tells me the nurses moved my incubator close to the radio because I'd kick my feet to the beat of the music.

My mother was single, which was frowned upon in the 70s. She was 26 at the time, and after helping care for her 10 siblings, she felt she was fully capable of raising her baby on her own. She was an attractive woman with short brown hair, cute dimples, and a wide smile. She took great care of herself and me.

I have been told I was a sweet and funny child, clever, and didn't sit still for very long. I loved my mommy, playing with friends, and swimming in the neighbourhood pool. My father was not around. My parents had a brief relationship off and on for a year, but my mother said he was only interested in the physical perks. He was not happy to discover she was three months pregnant and promptly disappeared.

I knew very few details about my father. The ones that stick out were that he enjoyed muscle cars, marijuana, and music. I met him only once. He stopped by one evening when I was three years old. My mom recalls that he didn't engage with me or pick me up. He borrowed $10 from her, and we never saw him again.

In the early 80s, when I was age six, we moved across Canada to Alberta. My mom heard of opportunities out west, and she wanted to get away from her large and chaotic extended family. She found a job at a grocery store and soon after met a handsome cowboy who was divorced with two teenage daughters. Over the years we had some fun road trips to the mountains and freshwater lakes for camping and sightseeing.

There was frequent arguing and resentment between my mother and his daughters, as they were used to being on their own with their dad. Nevertheless, he and my mom married after five years of living together. Shortly after their nuptial ceremony, I mentioned, "So you're my dad now, huh?" He walked away as my smile fell to the floor. I felt invisible. Unheard. Confused. I thought, *I don't belong.*

There was no wedded bliss, and an already fractured family was now my reality. There were many arguments about whose kids were worse and who didn't say or do what. I reverted to the basement bedroom with my music. My mother and I started to get into physical fights as I became older and more defiant; she was the aggressor. I was increasingly disrespectful and not willing to follow her strict rules. We weren't communicating or listening to each other. My parents' bickering was constant. I felt like an unwelcome visitor.

At the end of ninth grade, I lost my virginity to a boy I liked at school. It was nothing how I imagined it would be. Pretty uneventful, actually. He told everyone at school, and I was labelled as the town hussy. High school was difficult, and no one noticed my grades were slipping. My friend and I would often skip school to hang out with a group of boys who shared an empty apartment.

I quit school at age 15, halfway through grade 10, got a retail job at a little shoe store in West Edmonton Mall, and moved in with my 19-year-old boyfriend. At the time, it was a lot better than being an outsider in my own family. My boyfriend was funny and charming. I had big plans for us.

And then, two of his friends raped me.

I realized it was rape only after it happened. I said, "No ... please no." I was overpowered. I was violated anyway. The hot tears on my face and filthy contaminated feeling coursing through my veins and covering my skin told me I was raped.

I said NO! Why did they do that to me? Why? What should I do? What CAN I do? No one will believe me. I'm only 15 ... I don't belong here.

I couldn't tell my boyfriend. I was afraid of how he'd respond to me... or to them. My worst fears came true. He heard I had "slept with" his friends, so he violently assaulted me, using the steel pipe from his weight-lifting bench. It left me with bruised ribs, a twisted hoop earring, and a broken heart.

Maybe I had asked for it? Did I flirt with his friends? Did I deserve that beating? Does he love me like he says he does?

I had nowhere to go. I was hurt, angry, and all messed up. In turn, I assaulted a girl right in front of the store where I worked. She came at me with a group of five or six other girls to fight over a boy, and I wasn't going down easy. I landed in juvenile jail. The girls behind those walls taught me everything I needed to know about how to survive in the wild.

After being released, I was quickly devoured by street life. Sex trafficked and exploited at age 15 throughout Western Canada, I was passed around [among] pimps and two group homes created specifically for street kids. The safe houses offered structure, love, routine, safety, regular meals, and a reprieve from the emotional trauma and mayhem that is street life.

It was always a relief not to have to interact with sexual predators, deviants, and addicts. The social work ladies who worked with us were our surrogate mothers when we couldn't mother ourselves anymore. I was a sex worker at 15 years old, surrounded by other fragmented girls and women who had chosen drugs over their children, or who seemed to live to satisfy their pimp's demands. I was neither.

Pimps, like parasites, lived off the resources of broken women and girls with families who ached for their safe return. These vultures would drive around in silk and velour two-piece suits and detailed cars, while their stable of girls/women would rent their bodies to porn addicts, lawyers, mechanics, and farmers.

In fact, Canada's most vile and murderous serial killer, Robert "Willy" Pickton, was plucking unsuspecting women from the same area I was working. He would offer them heroin and lure them to his pig farm, where he would torture them and kill them and feed them to the pigs. He confessed to killing 49 women. Forty-nine women. The reason I was spared, I believe, is that I had never done heroin. I didn't look or act like a junkie. I looked like a child. I was a child. I did not belong.

At age 18, an acquaintance and ultimately a human trafficker transported me to Macau, Asia, with promises of fast money. He said I would get $10,000 when I stepped off the plane for starters. He sold me to a Triad (Chinese mafia) businessman who put me in a brothel. As soon as I landed, I had to sign an IOU to pay for my flight there, food and lodging, and the original $10,000 Hong Kong dollars he gave me. ($1,796 Canadian at the time). He placed me in a high-class gentlemen's club, "China City." Travelling wealthy businessmen from every corner of the world, and countrymen with bad breath, would peruse the place looking for a lady of the evening.

Most of us were barely 18. There were Russian, Brazilian, Columbian girls, and others from all over Asia. A handful of us would be corralled into a private room where the men were seated. A mamasan would shout our country of origin. "Canadaaaiiiii!" We were expected to feed the men fruit on sticks, be pleasant, and look sexy. We were also referred to by our number outside of the garishly decorated rooms. Mine was C07, "See-lang-chat!" As English was my native tongue, it was not difficult to speak with many of the customers, but there were so many from mainland China that negotiating prices and services was often frustrating, and no one wanted to discuss politics or world affairs anyway.

My agent took half of what I made at the club. The half I kept went to living expenses, and there was barely anything left for a plane ticket home. I had no way home for about five months. One of the Columbian girls had a sugar daddy who helped me get to the airport in Hong Kong for a long-awaited flight back to Canada.

Only one month back, I was raped for seven excruciating hours by a housemate where I was staying.

Again. Please, God, no. Are you there, God?

I finally had enough. I was an empty vessel floating in the ocean. I was so violated that I didn't even recognize myself anymore. A transgendered woman I had just met noticed I was going through some kind of internal storm and convinced me to press sexual assault charges. My assailant was picked up at the same house [where] the assault had taken place.

Two weeks later, I met someone who didn't want to hurt me, and I became pregnant. I went to court at five months pregnant for the preliminary hearing. I had just turned 19. It still blows my mind. The actual trial was so traumatic that I know firsthand why sexual assault survivors don't go through with testifying. The good news was that he was sentenced to seven years in prison for sexual assault and unlawful confinement.

I was finally able to escape the madness.

Fast forward 25 years. I raised a beautiful and smart daughter by myself, lived in a house I was able to purchase, and worked in the same field for over 20 years. I am also a portrait/visual artist and run a charity that supplies free products and services to women leaving the sex trade. I have been given much grace and support and feel it is my job to do the same. I am grateful for all my life. The good, the bad, and the ugly.

4.

JESSICA'S POEM: WHY?

Jessica, a mother of two, sold sex in Edmonton city-licensed "body rub" parlours for five years. Her bitter reflections underscore many social and public health issues that require examination, including wage parity, employment opportunities, economic support for children, improved police response, accountability for offenders, and trauma treatment.

WHY?

WHY ARE THERE WHORES?
To be or not to be (a hooker); *that is the question.*
WHY?
Because of the Wage Gap.
Because our rights as women have been stripped away.
Because the best way to feed and clothe your children is with a dick in your mouth.

Because some men do not take responsibility for their own children.

Because the world has robbed us of our sisterhood.

Because our pain has been taken away. We no longer allow ourselves to grieve.

Because Rape is a fact of life for billions of women and children every day.

Because the victims of sex crimes are treated with less dignity than phone scam fraud.

Because when I reported my rape, I was asked what I did wrong.

Because when I asked the police about the pedophile who wrecked my life, they told me there was "not enough evidence."

Because the trickle-down economy has me in chains and wearing cement shoes; when the tides come in, I drown a little each time.

Because when my body breaks, my friends flee.

Because I was the target of sexual interference and abuse, I learned to fight back.

Because fighting back meant exploring my sexuality at a young age.

Because when you start at age three, you are a fucking prodigy.

Because the slut shaming forced deviance and shame.

Because when push came to shove, I was a starving single mother with nothing to show after four jobs and eating at the food bank.

Because it was decriminalized and required only licensing
and police checks.
Because for the first time in my adult life, I was able to
buy an outfit for myself.
Because seeing the pain and suffering like a third world
country, I saw the whole thing in my back yard.
Because the Reservations are overflowing with crime,
drugs, suicide, murder, incest, deep generational poverty.
Because no one who hasn't stepped foot on Aboriginal
land can say anything.
Because when I asked for help, I was met with criticism
and resentment.
Because the world is a dark, ugly place.
Because my moral compass might be broken but it still
knows the difference between right and wrong.
Because I am broken, but money can help put me
back together.

5.

JUANITA'S POEM: FAMILIAL EXPLOITATION— LOYALTY OR LOVE?

Juanita Murphy is a woman of two cultures, African Canadian and Cree First Nation, who dedicated many years to helping create awareness of sexual exploitation. She received a Woman of Courage Award from CEASE in 2010, a YWCA Woman of Distinction Turning Point Award in 2012, and an Esquao Award in 2013 from the Institute for the Advancement of Aboriginal Women. Juanita worked as a public educator and peer mentor with CEASE until she retired for medical reasons. She was the recipient of a double lung transplant in 2022.

Familial Exploitation—LOYALTY OR LOVE?

Familial exploitation, one seed of property, servitude to family, loyalty is dark.
Familial exploitation, intertwined, amongst my basic needs of survival.

The seed feeds in umbilical poison of generations
of trauma.
Family blood is pumped into brain, scattering dysfunction
cell by cell.
Neglect is weaved into my muscles.
My heart was held together with money, pumping dollars
for a meal and love.
Lungs pumping like a coal-eating train, screaming *"save
me, save me, save me"* with each breath.
My eyes are forced to focus on men with money.
My brain walking through dog shit, needles, condoms,
empty alcohol bottles, drugs.
Just to hear my addicted father slur, "Where is Daddy's
little girl?"
My skin was never mine; it belonged to the family.
Crawling through rooms of pain, each session, each scar a
badge of honour. For being a good girl. I did not cry.
My voice groomed out my mouth, by power and control,
to keep family survival secrets.
My ears hearing family bartering my worth into dollars.
Putting me in that pretty pink dress meant I am sacrificed
for family honour.
Groomed into believing every stranger is a family friend.
Every man a family friend.
We all had a part to play in the wheel of familial exploita-
tion. Aunts gave sex trade tricks. Uncles were good-time
partners. Cousins were all on the block to watch me.

My daily assignment was to get the spoon, mix the dope, heat it in the spoon, help tie my daddy's arm, find a vein. I was proud to make Daddy feel better.

One day, I was told to put the tie on my arm. Being junkies together, that was family love.

Being the only girl in a family of men, I was told to be proud for being a girl. From the day I was born, I was reminded that I HAD A GOLDMINE between my legs.

I HAVE riches. That solidifies my place in family.

I was the lucky one?

I can hear my brother crying. I began to wonder, what price did he pay to establish his place in this family?

I forgive those who harmed me; what they did to me, someone had done to them.

The wheel of Familial Exploitation is a hard chain to break, but I did it.

6.

KATIE'S STORY: RESCUED

Testimony from Katie about her five-year journey, 2009–2014, exposes the suffering that can follow even a "voluntary" entry into the sex trade, the descent into mind-numbing trauma, and the challenges of a successful exit.

Rescued

I entered the sex trade months after I turned 20. My childhood had been difficult from the few memories I have, and my teen years were even more so. Despite a mundane, comfortable middle-class existence, my home life was marked with emotional abuse and parents who hated each other. This developed into a deep insecurity. I started cutting myself at age 11 (before it was in or "edgy") and slowly morphed from a quiet perfectionist to a teenager desperate to escape with alcohol and weed. I moved through a series of intense, volatile relationships, desperate for the attention, approval, and unconditional love of a man.

I had just left one such relationship when I met Eric in a remote work camp in northern Alberta. He was working on an oil rig, and I was the medic. He immediately noticed me ... and I loved it. Every day he came to talk to me, he listened to my relationship woes, my financial woes. Back in Edmonton, I was living in a friend's unfinished cement basement on an air mattress. The day we left camp, Eric promised to take me out for dinner and drinks, and he did. He opened doors for me, complimented me, made me feel special and important. Things moved rather quickly. I started to learn things about his life that should have been red flags, but instead, they intrigued me, and I wanted to be in that world—drug dealing, gambling, clubbing. All of it.

A few months into dating, he told me about a friend's wife who was opening a massage parlor. I knew relatively nothing about the sex trade, other than what I had seen in movies. He told me it would be a way for us to build the life we wanted, it would only be temporary, and we would emerge rich and live happily ever after. I was shocked when I spoke to the friend and found out it was not just massage and blowjobs; full sex with every client was expected. I pushed down my discomfort, and out of love for Eric and an insatiable desire to be in his world, I agreed.

The three years that followed are a blur ... trauma is strange like that. There are memories I can't bring into my consciousness at all, and others that are so deeply ingrained that it feels like I am reliving them nearly 10 years later. At first, I only lasted a few months before having a complete breakdown. I was having sex five days a week, with four to five men a day. I told Eric, in a fit of tears, I couldn't do it, it was too hard, too disgusting, too painful. He didn't care ... he callously said he wasn't going to be the only one in our relationship making hundreds of thousands of dollars a year. His response was such a departure from his earlier behaviour.

Eventually, I returned. This time was markedly different ... I rarely did a session sober. I was always drunk or stoned. I would smoke on the way to the brothel. After each session, I would shower the filth off and race to the back door for a joint and a drink. A few months later, I tried coke for the first time, which was really the beginning of the end for me. For the next few years, the only time I wasn't high was when I was in the hospital or treatment. Coke was the answer to all my problems, and my life became a vicious chase of money, coke, and pills ... trying to stay numb and forget the things I had to do behind closed doors.

I will admit that at first, I loved it all ... I loved the money, the partying, and my newfound "sisterhood" at the brothel. I loved the delusional belief that I was his "down-ass bitch" and together we would build a life. Slowly, though, that all faded away. Parties devolved into me using for days on end alone, nights bleeding into morning, police being called because I was suicidal or because Eric had beat me up, extended stays in the hospital for overdoses or suicide attempts, detoxes, and treatments centres. My behaviour was dangerous and erratic. Once I totalled my car on my way to my drug dealer; under my winter coat I had on only lingerie, as I had to go back to the brothel for a client. Often, I had no place to stay at night and would end up at a drug dealer's house or at a motel with them. I wasn't really living, and I hoped many nights that I would not wake up. I tried countless times to leave Eric but always found myself back in his grip.

Around the spring of 2012, I was back with Eric, and he suggested that I move to Toronto. His friend, who had several girls working for him, had moved some of them there and they were making a lot of money at a strip club. The idea of escaping my current life was appealing … Edmonton had become a nightmare. No one wanted anything to do with me; I had burned every bridge with friends and other working girls; even addicts thought my drug use was terrifying to witness. I lived only to use, and I was desperate for a change, so I sought to escape across the country.

I barely remember being on the plane or my first few days in Toronto. I eventually got a job at an escort agency and spent the majority of my days doing in-calls at condos around the city or going to clients' houses. I was again doing drugs every day and putting myself in dangerous situations—blacking out when on outcalls and passing out at client homes, sharing very personal information, not letting people know where I was or who I was with. I had more admissions to the hospital, where the staff first planted the seed that Eric was more of a pimp than a boyfriend. It took some time, but eventually I could admit that he didn't love me and was only using me. The staff started to share ways that I could exit and the support I could have, and for the first time in several years, I started to think seriously about getting out.

One night, Eric and I got into one of the worst fights we ever had. He hit me hard, and I went headfirst into the wall. When I woke the next morning, my face and arms were badly bruised. He would not let me leave the condo for days. Shortly after that incident, I went to the welfare office, where a kind worker gave me an emergency needs cheque that day. I found a room for rent, threw all of my lingerie and sex work paraphernalia down the garbage chute, packed up my things, and left. I knew nobody in the city and had not been sober or had any legitimate work experience in years. I never saw Eric again and never turned another trick.

Traumatic flashbacks those first few months were debilitating; suddenly my chest would tighten, my head would spin, my heart would thump and skip beats, and I would think I was going to die right there. I hated physical touch ... being hugged made me feel like my skin was crawling. My thoughts raced ... all of the unwanted sexual interactions, the years of abuse from Eric, him holding a gun up to me and threatening to kill me and my family if I left him. I had been raped in Las Vegas and very few people believed me; one person actually said, "Can a hooker even get raped?" My brain felt like it went in circles trying to organize the series of events over the past years, trying to fill in days lost to blackouts, thinking of all the people I had hurt.

I moved to a sober living house for young girls and worked with a social worker who specialized in helping women leave the sex trade. Slowly but surely, I began to reintegrate into society, though I could never free myself from the terrible burden that I had experienced and the ways I had victimized others. I continued to suffer from PTSD, depression, anxiety, dissociation, and self-harm. I suffered from extreme mood swings or total numbness and felt nothing toward other people. It felt as though my conscience had been ruined beyond repair.

It was in that state of absolute desperation that I came to a faith in Jesus Christ. Years earlier, a former stripper had told me how Jesus had saved her and restored her, and for the first time, I believed in God, the God of the Bible.

After that, I felt an immense weight lifted off my spirit. My mind rested for the first time in years, knowing that I was forgiven and could finally forgive others. I reached out to whomever I could to make amends for the pain I had caused. In the past six years, God has indeed restored me … He has given me back real emotions and real relationships and many opportunities to use my story to help others in addiction and show His power to heal the broken-hearted.

I am now happily married to a man who really knows and loves me, and we have a beautiful son.

7.

MARIA'S STORY: FOR MY SISTERS

Maria Elroy (her chosen alias) was once a struggling nursing student. She shares some of the trauma she experienced in less than a year trying to make extra money as a licensed provider in Edmonton in 2007. She was 23 years old at the time.

For My Sisters

I remember her hollow eyes, sunken into her angular and weathered face. Her emaciated body lay twisted in the bed, rectal tissue hanging from her anus. She was not 10 years my senior but had been living and working on the street since her youth. Years of drugs, physical and sexual abuse, hardships unimaginable had damaged her physical body beyond repair.

Here she was in the ER. The rectal tube, designed to hold her damaged bowel in place, was no longer adequate, leaving her skin sore and inflamed from frequent leakage.

We, the medical team, were trying to build her a new anus from hydrocolloid dressing. I think about her a lot. I wonder if any of the men who used her do.

Rewind a couple years earlier; shame overwhelmed me as I applied for my body rub licence. My hands shook so badly as I struggled to sign the city documents. How did I find myself in a position to be filing an application for student loans to attend nursing school while simultaneously applying to work in the city's licensed massage parlours? Massage being the sanitized euphemism for sex.

Debt and desperation.

I was so ashamed and scared. Before I started, I spoke with the owner of the massage studio where I would be working, and she calmed me with reassurances that I would not have to do anything that I didn't want to do. I would be provided a level of safety by working indoors, [and] there were security cameras and other women there to help me with difficult situations.

What difficult situations?

Well, it turns out that when you are new to the business, every creep and perverted weirdo patrolling the review boards wants to come take the new ride for a spin. Because that's all you are—a product experience. They know that you're naive and scared. They want to try their bullshit on someone new. Try to convince you to undercut the other girls, blow them without a condom, kiss their disgusting mouths, slip the condom off, choke you out, hurt you, traumatize you. Whatever they think they can get away with, they'll try it.

Always with some bullshit excuse, "If you let me do this to you, I'll be your regular. I won't see anyone but you." They manipulate and abuse you, using your lack of experience and fear to control and extort you for their gratification. Like a rapist, control and trauma seem to gratify them as much as an orgasm, maybe more.

Fortunately for me, through sick and twisted fate, I was selling my body alongside one of my best friends. She protected me from many of the creeps and perverts, but even she couldn't prevent the occasional, terrifying choking. Or the sneaky attempts at condom removal that were so revolting I wanted to peel my skin off and vomit my insides out. I never knew what a man would do once the door was closed. Some of the verbal degradation was even worse than the physical.

One guy tried to remove the condom while he pathetically attempted to hammer my vagina. When it slipped off, he kept trying to penetrate me, even though I could feel it was gone. I pushed him off me and ran to the bathroom, tears welling up in my eyes. I had to fish the thing out of myself, unsure if there was semen in it or not. He was banging on the door demanding to "see the trap," because he "paid money to finish," and goddammit he wasn't "done yet." I was just a product to be consumed; it wasn't even a human experience. All he wanted was to get his money's worth. To finish. When I wouldn't leave the bathroom, he ranted about me being a useless whore, who couldn't even get him off.

Never mind the man was practically impotent and even trying to get him hard enough to put on the condom was like being a bird trying to pull a worm out of the ground. But I was the useless one. In hindsight, I laugh at his shriveled old body and impotent rage, but in the moment, I was terrified and disgusted with both myself and him for putting me in that situation. If I'd had a knife, I might have killed us both right then and there.

There was a kind of comradery between me and my friend. Our new common ground was so incredibly painful and grotesque [that] it gave us incalculable amounts of dark, raw, comedic material. Some of our experiences were so disturbing and humiliating the only way to cope was to make a joke about it. Or better yet, make a joke of the trick, the punter, the f**king loser who couldn't achieve real consent from an actual adult female. There were plenty of those.

Plenty of freaks would probably have frightened a normie gal with the kind of requests we received. Like, who wants to jerk a dude off with their toes and then let the man f**k their feet while he screams about how sexy they are. All while wearing female lingerie. It's not exactly a first date conversation: "So, how freaky are you? Like, crossdressing foot-fetish kinky? Or am I wasting my time?"

Now there are websites for that sort of thing, so I imagine the buyers have really upped their game behind closed doors. Now it's paying for things **no one** *would let you do without some kind of transaction. I don't even want* to imagine. I never had one of the sickos wanting to role play pedophilia. I guess I wasn't petite enough for that.

Trying to sleep was the worst. I started mixing alcohol with Ativan. That's when I couldn't escape myself, my thoughts, the violent disgust that shrieked inside my head. Relentlessly tormenting me and telling me what a worthless scum bag I was. I didn't deserve to live; I was a whore. What if everyone knew? What if everyone could tell at a mere glance that I was damaged and discarded, unworthy of love and respect?

Because that's how it feels.

That's how it feels every time a woman's body is dragged out of some gutter or cheap motel room. That our lives are meaningless, unworthy of love. What did we think was going to happen, living a "lifestyle" like that?

A LIFESTYLE LIKE WHAT?

The lifestyle of a student, barely getting by and accumulating more debt than any bank should even allow? Or the life of a single mother who can't meet the financial needs of her children, working two jobs, and even if she could, having *zero* time to meet their emotional needs?

Or is it the lifestyle of an abused runaway who's never known love and care, who now finds those comforts in drugs or alcohol? What lifestyle is it exactly that makes prostituted women supposedly disserving of such cruel brutality? To be disregarded as merely subhuman detritus? Those lucky enough to be warm, well fed, and worry-free have no right to cast such judgments on others.

8.

TANYA'S STORY: OUT OF THE SHADOWS

Tanya Michelle is a remarkable survivor now living in Edmonton who shares her story in *Out of the Shadows: A Memoir of a Childhood Lost, Modern-Day Slavery, and a Life Reborn* (2018). She dedicates her time to providing support to other women still caught in the despair of sexual exploitation. Tanya wrote and published her own book for personal catharsis and to help raise money for her Made for More project. Excerpts from her memoir are shared:

Out of the Shadows

I was the girl who was brutally victimized, I was the loner at school, the outcast of my family, the one who felt unloved and unworthy most of my life. My childhood in northern BC was one of pain and violence with an indifferent mother and a giant scary stepfather. As a child I did not understand depression; I only knew our mother did not protect me and my two younger brothers from the cruelty of our father. We all lived in fear of his rages.

I was groomed at age thirteen by a girl my same age. I had run away from home, ended up in a group home, been raped on two different occasions, and attempted suicide. Then, miraculously, I was befriended at a treatment centre by another resident, a beautiful bubbly confidante who listened to me and promised we would be friends for the rest of our lives. I realized later she had probably targeted me before we even spoke.

One day on a pass, my new friend insisted on showing me the bright lights of Vancouver. She introduced me to a group of friends including a man she "worked for." Later she encouraged me to share an apartment with her, and the pimp quickly made his intentions clear. Still aged thirteen, I was introduced as his new "wifey" and told my job was to earn $500 a night. That was 1989.

Days turned into weeks and life took on a schedule and routine. I knew what was expected of me; I needed to make money, but for the most part, I felt like I belonged. I belonged to my man, I belonged to our family of girls, and to this life. I no longer had to worry about where I fit in or where I would stay or how I would eat.

The downside was all the men. At first, I didn't know how to handle it; I could feel my mind, heart, and soul going numb. Eventually, while my body was being used by sick perverted men, I would just float to the top of the room, completely leave my body, and separate myself from the horror that was my life. Just so I could survive.

The weeks quickly turned into months. Soon it had been a couple of years and I continued to work on the streets of Vancouver. Later, at age sixteen, I was sold to another pimp for drug debt and extra cash. This man was exceptionally violent. He expressed rage and displeasure with his Pimp Stick, a wire coat hanger used as a whip. Frequently, I was forced to continue work after covering bruises on my face and body with make-up as much as possible.

Resentment and rebellion were building deep in my soul. I hated this man when he beat me and called me vile names. But then it would feel good when he told me he loved me. He was always so happy when I gave him the money I made each night. He took care of me; he fed me, housed me, clothed me, and truly made every single decision for me.

He reminded me daily that I had nothing without him, was nothing without him, and that "square" people hated me because of what I was doing. Only he would love me and accept my darkness.

Every hand that touched me seemed to be slowly rubbing me completely out of existence. I had been with so many strangers that, as time passed, they became a blur of bodies, hands, dicks, and hundred-dollar bills. Any act of kindness was a shock and I responded with disdain. I didn't trust anyone and believed I was nothing more than a worthless whore, good for only one thing. The whole time I was bonded in fear. When I look back at that time of my life, I felt like a caged animal, just wanting to escape and survive.

Somehow, we ended up in Edmonton and I became pregnant. He wanted his own child and I had managed to avoid that possibility for four years. My pregnancy was a complete blur. The whole time my belly grew, the violence increased, beatings became more severe, and I feared I was going to die. I was so terrified for myself and my unborn baby. She stayed very still inside my belly, as if trying to stay hidden from the monster that was her father. He began to talk about taking her and ending my life.

I was forced to work the street all through my pregnancy and had one night in the hospital alone with my daughter after she was born. Then I lost everything. He changed her name and our lives the next day. I continued to work every day while he refused me any time with our daughter. This time I realized he would ultimately kill me rather than have me beg for my life over and over.

Beatings continued and he eventually forced me to sign away my parental rights, allowing me to escape barely clothed. I was a twenty-one-year-old girl, beaten to a pulp, with no one to call for help. He had stripped me of everything.

Fortunately, I was able to find shelter in a safe house and had support in giving a statement to police. Days turned into months before he was located. In the meantime, my support system helped me with housing and funding for school. Although I temporarily gained custody of our daughter, he continued to harass me, and I was not able to prevent his access. After a final serious assault, I quit fighting. He continued to control and extort me by allowing visits only for large sums of money.

It was not until after the birth of my second daughter, four years later, that I finally said "No more! No more money, no more drugs, no more control!" I also made the difficult decision to spare my first daughter continued conflict and did not see her again for thirteen years.

HUMAN TRAFFICKING! Watching a documentary one evening years later awoke something in me. I sat in almost a trance-like state, staring at the screen, listening to each and every word. People were preying on young girls, telling them all the things they wanted to hear, making them feel loved. Then these girls were manipulated into selling their bodies and souls. It sounded all too familiar to me.

So many feelings washed over me as I listened, so much sadness for those young girls, so much anger for what they had to endure. I was shocked that it was still happening to so many others. A sudden feeling of acceptance and validation swept over me. For most of my life, I believed I needed to keep those early missing years of my life a shameful secret from the rest of the world. For so many years I truly believed all the bad things that happened to me were my fault.

At that very moment, I began to see the truth; I'd been the Victim! I had carried shame and guilt for so long that I no longer needed to carry. I had been TRAFFICKED, sold, and placed in SEXUAL SLAVERY, and now I finally had a name for it. For decades, I called myself a survivor but was unable to put into words what I had survived. Sexual exploitation? Yes. Domestic violence? Yes. The system? Yes.

Now I had a new name to identify what else had happened to me: TRAFFICKING.

For the first time, I began to feel justifiable anger toward the people who had exploited and abused me, rather than at myself for making wrong turns and huge mistakes. A sense of forgiveness washed over my whole sense of self. I wanted to reach out and hug each of the young girls and tell them they were worthy of real love.

I also wanted, for the first time, to share my story with the world, my REAL story. The good, the bad, and the ugly. I was done being silenced. I wanted to ensure others understood about Human Trafficking and what is being done to our children across our country. I have learned that trauma bonding takes full advantage of victims and creates slaves. Human Trafficking uses a complicated mental process to entrap victims.

I spent twenty-two years of my life shackled by shame. I am now a strong woman with an even stronger voice, a voice to educate others right here in Canada. My story demands to be told. Shame loses its power when it is brought into the light and out of the shadows!

9.

WENDY'S STORY:
WHEN I CLOSE MY EYES...

Wendy's manuscript in progress shares her memory of being forced to sell herself for sex after travelling across Canada to join her new "boyfriend" in Edmonton. She thought it would be a summer adventure. Little did she know what he and his friends had planned for her and how quickly her life would change. Some excerpts are provided:

When I Close My Eyes ...

All three were up and waiting for me when I awoke. I do not remember who mentioned it first. The idea that I could sell sex for money. I laughed it off, a simple, "No, I do not think so." This was a joke; they were not serious. They could not possibly be serious.

They continued all day, telling me how much money could be made. "I don't care. I am not going to be a whore." I could not believe they were even suggesting this, but I was not scared. I just kept saying no I wasn't doing this. I still felt I had control, agency, over myself.

I could not believe that they really wanted me to do this. All day, on and on they went trying to convince me. My answer was always the same, "I will not." I am adamant, there is nothing they can say that will change my mind, I will NOT do this. They can talk until they are blue in the face. THIS IS NOT GOING TO HAPPEN.

From the outset, this should have told me where I fit in my boyfriend's world. I meant nothing. I was less than nothing. In that moment, though, all I could think was how do I stop this, how do I get out of this? Looking back, I see how vulnerable I was to having someone control me. How easily manipulated I was, and so blind to it. If not for such dire consequences, I could almost laugh at how naive and ridiculously unworldly I was ...

The first night he tricked me into getting ready to visit a friend. Instead, he stopped the car in a laneway and made me get out. In that moment, I was lost. I did not know what to do. I could not think. I has no idea where I was, alone in the dark, in a strange city. I can still close my eyes and feel the terror. A car pulls up and I get in. The man is so disgusting. He wants a blow job. I tell him $200. He refuses and drops me back in the laneway. I feel desperation set in. Another car stops. It is a young man about my age, clean and as nervous as I am. We agree on $40 for a blow job. He drives somewhere and we are only parked a few minutes when a police car pulls up. I pretend to be his girlfriend; he drives me back to the laneway and lets me keep the money. The guys pick me up, ask for the money, and we all go to the bar.

Back at the apartment, [my boyfriend] starts to say about tomorrow and I blurt out, "I cannot do this again." He turns on me and shoves me into the bathroom, up against the shower doors. His arm is underneath my chin, pushing my head up and against my throat. "YOU WILL DO WHATEVER THE FUCK I TELL YOU TO DO."

He is staring right into my eyes; this is not someone I know. This person is a stranger, and he does not care about me at all. His eyes are cold, and he is shaking. I am terrified of this man. He gives a little push against my throat/chin, so my head goes back just a little and then walks out.

Even then he is not finished. To make sure I understand, he and his friends come into my room, and they all rape me ...

I was broken.

The next day they took me back to the laneway.

The shame I felt was something I could taste ...

When I close my eyes, I can remember that I am not angry. I am not panicked. I am nothing. I am frozen. My brain cannot think. I cannot feel anything. I am not thinking of how to get away. I am not thinking about where I can turn to. Nothing. I am frozen. I cannot explain this. I do not know why. To anyone who says I would do this, or I would do that, if this had been them. No, no they would not. They do not know what they would do if it had been them. My reactions were my reactions. I cannot explain and really nor do I have to. I was not the guilty party in this. But I did not know that. To me I WAS guilty. This was my fault. I did not save me.

For the next few months, all I remember is customer after customer. Man after man. I cannot remember how many, or what they wanted to do to my body or for me to do for them. As long as they paid the asked price, I went with them. I performed sex acts in vehicles, in a park beside the river, at men's apartments.

One night I was raped with a knife at my throat and dropped off in an area I did not recognize. I was alone and lost. I had no idea where I was or how to get back to the laneway. All I could think of was that I had to get back to the laneway. I ran, terror at being lost and alone driving me to run. Run fast and find your way. I have no idea how long I ran or where I ran. I know I was going in circles and then ... there was the car. My boyfriend's car. Relief poured through every pore of my body. I was going to be okay. I was back with them. I was not lost anymore.

When I close my eyes, I can still feel the power of that relief. The utter overpowering of emotion at finding my way back and seeing them. No one can possibly understand how I could feel this way. These men were abusing me. I know that. But they were the safest of all that was unsafe. Of everything that is unsure, I know them. They are all I have in this world. They are all I have as in a connection to home. I cannot go to the police; I am a criminal. I am a prostitute. I would be arrested. I would go to jail. I have NOTHING and NO ONE, but them.

How do I feel? I feel grateful. I am GRATEFUL. Grateful this man is not beating me. Grateful this man is being nice to me. Grateful I have survived another day. I am not thinking about having been raped less than two hours ago. I am not thinking that I was made to swallow the ejaculate of a stranger who might have AIDS.

I am thinking that I am grateful that my boyfriend who asked me to cross the country to live with him, and is now making me sell sex for money, is not going to beat me. Grateful …

The days go by. The guys go out, I clean, they come back, I get ready, we go out, and I sell sex. I have no idea how many men I have had sex with or performed oral sex on. It doesn't even matter anymore. The number doesn't matter. All I care about is not getting arrested.

Each night, in the laneway, I pray that God will send men that will not hurt me. Ones that will not rape or beat me, murder me. I am ashamed that I would even pray this.

Another time I was viciously assaulted and robbed. I had no way to call the guys and no money for a cab. So, I called the police …

I have no choice but to tell them how I came to be in the car with the man. I am still crying, nearly hysterical, and one of the officers says to me, "Well what did you expect when working on the street?"

I have to write out a statement of what happened. I tell them how long I have been here and that I live with my boyfriend and his two friends. One officer asks me if my boyfriend is my pimp. I tell him no. He is my boyfriend.

In my mind, how can a boyfriend be a pimp? A pimp is a guy who has lots of girls working for him. Not his girlfriend. My boyfriend is not my pimp; he is my abusive boyfriend who I want to escape but he is not a pimp. Not in my mind.

I look back now at the naivety of this thought process and want to shake that stupid girl. I want to scream at her and ask her how she could be so stupid not to realize that not only was he a pimp, but his friends were also too. That I not only had one pimp, I had three ...

What people do not understand about girls like us is this. We have no one. No safety net to fall on. No one to help us and fear permeates everything, to the point we trust no one. Even the people we used to trust are suspect now. How can we trust people that we KNOW look at us in disgust? How can they not look at you in disgust when the image of your face in a mirror makes you feel disgust about yourself? ...

Prostitution is falling down the rabbit hole unwillingly into a world of degradation, filth, fear, danger, drugs, and jail. There is no landing at the bottom and working your way back home. You NEVER get to go back to the beginning. The beginning is gone. Your past life is gone. All you have now is tumbling down and down. Desperation to find something or someone to anchor to will cause you to make horrible decisions.

Significantly, Wendy's story happened before Canada's *PCEPA* legislation. After 2014, she would not have had to fear being arrested and would hopefully have been treated more respectfully by the police.

10.

WENDY'S VICTIM IMPACT STATEMENT

An unusual sequel to Wendy's story was that her pimp/boyfriend and his abusive buddies were charged and convicted for several offences, including procuring, living off the avails of prostitution, and sexual assault in a unique historical case brought forward 24 years after their initial assaults and exploitation. Wendy returned to Edmonton in February 2015 to present her Victim Impact Statement to the court prior to the sentencing of the three men. A summary is provided:

> My process of seeking justice was not about revenge. It was not out of malice or hatred. It started from my extreme need to gain some sort of closure and healing from the abuse I suffered. It started from my need to show myself and the people in my life that I was a victim, not a criminal. It was to show myself that I was not, am not, and never will be complacent about the abuse I suffered. I needed to show my abusers what they did to me was wrong. I

wanted to force them to understand and take responsibility for what they did to me.

Abuse does not stop when your abuser is done with you. The long-reaching effects continued through my life, permeating everything. I was eaten up by its malignancy throughout, the black horror that I have lived with all these years.

Nothing in my life prior to meeting these three men prepared me for what they did to me. Adult men saw an opportunity in a naive teenage girl and they acted with calculating forethought and no mercy.

I am unable to adequately convey or do justice to the disbelief, horror, terror, and panic at what was happening to me. There are no words to describe the terror that they really meant to do this and the helplessness that still leaves me in shock nearly twenty-four years later.

Looking back, I can see what I might have done to save myself. That does not change the abuse I suffered or make me an accessory. My worst fears were that people would find out and hate me because I was so disgusted and revolted at myself. I had been prostituted and I felt worthless.

The men who paid for me thought nothing of me other than what they paid to do. They saw me as human refuse. Rape, sodomy, violence, strangulation, being thrown from a moving vehicle, being left in the prairie in the middle of winter, being left naked and bleeding in an alley were part of my constant terror. And even worse was not coming back with money. Even fear of the police was paralyzing. There was no safe place. Ever.

289

The first time I was arrested, an officer asked me if my grandmother was a whore too. That is exactly how he spoke to me. He looked at me and saw a whore, not a teenage girl with no criminal record, not a victim in need of help, not a young girl far from home and alone. He only saw a whore. Who I used to be and where I came from no longer mattered.

My former world is lost to me. Guilt and shame have been my companions for so long it is hard for me to just let them go.

There are physical ramifications from the abuse I suffered. Many bladder and kidney infections resulted in scar tissue that affects their functions. I had to undergo multiple surgical procedures and have permanent damage. Years of blood tests and worry about HIV and Hep C. Missing teeth from being punched and teeth damaged. Debilitating headaches from stress, anxiety, and insomnia. I am also certain that having my head punched, smashed off the steel frame of a bed, floors, and walls have contributed to the chronic headaches. Scars from injuries during beatings add to the list. Constant nausea and fatigue.

The career I could have had, the life I could have lived, was stolen from me. I have a high IQ and could have done so much with my life. I was robbed of the opportunity. While my abusers lived the life they wanted, I was chained to a past I could not escape.

I can say I am luckier than most. I am alive. I am here to be able to tell my story. I think about how my bones could be scattered in a field by animals and my family left with no answers as to what had happened to me. No answers, no closure, no grave to visit. Would my abusers have cared? I think not. Their only concern would be about where they could get money. A new girl would have to be found.

I am angry. Angry that three men thought the abuse and misuse of a teenage girl was acceptable. In essence, they murdered who I was and who I could have been. I grieve every day for that girl. I want to save her, protect her, but I can't. It's too late. All I can do is try to salvage the life of the woman I am today.

I am angry at a system that failed to save me. A system that saw me as a criminal rather than a victim in need of help. A system that further victimized me and does the same to so many girls. I am angry that society turns a blind eye to sexual exploitation. I am angry that my family had to suffer. I am angry that I will have to spend the rest of my life struggling with the memories and effects of what was done to me.

I am angry that this trial had to happen, that I had to endure the humiliation of describing all the disgusting and debasing things that happened to me because of you. That you treated me as disposable.

I am NOT disposable. What the three of you have done to me—the trauma, hurt, anger, pain, destruction, degradation, stolen years, stolen hope—will NOT be the end. I will move on and help others. This is NOT the end of my story. I am a survivor. I will make MY life mean something.

PART SIX:
GUEST CONTRIBUTORS

1.

ANONYMOUS:
MY TANGLED WEB—A JOHN'S STORY

A former buyer chooses to write his story under the pseudonym of John. While this may seem a bit cliché, considering the subject matter, he believes it to be very apropos.

My Tangled Web—A John's Story

She told me her name was Debbie. She was quite tall, with brunette curly hair, and in her late twenties, and she was dressed very nice. We had just made a date, but she said she didn't get into a stranger's car. She quickly flagged down a nearby taxi, and the two of us got into the cab. The truth is, Debbie was a hooker. She propositioned me on a cold November night in the downtown core of the city. I was 17 years old at the time, and this was the day I lost my virginity and the first day of my 35 years as a sex buyer.

"Sex buyer." On the surface, it is a very appropriate term, but today it repulses me, as it should. It should have repulsed me on that first day, but here I am. How could I be one of "those guys?" All in all, I was a decent young man at the time. I had a relatively normal upbringing in a large family from a rural home with no reason to believe I wouldn't grow up to be a responsible and trustworthy man.

The day before this first encounter, I had a heated argument with my father, and I left home. I had recently graduated high school and was living at home trying to save money to further my education. This is where my "decent guy" persona begins to show some cracks. Beginning in junior high school, with puberty raging through my body, I started the typical acting out and testing the boundaries most young men do at the time.

Prior to this, I was a solid A to B student with a zest for learning. Not particularly strong in athletics, I was more of the artistic type and enjoyed drawing, painting, and woodworking. Now for the other boys my age, it was all about styling their hair, smoking at recess, punching each other in the shoulder, cars, and noticing girls. This appealed to me, and I was desperate to be one of the guys. I joined all of the sports teams, went to weekend parties at the lake, and tried hard to fit in. Slowly my grades in school began to slip as I tried to carve out a niche for myself.

I coasted through high school, and while I graduated with a surplus of credits, my academic c.v. was rather lacklustre. During grade 12, I met a beautiful girl from a neighbouring town and fell head over heels for her. Unlike myself, she was grounded in life with a clear path laid out for her. My continued acting out and lack of seriousness about my future led to me getting into trouble with my peers. I wanted so much to be the cool guy, but in hindsight, I was undisciplined, immature, and living in the moment. This led to the eventual breakup with my girlfriend, and I was devastated. Although I eventually recovered and carried on, I was still rudderless in any meaningful direction.

I eventually returned home, flat broke, defeated, and embarrassed, but determined to get an education and away from the mundane boredom of small-town life. I worked for two years before leaving home again, this time with what I hoped was a plan for adulthood and my future. Arriving in the big city was exciting for me. The fast pace seemed to spark something in me, and I was thriving. Enrolling in and doing well in college was the fuel that kept me going.

I don't know if it was the fact that I was in a new situation (city life) that sparked it or the fact I was on my own, making my own decisions, but sex was an ever-consuming obsession since my first time. I often thought about how easy it was to engage in so-called transactional sex, and I quickly and deeply descended into it. I sought the company of girls on the street, both in the low track area of Edmonton, referred to then as "The Drag," as well as the higher-end girls on "The Stroll," where I had my first encounter. I chose this rather than cultivating a normal, organic relationship with the opposite sex.

Exotic dancers started showing up in what seemed to be every second bar. Massage parlours and independent escorts, both in and outcall, were popping up almost daily, with risqué advertisements in the newspapers. I fell for it all, hook, line, and sinker. Over the next few years, I saw the entire gamut of the sex trade. You wouldn't know it to look at me or talk to me. I was one of those guys who seemed to have his act together, but in truth, I was living a secret life of sex addiction.

With the advent of technology, namely the internet, it was only a matter of time before I became addicted to pornography as well. I became a frequent user of escort review websites, where members would discuss and rate the "looks, attitude, and service" of various women throughout the city working independently, as escorts, or in massage parlours.

To analyze it today, the concept of such a rating system is akin to that of the prices of meat posted in the grocery store window, but at the time, I justified to myself that this would be a safe place to gather information. I got to know some of the men posting on this site by way of private messaging. I can't say I developed any friendships there, but I was able to discern who seemed to be of like mind and in a similar situation as myself.

Many service providers were also members of this site. Most of them actually advertised there, and a majority of them chatted with the men, both in open forums and private messaging. Dates were arranged on this site, as well as group meetups in social situations for both the men and service providers. I never attended any of these functions. On the seedier side of things, I also noticed that, occasionally, groups of men would organize group sexual encounters with several of the ladies.

There were several types of men who frequented the review site. I suspect the majority of them used it for information only (voyeurism?) and never participated in any of the conversations. A small group would ask questions of others but not offer any personal experiences. The active members who wrote the majority of reviews were all very prolific in their participation. Of this last group, there were several subsets that were generally behind the scenes. They would include the website administrators and moderators and groups of men who met one another in person, as explained earlier.

While many of the men kept personal information private, the makeup of this group spanned across all societal, cultural, and socioeconomic groups. There were construction workers, professionals such as doctors, engineers and accountants, government workers, lawyers, and even rumours of the odd celebrity and politician hiding behind fake names and avatars.

There was a service providers section where only the women could interact with each other. This was purported to be a secure section where the ladies could verify the identity and past interactions with any of the male members.

Looking back, and not just in reference to the escort review boards, it's almost unfathomable the amount of "infrastructure" around the sex industry today. Be it custom software to host review boards, image verification software whereby you can upload a photo from an advertisement of a sex trade worker to verify it as genuine, to offshore websites hosting various sex sites, and long before the final exploitation of the worker actually occurs, there are endless hours of human capital expended in the forging of countless cogs on the gears that keep this industry chugging along.

Throughout these years I never had a brush with the law and thankfully contracted no sexually transmitted infections, but I did also see the ugly underbelly of the sex scene. I witnessed a prostitute, unable to find a vein in her arm, shoot heroin between her toes in order to numb herself enough to have sex with me. One would think that might have been enough of an event to stop me in my tracks, but it disgusts me that I just brushed it off and had sex with her anyway.

I recall another time when a young lady paused while giving me a blowjob to say, "Hey, my mom is working the streets tonight too; maybe you saw her." At the time, what she just said should have served as another "what the hell was wrong with you?" moment, but instead, I let her finish the blowjob.

Not too many men can say that they've witnessed a woman move her baby from its crib to a separate room to have sex with a John, but that was me, and there I was. She handed the baby to her mother, who lived with her.

One evening during the summer of 1987, I picked up a prostitute working the streets, and we went to a nearby motel. After agreeing on a price, she turned out the lights and said she needed to get something from the bathroom before we started. Sensing something wasn't right, I ran from the room, somehow fumbled with my keys unlocking my car, and flew out of the motel parking lot in reverse, then swinging the car around in a "J-turn" or "Rockford Slide" just like the movies. From my rear-view mirror, I saw no fewer than four or five men running out of the room where I had just bolted.

Eventually, the sex addiction wasn't working to satisfy whatever I was looking for, and after every encounter, I started feeling shame. Coupled with the fact that I'd struggled for years with being overweight, I was now self-medicating with food. It wasn't uncommon for me to gorge myself at McDonald's drive-thru after spending hours cruising the streets or visiting a massage parlour or escort. The food helped pile shame on what I was doing. I guess I told myself if I was going to live like an animal, why not wreak havoc on another area of my character I was ashamed of and worsen that too.

On several occasions, I seriously contemplated suicide. I hated myself. I hated what I was doing to myself, let alone the lives of others. I was a narcissist, thinking I was entitled to any pleasure I desired; then I was appalled by myself when acting out, only to repeat this destructive behaviour countless times over. How could I possibly feel both of these emotions? A remorseful jerk seems a bit oxymoronic because everything I did, I did willingly.

Throughout this period, I had a long-term girlfriend, and we eventually married. I was still purchasing sex, but after we got married, the frequency of my cheating decreased. After five years of marriage, the shame of my actions caused me to leave my wife. While we had our own issues, be it sex, money problems, and careers, I left because of guilt. It was a gut punch for her, my betrayal.

After a year we reconciled, and for the next 25 years, life moved along. The first years I remained faithful, but I eventually returned to my old ways. For some spells I was buying sex once a week for several months, followed by perhaps once every six months to a year. During this time, my marriage remained stagnant, but to people on the outside looking in, we appeared to be a normal couple. My wife had lost all interest in sex, and this was the only excuse I needed to step outside our marriage. She didn't want to seek counselling and didn't feel we couldn't work out any of our problems on our own, but these issues were always shelved, as life has a habit of getting in the way. It's much easier to ignore and avoid conflict. Over the next five years, I fell deep into sex addiction once more.

My workdays were consumed with thoughts of sex. Having an office with a managerial position, few coworkers, and little supervision, I could hide behind my computer screen searching out porn and sex provider ads, then act out with no suspicion as I told my coworkers I was leaving for a few hours for a "meeting with potential new clients."

It was during the end of June of 2017 that I decided again to leave my wife. My birthday was the next day, and I selfishly thought I'd go out with a bang, return home, and announce to my wife I was leaving for good. Using an anonymous texting app on my smartphone, I arranged a date with an independent escort advertising on the now-debunked Backpage website. I quickly set up a meeting with an escort at a local hotel.

Upon opening the door, the woman walked quickly to the far end of the hotel room and invited me to come in. As I passed the washroom and entered the bed area of the suite, from behind the wall, a blur of men rushed me. I flashed back to the time I ran from the motel suite years ago, believing I'd soon be dead or seriously beaten for my wallet.

I still can't recall the words said by the men around me, but I was soon in handcuffs, noticed the badges and sidearms on the hips of these plain-clothed police officers, and quickly realized I was being arrested. I was led across the hall to another room, where I noticed a couple of uniformed police officers and other men also in handcuffs. I was informed that I was under arrest for communication for the purpose of obtaining sexual services.

I was then led to an adjoining room and ordered to sit on the side of the bed alongside two other men. I cowered with my head down the entire time. My phone and money were taken from me. The money in my wallet was counted. After what seemed an eternity, a soft-spoken officer entered the room to talk to me. He explained why I was arrested and what my options now were.

Thankfully, he said I'd soon be free to go, and I would not be taken to jail that day. I was written up and handed a document showing the charges against me. While it was all a blur at the time, he informed me that while I had broken the law, I was also being offered a second chance. If I paid the fine, met with a probation officer, and attended a day-long "john school," the charges against me would be dropped. I was then instructed to leave by an emergency stair exit. I later learned that their sting operations resumed, arresting a steady stream of men for the remainder of that day.

I lived the next six months in complete fear. Who was going to find out? Would my name be on TV? What was I going to do if this got out among my family and friends? What about my son? Eventually, the day of john school arrived. I lied to my wife, explaining that I was helping a friend move that day.

I arrived at the meeting place with my head down as I met the facilitator, Kate, who took my name and the money order for my fine. What struck me was her friendly attitude toward me, something I wasn't expecting. I was positive I was there to be berated and scorned, which would have been fully justified. I entered the meeting room and was told to take one of the empty chairs. Slowly glancing up, I saw the room full of men of various age ranges, then quickly returned to looking down at the carpeted floor as I made my way to my seat.

Throughout that morning, a host of different presenters spoke to us. It began with the police officers, including those who had arrested me, explaining why we were there and how the john school was offered as an alternative to formal charges in the hopes that re-education on the effects of the sex trade would impact not just those who had been arrested, but society as a whole.

A representative from the Crown explained in detail the seriousness and consequences of various degrees of sex crimes, while the probation worker laid out how being charged with a sex crime can affect one's life. Prior to the break for lunch, a nurse from the Sexually Transmitted Infections clinic gave a presentation, and free STI testing was offered to all in attendance.

The school in Edmonton was hosted by CEASE, the Centre to End All Sexual Exploitation. As opposed to payment to the Crown, all of the fines from the attendees were payable to CEASE in support of their community efforts to help reduce the harms of sexual exploitation. During the lunch break, I sat quietly by myself, finally comprehending the gravity of my situation and the realization that I was at a serious crossroads.

I wasn't prepared for the afternoon session of the school. During this time, we were asked to reflect personally on how our life was impacted as sex buyers. A psychologist spoke on the reasons men purchase sex and asked us to consider making productive, meaningful life choices.

We heard the tragic story from the mother of a girl who had been murdered. The young lady had lost her way in life and became a tragic victim to the underworld of street life. The presenter reminded me of my own mom, similar in appearance and mannerisms. I was so ashamed to sit in her presence.

The next two presenters were former sex workers. Thinking I was well versed in what prostitution is, any knowledge I thought I had was soon dashed as both ladies laid out their respective life stories and offered anecdotes of unspeakable horror I never could have imagined. I quickly realized how little I did know and how my years of purchasing sex had a negative effect on those women I engaged with.

One of the ladies presenting had a familiar life story, and a few things she said sounded familiar. I finally made the connection that she and I had communicated several times on an escort review website, although we had never met in person as a john/service provider. After listening to her presentation, I was thankful that I wasn't a direct part of any of the anguish she experienced as a former sex trade worker, but then again, I was an active participant just being a sex buyer. Even though we'd never met, I was still a component of a large machine.

Late in the afternoon, at the conclusion of the school, Kate asked all participants to reflect on and share what we had learned from the day, and what actions we were going to take to not take part in the sex trade again. My turn came to stand up and speak. I apologized for why I had to be there that day and declared that after 35 years, I was finished with being a sex buyer.

Following the meeting, I approached Kate and asked her if there was anything I could do to help her out. I finally realized that I needed to atone for my actions and find some way to make amends for my involvement in perpetuating the sex industry. She asked me to return to john school and tell my story. Kate and I met for coffee, where I opened up about my past. She encouraged me to simply share my story.

The first time I spoke was very difficult. When I arrived at this meeting, I was welcomed by Kate and the police officers and made to feel quite comfortable. It felt strange to address the men, being that only a short time prior to that day, I sat among them.

I've returned and spoken at eight meetings since I first attended as an arrested john four years ago. Admittedly, on some days it's difficult to speak to the men, but it's my continued hope that something I might say during my presentation might strike a chord with one of the gentlemen in attendance, which will lead him to make some changes in his own life.

The four years since my arrest have been a time of deep self-reflection. I've looked beyond myself and have found satisfaction in helping others, be it going the extra mile at my job to offering a listening ear to a friend or family member. I've not forgotten my past. I admit there are days when I can't fathom what I've done, but I have to set that aside in order to become a better person.

In the end, only truth matters. Truth in speech, but more importantly, truth in actions. The truth is, I willingly participated in actively purchasing sex, regardless of the consequences. I had sex with hundreds of strangers, spending thousands of dollars along the way. The greatest expense was not monetary. It was the residual mental harm I did to myself, but more importantly, the harm I inflicted on the women I exploited. I added to the problem. That is the truth.

I hope that one day I can feel that I can be viewed by others as someone who can be counted on, to be valued, and be considered a gentleman. I hope that by speaking and conducting myself with honour and humility, it will have a net positive effect on others. I've decided to maintain the secrecy of my arrest. The only people who know are the facilitators and participants I've come to meet at the john schools. At this point in my life, I felt it best to abandon the old me and embrace this second chance I'd been given.

As far as what defines who a john actually is, I don't believe there is a good answer. Sadly, you might say they could be anyone. It crosses all boundaries of race, culture, socioeconomic standing, education, intelligence, and vocations. Sex is still a very taboo subject, more so in the context of sexual exploitation. It isn't a comfortable subject to discuss in casual conversation. It's not something anyone really wants to talk about, whether you are an anonymous john, a lawmaker, or a layman. This lack of exposure drives it further underground and hardens its shell.

I failed as a husband. I failed my character. I failed as a person. Despite this, I did have a part in raising an exceptional son. He is now grown and on his own, professionally employed in a rewarding career. While I know he is grounded in life and is an exceptional young adult, I can't help but pray he doesn't repeat the dreadful sins of his father.

How did this all happen? While I've never totally subscribed to the concept of repressed memory, I recently recalled that growing up in a farming community in the 1970s, it wasn't uncommon for children as young as 10 or 12 to babysit their siblings or the neighbour's children. At the age of 10, I was called on several times to sit with children a few miles from my home.

On two occasions while sitting late at night, I was awaked by an attempted molesting at the hands of the children's 80-year-old grandfather. I will omit the details, but simply say that these memories were locked away for over 40 years. Could the events have helped form who I am today? Perhaps, but I was an adult while a habitual sex buyer, and regardless of events leading up to that point, I knew right from wrong. I owned my choices because I alone made them.

Moving forward, I have done an extensive amount of reading and research in the hope of understanding my past. I've seen psychologists as well who have been of great benefit. Looking back, my arrest was the best thing that could have happened to me. It was the one reality-defining moment as a 35-year sex buyer. I'm hopeful and gaining confidence that this former life is behind me and that I will be successful in rebuilding my character and worth.

It is said that we are a sum of all our parts, and we must not let one small facet define us, but I spun a web of my own making. I sincerely hope that any pain I've caused by being a willing participant as a sex buyer might one day be outweighed by some of the good I have yet to do.

As I move forward, this quote helps provide me with inspiration:

"Being male is a matter of birth. Being a man is a matter of age.
But being a gentleman is a matter of choice."
—Vin Diesel

2.

DOLTZE, HENNES: ENGAGING MEN AND BOYS

Hennes Doltze managed the Prostitution Offender Program (POP) with the Salvation Army Correctional and Justice Services (SACJS) in Winnipeg, Manitoba, between 2013 and 2020. POP has operated as a restorative justice program in Winnipeg since 1997. Hennes believes it is essential to include men in combatting sexual exploitation and domestic violence in order to create safety for women and girls.

Hennes has a strong interest in social justice and advocacy and has held various positions in the justice, child welfare, and mental health field in Canada as well as Germany. He is currently (2022) leader of the project "Empowering Men—Engaging Men and Boys to Prevent Sexual Exploitation" with the Ma Mawi Wi Chi Itata Centre in Winnipeg under executive director Diane Redsky.

The name Ma Mawi Wi Chi Itata translates from Ojibway into the phrase, "We all work together to help one another."

Engaging Men and Boys

"Men too make choices. When will they choose not to despise us?"
—Andrea Dworkin, Intercourse

I have worked many years with men who purchase sex from other people and, over the years, have given many presentations about my work. Before beginning a presentation, I look through the audience to see how many women and men are in the room. There are usually about 85% women and 15%, sometimes fewer, men in the room. The reality is that most of the work to address sexual exploitation, prostitution, and sex trafficking is still shouldered by courageous and strong women. We, as men, have a long way to go in doing our part to address the ongoing injustices brought on by sex buying.

When it comes to the gender difference regarding who pays for sex, the numbers are even more staggering. During the seven years that I managed the Prostitution Offender Program (POP) in Winnipeg, not one woman was arrested. This highlights that buying sex is almost exclusively a male activity, not just in our city but anywhere. I believe we need to expand our view of prostitution and focus much more on the reasons, motivations, and activities of men as sex buyers.

At the beginning of the POP seminar, we would ask: "Why do men buy sex?" The answers that typically came up were: "Because of frustration, boredom, or stress; it's a novelty, and I can live out my fantasies; it's convenient; there is no commitment necessary and no emotional investment required; for entertainment; or to satisfy an immediate sexual urge." Other answers were more disturbing: "Practising sex acts seen in pornography or that their partner will not do, to feel in control, or to dominate the other person." Others mentioned loneliness, poor self-esteem, conflicts with their partner, male bonding, and peer pressure. We created a space where participants could talk and be open to listening and receiving information from different presenters.

Many men have very ingrained attitudes, justifications, and beliefs about prostitution and the impact of their involvement. Our discussions still focused on the dominant narrative of prostitution as a victimless or even enjoyable activity for women. Many men believe they are helping the women with their money, that women enjoy having sex with multiple men every day, or that it is the women's job to satisfy their sexual desires. Some men realize women may be in the sex industry because of poverty, abuse, or coercion. However, this does not prevent them from wanting to purchase sex. The men often experience a level of cognitive dissonance, choosing their own personal gain over the well-being of the women. They see women in the sex industry as objects rather than human beings with personal stories of financial, emotional, social, and spiritual desperation that led them to this place.

At the same time, most men believe they are treating the women with respect and dignity, that they are the "good johns" and not creepy or abusive as some "other" guys. This allows them to justify and continue their own behaviour. In our work with sex buyers, the program focuses on exposing those contradictions and on humanizing the individuals who sell sex so that buyers understand the reasons why women enter the industry in the first place.

It is also helpful to increase the level of empathy amongst buyers. The most powerful impact usually comes through the testimonies of women who have exited the sex trade. These stories are honest, raw, and highlight the struggles and resiliency of the women. They touch men's hearts and feelings in deeper ways than any other presentation. They show the human side of a dehumanizing activity. Since most of these men are not hardened criminals but regular men who have women in their lives, the stories touch closer to home when we ask them: "How would you feel if she was your daughter, mom, or aunt?"

Another aspect for men to understand is the impact of prostitution on the wider community. Men often have the very limited view that buying sex only involves two people. Many more people are impacted, including profiteers such as traffickers or drug dealers. Children are harassed when being prepositioned for sex on the way home from school. Partners, parents, and children of the exploited are also affected as well as the families of the men. Many men also don't consider the potential effects on their own health and well-being, criminal records, or not being able to coach their kids' sports team with a conviction, or the impact on their ability to travel. Raising these topics with men often comes as a surprise to them. The wives, girlfriends, and partners of those who buy sex is probably one of the most overlooked groups of people who are impacted in the sex industry.

The responses from men who participated in the program were very diverse. Some remained resistant to changing their mindset about their own behaviour and may never do so. They believed prostitution is inevitable and that paid sex is a service that men should have access to. Others were shocked about the harms the industry creates for women, and they no longer wanted to be part of the exploitation. A third group of men understood they needed to examine their own lives, that paid sex isn't necessarily what they're looking for. They saw that connection, intimacy, and a sense of belonging were missing in their lives or that they bought sex as a coping mechanism to divert themselves from the struggles, disappointments, and stressors.

I believe an approach that recognizes those deeper factors in men's lives is important when creating meaningful strategies to engage men and boys to prevent sexual exploitation of women, girls, and LGBTQ+ individuals. We have recently started a new and innovative project to develop such a strategy at the Ma Mawi Wi Chi Itata Centre. We are an Indigenous and community-led organization on Treaty 1 territory with a long history of supporting Indigenous women and girls who experience sexual exploitation and trafficking.

After many consultations with survivors, community, and law enforcement agencies as well as men themselves, we work on education, online engagement with men who buy sex, support services for men and their partners, demand-related research, as well as building new relationships with law enforcement and the corporate sector. We believe that it is time to focus on the demand for paid sexual service as a driving factor for sex trafficking and sexual exploitation of vulnerable women and girls, particularly those who are Indigenous.

Men play a major role in the economy of the sex industry and contribute to the market that demands more and younger women and girls for paid sex. Through the project, we hope to reach boys and men of different ages and backgrounds, and in different settings, to highlight their responsibility to prevent exploitation. We will do this through workshops in schools, training in social service and health agencies, and deterring men when they are in the process of buying sex online. We also want to engage with the corporate sector and other employers to take steps to address illegal sex buying and trafficking. Since there is a lack of research about the demand for paid sex, we will conduct Canadian-focused research through surveys and interviews amongst men about their reasons, motivations, and behaviours.

We believe these activities can contribute to a cultural shift that recognizes the role and responsibility of males in addressing sexual exploitation and sex trafficking. There are many men who do not purchase sex. But there are men who do, and they contribute to the harm to individuals and the community. Let's put our emphasis on challenging those men to rethink their attitudes and behaviours. We can also help boys to critically assess and reject the values and narratives of the sex industry and the objectification of women and girls as sexual objects. After all, it is men and boys who make the choice to buy or not.

3.

NIXON, KYLEE: MAKING SENSE OF THE INERTIA

Kylee Nixon, a former resident of an Edmonton inner-city neighbor-hood, shares her experience of living for several years in an area surrounded by visible sexual exploitation.

Making Sense of the Inertia

Why is it the prostitution of women by men is so hard to stop? Why is it that we are moving counter-productively toward official institutional-ization despite federal legislation that makes the buying and pimping of women illegal? From men's perspective, the practice makes sense; it is useful, in an immediate sense to profiteers, to have women available in various parts of the city. It is also useful to men generally (those not profit-ing directly from the exploitation of women) though they would likely not admit to it, to have women being prostituted in every spot in the nation. The practice has the effect of keeping all women and girls in check (being nervous about the ubiquity of predatory male behaviour), consciously or not. The very existence of our commodification forces dehumanizing sexualization upon us in all milieus including the workplace, the family, school, and the community.

In places in the world where prostitution has been officially curbed, it was women who effected this change: feminist groups in Sweden, women in government in Iceland, women-led societies in traditional Indigenous tribes. Men have not historically or currently ushered in anti-prostitution change. Thus far they have not, nor do I expect they will.

The more puzzling and upsetting point on this issue is women who are seemingly complicit by lack of protest. Even worse is the betrayal of women who actively promote our prostitution, for example, a female city councillor who was swayed to think licensing brothels somehow sanitized prostitution and made it safer for women. Her support came from the false idea that "stigma" is to blame for the harm that comes to prostituted women, rather than them being subjected repeatedly over time to unwanted sexual contact with many men to earn money to survive.

The fact is that prostitution has never been a safe practice for women, historically or currently. This has not changed over time; according to some women involved in the sex trade, it is more dangerous than ever due to mass influence over men from sexualized domination/violence scripts that are shown in garden-variety pornography. Pornography is played constantly in virtually all spaces in brothels.

The despair at this situation crosses my mind often. I start down the rabbit hole of why, why, why can't we change this? Because women as a class are oppressed. We are groomed from our youngest years to make up for male behaviour and to take on men as life-long projects (boyfriends and marriage) when we grow up. When a woman is busy trying to keep the peace by spending her energy keeping the men she knows happy, keeping them calm, supporting them to be good parents, how can she simultaneously focus on her own and other women's best interest in fighting male domination and exploitation?

The evidence that this situation continues to occur for women has become apparent to me throughout my personal life, but the universality of this impossible dilemma for women became most clear when I lived in an inner-city neighbourhood, and in my work as a therapist.

Living in Edmonton's inner city came before my counselling/therapy work. I moved with my young family of five, three kids, a spouse, and myself, to an old downtown neighbourhood in 2007, to be near my dad who still lives there. I knew we were moving to an "interesting" and "colourful" neighbourhood. Our realtor showed us houses while actively discouraging us from considering any of them. The one we finally landed on was about six blocks from my dad's. The day we looked at it, four women were standing on each of the four corners of the closest intersection, and in the other direction was a giant lineup of people waiting for supper to be served at a church nearby.

I really thought at the time that this would be an "exciting" neighbourhood full of "grit" and "reality." I soon experienced these frightening qualities when being followed and propositioned by men through the windows of cars whenever I went anywhere on foot without my dog or my children. I experienced this when there were frequently women outside screaming at night, and people fighting. We called the police many times and were usually told variations of "What did you expect living in that neighbourhood?"

Prostituted women became more and more apparent to me over time. I was raising young daughters and a son. I discovered through research that the neighbourhood was highly imbalanced with men far outnumbering women as residents. The ratio of children was low. The number of services for the extremely poor was the highest and pretty much all that was available in Edmonton and for the whole northern region of the province. The average household income was extremely low. The rate of transience was much higher than in other neighbourhoods.

This is the context in which I discovered the theory and analysis of the sex trade from a feminist perspective. I was searching, trying to find out why there were girls of thirteen through women of over fifty on the streets. I became increasingly appalled and distressed about knowing girls in the neighbourhood and then seeing them prostituted. Some friends, the community league, and I started a swim club for neighbourhood children at one point. One of the members was prostituted when she was only thirteen. I worked at a provincially mandated nine-day detox for teens during this time; I saw girls from the program prostituted. I worked at a psychiatric hospital and saw patients, chronically ill adult women, and transgender women, prostituted in the neighbourhood. I saw teen boys prostituted.

Alongside all the street prostitution that carried on day and night, it also occurred within several of the old-world cafés frequented only by men and exploited women. It was happening and still happens in the three body rub parlours in the neighbourhood (there may be more). I could not wrap my head around how all of this could be going on, given all the well-documented evidence of the harms of prostitution I was reading about. How could the residents of the neighbourhood, which included women and children, grandparents, and seniors, possibly put up with all of this?

I still grapple with that question. However, the feminist analysis that women are oppressed as a sex class and are busy keeping the peace, keeping themselves and their children safe, and keeping the men positively involved, is the answer that is realistic and accounts for the situation. Contributing factors for street and parlour prostitution are systemic poverty entwined with systemic racism. This established, culturally rich neighbourhood, full of beautiful tall trees, is much more diverse than many neighbourhoods in Edmonton, but some of its patterns are legacies of historical injustice. The street-prostituted women are often Indigenous, as were the street-poor people generally, while "Asian Massage" brothels abound in the inner city and other areas of Edmonton.

One morning in 2011, I was at the park with my kids. It was a school day. There were two others there I recognized from the park. I asked the girl I knew best why she wasn't at school. She indicated that her mom had just died. She hung her head. I asked what had happened. She said her mom had died in the hospital of a disease. Then she spoke again and said her mom died in a hotel. That was devastating news. This child was Indigenous, and I knew immediately that the chances were high her mother had been murdered. That was the case.

I had discovered Sheila Jeffreys' *The Industrial Vagina* by this time, as well as Vancouver's Rape Relief website, Asian Women for Equality, and the Feministas of Canada Facebook page. The relief from knowing there were women who cared about prostitution in Canada and around the world, relief from reading these and other feminist resources, the sadness, the new understanding—all these have changed me and remain with me. I started to be more active in anti-prostitution work. I went to City of Edmonton public meetings to oppose further entrenchment of the industry through licensing. I attended CEASE's events. I saw Rachel Moran speak at the library downtown. I started a social media group with friends (EWAASI: Edmonton Women and Allies Against the Sex Industries), which is still operational, a cataloguing of sexual exploitation-related news items.

My work as a clinical social worker/therapist offered me plenty of opportunities to meet and talk with women and girls affected directly or indirectly by prostitution, in clinic work, a women's shelter, and the aforementioned youth detox. I have worked with children whose mothers are or were prostituted, some of whom had been killed, and children whose fathers are or were pimps. There are no firm statistics (estimates range from ten to fifty percent) on how many men pay to sexually exploit women in Edmonton. I have yet to have a male client express concern regarding this issue, except for one teen boy who was aware of his mom's prostitution history, and his estranged dad's pimping of her.

I have met men through work and in my personal life who bragged about using prostituted women. I have worked with mothers who are or were prostituted while supporting their children and other family members. The misplaced guilt and self-loathing (it should be with the johns) these women have is profound. The anger about childhood molestation in various forms, the inability to get and keep a "regular" job, resulting poverty, and the struggle with the extensive mental and physical suffering, especially autoimmune diseases caused by too much cortisol induced by repeated trauma from many assaults, are also profound.

I and other Canadian feminists were overjoyed when the Canadian *PCEPA (Protection of Communities and Exploited Persons Act)* law was passed in 2014. We were hopeful that finally there would be a tool in the toolbox for prostituted women, for police to have for curbing the demand. At the time I was still living in the inner city, and for a whole month after the law was passed, I saw no prostitution activity whatsoever on the streets of the neighbourhood. I was watching for it. I started to feel a weight lifting, but the activity resumed, and nothing changed. Police continued to fail to intervene.

During this period, one city councillor, alleged by women in the trade to be a confirmed john himself, and the mayor continued to support city licensed prostitution outlets where buyers remain anonymous. The city licenses women operating as escorts. This policy is precisely the opposite of what *PCEPA* set out to do, which was to identify and charge the buyers, decriminalize the women, and provide them with meaningful exiting services. Our municipal government has made it clear it has no intention to abide by the federal legislation, using the same excuse for seven straight years, that the feds are "considering revisions" to the legislation. This has been depressing for women active in anti-exploitation in Canada. Still, we press on, in small groups, and collectively by connecting through social media, organizing, attending events, and supporting public awareness initiatives such as this book.

I have now been away from the inner city for five years. I live in a middle-class south-side neighbourhood with no visible street prostitution and no obvious commercial body rub parlours. Overt commercial activity would not be tolerated in this neighbourhood, though I have seen it happening in the parking lot of the nearby mall. I am permanently hyper-vigilant. There are body rub parlours not too far away; they are in commercial strip malls, in areas where there is not an active community league to put up any meaningful resistance.

As I write this (April 2021), Cindy Gladue's murderer has been finally found guilty of manslaughter. This followed an appeal filed after his being found not guilty several years earlier. Cindy was the mom of the girl I knew in the park. It is bittersweet, way more bitter than sweet, that the man responsible will be behind bars for a while. The hope is that his conviction will send a message to exploiting men in Canada. But what kind of message do men and boys get when a man who has injured a women's vagina, causing her to bleed to death, is guilty only of manslaughter, and only after a retrial, while all the while there are forty city-licensed body rub parlours with women available to rent with complete anonymity for men? The women are expected to register with the city. It emerged that Cindy Gladue's killer had searched for violent internet porn featuring damage to women's vaginas. What does it say to men and women, to boys and girls, that governments at every level say and do nothing about readily available violent pornography?

Mainstream pornography features men who are pictured as superior, powerful, and lacking emotion while clearly despising, scorning, and harming women who act out opposite emotions of fear, submission, and faked happiness, all piped in for any child or adult to view freely at any time of day, from anywhere a phone with Wi-Fi can be held in hand. There are so many wrongs in this picture, it's overwhelming. Is it any wonder we as women don't know quite where to start to make life safer for ourselves and each other?

We continue to work on our own consciousness raising while encouraging it around us where we can. The efforts to make us accept the myth that prostitution is inevitable, that it is empowering for women, has all the force of the multi-billion-dollar industry behind it. This is the well-funded backlash to any progress toward liberation we make, the never-ending push to continue to commodify women's bodies and male access to them. This push is relentless and what was learned and taught by the women before us is scuttled away from us at every turn.

Ironically the internet and social media that led to a proliferation of the global sex industries also enables women to connect more than ever before across this gigantic, unwieldy country. This connection, the friendships, the planning and organizing, the letter writing, the spreading of information, the opportunities to support women's safe spaces in shelters and exiting services, all allow us to continue to share, to work, where we continue to draw strength and hope for change. There is forever work being done to invite women to join the anti-exploitation movement; the survivor/exited voices of women with lived experience of exploitative violence are sobering and unwavering, a candle in this mess where we find ourselves. We honour their strength as we move forward toward a safer life for ourselves and our daughters.

4.

PEREZ, TOMAS: EPIK

Tomas Perez, founder of the organization EPIK, with a branch in Alberta, shares his personal journey of transformation as part of his work in tackling sex trafficking.

EPIK: change extending beyond the usual or ordinary, especially in size or scope

We live in a supply and demand world. If people want yellow shirts, someone will sell them yellow shirts. If they want a bacon-wrapped doughnut, someone will sell them a bacon-wrapped doughnut. In the end, you can tell a lot about a culture by what people are asking to buy.

In 2010, I began hearing more and more stories about children and vulnerable people being bought and sold for sex in America. I'm not a cop, mental health worker, or celebrity who brings a large platform to this work. Those who know me often describe me as a "guy's guy." I ride motorcycles, work out a lot, and enjoy many of the things our culture associates with the idea of manliness. So when I saw what was happening, I did what you would expect a normal guy to do: I got angry.

My anger motivated me to act. I organized motorcycle rallies; I told everyone I met about what was going on. I recruited like-minded guys, calling them to be real men and to fight to save and rescue the victims of exploitation. When confronted with a dangerous situation, the human body is hardwired with three primary responses: fight, flight, or freeze. My instinct was to fight; as a dad, coach, and community leader, doing nothing was not an option.

I envisioned alongside me an army of like-minded and well-equipped men who would rise up and save children from the forces of evil. We would simply fight for the safety and security of our communities, and sex trafficking would become a thing of the past. I started my own non-profit and called it "EPIK," initially short for "Everyman Protecting Innocent Kids." I believed that if good men only knew what was going on, they would surely answer the call.

During these early years, my response was to tap into the masculine nerve that saw men as warriors. I repeatedly appealed to the notions of defending and protecting because that's how men typically think. That's how I thought. I used battle metaphors to communicate a sense of urgency. I spoke of our effort to engage this issue using vivid militaristic references. In my mind, this made sense and would obviously lead to real solutions and real change. In many ways, I saw this issue as a binary landscape of good guys versus bad guys. All that was needed was for the good guys to step up and expose the bad guys.

The solutions to the problem seemed plain as day. I couldn't see it then, but I've since learned that the roots of sexual exploitation are deep, intractable, and systemic. When talking about evil, the late Russian dissident Aleksandr Solzhenitsyn said,

> *"If only it were all so simple! If only there were evil people somewhere insidiously committing evil deeds, and it were necessary only to separate them from the rest of us and destroy them. But the line dividing good and evil cuts through the heart of every human being. And who is willing to destroy a piece of his own heart?"*

I've come to realize that framing sexual exploitation as merely bad guys vs. good guys does nothing to change its traumatic outcomes.

About four years into this work, I encountered an unexpected change. I had been invited to join the Multnomah County (Oregon) Commercial Sexual Exploitation of Children Steering Committee. This was a multi-disciplinary task force composed of law enforcement, local and state officials, and faith and mental health communities. Eventually, I was asked to join the executive team and tasked with developing a strategy aimed at the demand driving the local exploitation market. I was happy to do whatever I could but often felt like I wasn't making a difference.

One day after finishing what felt like my 500th task force meeting, I cornered a district attorney in the hallway and said to her, "If I could bring you a dozen or so trustworthy guys, could we sit down and brainstorm ways we might be able to help change this situation in our community?" Hesitantly, she said yes, and I later learned that her apprehension stemmed from a justifiable fear of having to deal with a bunch of uninformed social justice zealots, think the angry-villagers-with-pitchforks in the old *Frankenstein* movies.

A week later, we met. She began by telling us she had been monitoring the online ads selling sex in our community for the past three days. She had printed the postings and taped the papers end to end. She then lifted the pile of paper and let it cascade to her feet and across the floor. The list was more than eight feet long, and she said, "This is what the market looks like. If you guys are willing to explore ways to disrupt it, we might be able to make a difference. The smartphone in your pocket is the brothel of the 21st century. The vast majority of commercial sex transactions are advertised, initiated, or somehow facilitated in the digital world."

EPIK took up the challenge and, with a cheap phone and donated laptop, we began posting fake sex ads on Backpage. The first night we gathered to do this, I posted an ad at 7 p.m. The phone rang nine minutes later and kept ringing every other minute for over an hour. We had no idea how quickly we would be inundated with calls from sex buyers eager to deal.

Our repetitive process began with a long, heavy-handed, and shaming "script" that our volunteers were trained to use when they caught an unsuspecting buyer on the phone. Some buyers stayed on the calls, but only to argue, ridicule, or make death threats. However, the longer we persisted, the better we became at simply talking, "man to man," about what their action was doing to the sellers, their communities, and even to themselves. We reached out to survivors and asked them what we should be talking about. In response to their input, we tossed our first script and settled on a shortlist of persistent myths that buying sex was acceptable.

That was over nine years ago. Since then, we've disrupted more than a quarter-million attempts to buy sex online and had tens of thousands of text and phone conversations with active sex buyers at the point of sale. Slowly, more and more men (not all) began to engage in actual conversation. Though we didn't know what was happening in the hearts and minds of those buyers, we knew that while they were talking to us, they weren't buying a vulnerable person.

When I first began talking to sex buyers, I imagined a "gotcha" scenario where I would scare poor unsuspecting sex buyers into immediate and profound shame and remorse. Safe and secure in my moral high ground, I assumed they would have no choice but to repent or face the consequences of arrest at some point in the future. At the very least, they would experience the shame of having their behaviour discovered by at least one other man. In other words, I would try to morally bludgeon the unsuspecting buyer into submission. We've come to refer to this as "the baseball bat approach."

The strangest thing began to happen as I continued to interact with men seeking to buy sex; I realized that they were more like me than they were different. You see, in the process of disrupting their purchase of online sex, I began to experience an unexpected kind of pondering. It's important to note that I wasn't the only man experiencing this epiphany. We had been running this intervention for more than four years at this point, and our network had grown to trained teams of volunteer men in over a dozen cities.

Volunteers began giving unsolicited feedback about how this work was impacting them. While the intervention itself was useful in disrupting local sex markets, our guys were voicing a growing desire to go deeper, to do more to get to the roots of the problem. Disrupting sex buyers at the point of sale was innovative, and it was drawing positive attention to the issue, but it wasn't doing anything to address the deeper systemic sources of exploitation.

By this time, our guys had developed an authentic curiosity and even compassion toward the men we encountered. We had become experts in using everyday technology to disrupt commercial sex transactions, but it felt like fighting a forest fire with a garden hose. The longer and more closely we looked at the commercial sex ecosystem, and the harm it unleashed on the victims, communities, and even the buyers themselves, the more we began to see that there was a distinct narrative driving this pernicious market. That narrative itself had to be disrupted.

We began to understand how cultural expectations of masculinity perpetuated evil; stories about men as violent, sexually entitled, and powerful had to be called into question. This kind of deconstruction became personal when we realized so much of how we moved about in the world was based on the same kinds of privilege, power, and position that other men used to justify renting other people's bodies for sex.

For the first time in years of "fighting" sex trafficking in America, we began to realize that our own unexamined and potentially toxic views of masculinity had to be challenged. But more than deconstruction, we also saw clearly that we needed to offer men a clear and compelling path of change. What was needed was a vision of masculinity that was generative or life-giving rather than life-destroying.

What began as a simple tactic to disrupt the online sex market forced us to look critically at the culture that was enabling this exploitation, and as we stared that reality in the face, we were confronted by our own complicity in the problem. As we began to identify and more clearly articulate this three-fold disruption of the sex-power-violence paradigm, what EPIK stood for became more and more clear. We wanted to facilitate a change away from *toxic*, destructive masculinity and toward *generative*, health-sustaining masculinity as the preferred alternative. This meant we needed to learn to stand alongside women. We believe that women and men are made to flourish together and that they share a fundamental right to equality.

More importantly, when we insist on assuming the role of protector, we devalue the power and resilience of the survivor herself. Trafficking survivors need the opportunity for equality; anyone who's endured that kind of trauma should be honoured for their strength and not kept in a state of perpetual vulnerability.

It's been more than 10 years since this journey began, and while I do believe our work has been helpful, there's still so much more to do. The roots of sexual exploitation are deep and deeply ingrained in Western culture. Substantive change for the better will likely take generations to achieve. That being said, generative men—humble, empathetic, possessing true strength, and with an appetite for justice—are our best hope in seeing an end to the commercial sexual exploitation of vulnerable people.

Initially, "EPIK" was an acronym that stood for "Everyman Protecting Innocent Kids." It doesn't mean that anymore. Yes, we will always be there to provide protection for vulnerable children and youth when and if called upon, but I believe more is being asked of us as men; we're being asked to change.

The narrative arc of any great story always introduces us to a character who undergoes change; when we first meet them, they are young, unaware, or perhaps broken, and believe they're beyond redemption. These characters will inevitably face a crucible that may destroy them: Odysseus leaves home, Luke Skywalker enters the cave where he meets Darth Vader, Frodo decides to carry the ring. And the person they are on the other side of the crucible is most often a fuller, truer version of who they were meant to be.

An "epic" story is one that speaks of a dramatic change extending beyond the usual or ordinary, especially in size or scope. EPIK is just that—a story about men committed to pursuing a fundamental change in the way they move about the world. It's a story about humble, clear-eyed men who see themselves as they truly are: flawed, prone to failure but capable of growth, and with the agency to inspire other men to change as well.

EPIK is a story about men whose hearts break over the brokenness in the world. It's a story about how that brokenness draws out of men a deep kind of strength that, unlike the raw power we were taught to wield, is spent on behalf of others. In my experience, this kind of strength is reflected in the ability to serve the more vulnerable and advocate for them.

It's the story of men who know that change won't come quickly or easily and who have therefore cultivated an insatiable appetite for justice. Sometimes, and this is one of the hardest things for men to do, it means being willing to simply shut up and listen to others with less power and privilege.

This is what EPIK now means; we are characters caught up in an EPIC saga. We are men individually and collectively confronting the roots of exploitation, men who willingly challenge the view of manhood that normalizes and even sanctifies exploitative ideologies and systems, men who are willing to allow this experience to change ourselves, which ultimately also changes our relationship with women and with the world.

5.

RUBNER, PAUL: CHANGING PERSPECTIVES

Early intervention with young people, who may be sexually acting out without realizing the potential danger of their actions, is one way of deterring them from further exploitation. Paul Rubner, formerly with Calgary Police Service, shares his experience of working with vulnerable youth as part of his service in policing. Paul was named a 2022 Man of Honour by CEASE in Edmonton for his ongoing support of vulnerable people.

Changing Perspectives

"Have you ever thought of working in Vice?" This came from a co-worker as he and I were discussing career options. It was 2009, and at the time I had spent my entire 17-year career wearing a uniform: in patrol, instructing, in charge of patrol officers, and in administration. I honestly had no idea what Vice did, except in general terms, and had never worked in a plain-clothes, investigative area. After discussing the idea with my wife, I met with the inspector of the unit, was offered the job, and immediately accepted. Sort of like buying a car sight unseen and without a test drive. What could go wrong?

To say the learning curve was steep is a significant understatement. There were investigative techniques to learn (none of which will be discussed here), undercover operator training, surveillance training, and new (to me) legislation. After all of that, I was able to join my new team, which was in the middle of one of the most complex, undercover investigations into human trafficking in Calgary's history. (Our work ultimately resulted in the rescue of two foreign nationals with the arrest and conviction of their female trafficker.)

Shortly after arriving in Vice, later re-named the Counter Exploitation Unit, I was tasked with becoming the resident "expert" on the *Protection of Sexually Exploited Children Act*. This is protective legislation, unique to Alberta, that allows police officers and social workers to intervene if they reasonably believe a youth, anyone under the age of 18 years, is "engaging in or attempting to engage in prostitution."

"Prostitution" was defined as performing any sexual act in exchange for something else. Two examples would be a girl exposing her breasts for money or trading oral sex for weed with a peer. Although some adult offenders were arrested, our interventions primarily involved youth.

I realize the "p" word is generally not used when referring to sexually exploited youth; however, when the Act was drafted and eventually proclaimed in 1999, it was done to mirror language in the *Criminal Code*. Originally called the *Protection of Children Involved in Prostitution Act*, the legislation was re-named *Protection of Sexually Exploited Children Act* in 2007 for a variety of reasons, including appropriateness of language. (The provincial *PSECA*, protecting Alberta children, is different from the federal *PCEPA*, protecting communities and exploited persons.)

People often think sexual exploitation is something that happens to "other people"; it could never happen to them or their children. They ascribe certain attributes to those they believe to be vulnerable or at risk: they come from a certain part of town, their parent(s) can't or won't provide for them, they live in group homes, and education and mainstream society are not high on their priority list. All true, but the list is incomplete.

Throughout my career, I've worked with youth who came from both single-parent and two-parent homes. Some parents struggled with their own mental health or addiction issues; other parents were successful engineers, lawyers, and, yes, even social workers. In fact, I've had the opportunity to work with youth and families from every quadrant of Calgary and every socioeconomic stratum.

What I soon discovered was that a youth's address, or their parents' bank account, had very little to do with their likelihood of being exploited, or in some cases, self-exploiting. What really mattered was whether their basic needs were being met. In 1943, the American psychologist Abraham Maslow published what became known as Maslow's Hierarchy of Needs (https://simplypsychology.org/maslow.html), a very basic list of what we as humans require to survive and thrive. What I found was that exploited teens were missing at least one of these most basic needs: food, water, warmth, rest, security, and/or safety.

In addition, the psychological needs of love and belonging, ideally provided by family and friends, were often missing as well. When basic needs are not being met, a person is more vulnerable to outside influences. In the world of Vice and *PSECA*, that meant exploitation. And if multiple needs were not being met, which I found very often to be the case, the youth was exponentially more vulnerable.

Although *PSECA* legislation was a terrific tool to keep youth safe from predators, I soon came to realize there were serious gaps in its use. Most significant was a general lack of knowledge about the legislation among those who were best positioned to recognize children at risk. I'm referring to police officers, social workers, teachers, and parents.

This was illustrated in 2015 when I was asked by the RCMP National Human Trafficking Coordination Centre in Ottawa to participate in a province-wide training initiative. I agreed to present a case study of human trafficking with the provision that I also be allowed to review the *PSECA* legislation. Since the target audience was RCMP, municipal police, and social workers, with a few Crown prosecutors as well, it seemed like a perfect scenario.

We presented to audiences in Calgary, Edmonton, Medicine Hat, Lethbridge, Grande Prairie, and Fort McMurray. When asked if anyone either (a) knew of Alberta's *PSECA* legislation or (b) used it, less than 20% indicated they knew of it, and even fewer had utilized it. However, when the presentation covered signs of grooming, luring, and other risk indicators, almost every social worker or police officer in attendance could think of a youth they had encountered who met the threshold for vulnerability and exploitation.

In addition to police and social workers, perhaps the largest group who must be aware of youth sexual exploitation is our teachers, as they are uniquely positioned to recognize signs, perhaps sooner than parents. From September to June every year, teachers see our children far more than us parents, and they may notice changes that occur when something is wrong. They might observe decreases in attention or academic performance, changes in social groups or styles of dress or hygiene, and so on.

The key for teachers is to know who to contact to initiate the process of investigation and intervention. But teachers won't know what they're seeing unless they know what to look for. And while this may seem fundamental, there are still a surprising number of adults who either don't know the level to which youth sexual exploitation exists or refuse to admit that it does.

Winston Churchill said, when he paraphrased Santayana, "Those who fail to learn from history are condemned to repeat it." This is true in the world of exploitation. It is important to educate ourselves on the realities of sexual exploitation and to take appropriate steps to intervene early with high-risk youth.

In addition to hundreds of exploited youths, I had the privilege of working with dozens of adult women, all of whom were survivors of exploitation and, in some cases, trafficking. The common theme was trauma at a young age—sexual, emotional, physical, spiritual, residential, and any combination imaginable. It always made sense to me that if we could have an impact on our youth, we might not have as many traumatized adults.

It's a well-known biological fact that brain development, especially in the prefrontal cortex, isn't complete until we reach our early to mid-twenties. As I understand it, the prefrontal cortex is responsible for, among other things, predicting the consequences of one's actions, impulse control, managing emotional reactions, and planning for the future. If a youth is lacking basic needs, experimenting with substance use, and engaging in high-risk sexual activity, timely intervention is imperative and can change their lives.

While exploited youth took up much of my time, I also worked with, and learned to respect, the high-risk population of exploited and trafficked women either still in or escaping from "the game." It was this group that was the biggest catalyst for change in my way of thinking and how I became an advocate.

The challenge in dealing with youth was usually their denial and overt resistance to any change. The women with whom I worked were the exact opposite. They were unbelievably open about their experiences and, once in a recovery program, were more than willing to examine themselves and begin to make changes as part of their recovery process. That is not to suggest any of their experiences were their fault, but they began to see they had inner strengths that were previously untapped.

The first time I had the opportunity to sit down with a group of survivors was when I was asked to write an opinion for the Crown during the trial of a man accused, and later convicted, of killing a woman in the sex trade. I met with seven survivors, all in varying stages of recovery from their trauma, who spoke quite openly with me about the scenario presented and why it would not have occurred as the accused described. Their honesty and rationale provided a perspective that could only have been added by someone who had "been there and done that."

And it opened my eyes to something else. Even though they knew I was a cop, they felt safe enough to talk openly to me about personal matters in terms of crimes committed against them or, in this case, personal experiences like the victim of the homicide. This was something I noticed with youth as well. After they got over being mad about being confined, they were willing to talk with me about their circumstances.

The next opportunity I had to speak with survivors was at a life-skills recovery program in Calgary, whose purpose was to help women recover from the trauma of exploitation and trafficking. On the scheduled day, I arrived and met with the women, understanding the program had added an hour to the schedule for me. Two-and-a-half hours later, we wrapped up, with the women asking when I was coming back! We covered anything they wanted to talk about; nothing was off-limits. It probably helped that I was in my usual work "uniform" of jeans, t-shirt, and ball cap, but I have to believe that my approach and demeanour played a role as well.

I had learned by then that judgment and pre-conceived ideas would only sabotage any potential relationship between us. And since I was working in an area that is so relational, the cop I had been 15 years previously couldn't be the cop who worked with this new population. When you are investigating sexual exploitation, it's necessary to ask about intensely personal and private experiences. Without first building a relationship based on trust and non-judgment, you're not going to be very effective.

It was during meetings with these women, generally weekly for several years, that I discovered what true resilience looked like. Each day I would listen to someone, hear their story, and think to myself, "*If that had been me, would I even still be here?*" There are two things I've learned over the years. First, there is no end to the depravity of certain segments of the human race. Secondly, and more importantly, most of us are stronger and more resilient than we could ever have imagined.

I also discovered an uncomfortable truth about myself, one that I've admitted to the thousands of people in presentations over the last decade or so: my attitude toward exploited people, in general, was complete rubbish prior to coming to the Vice Unit. As a uniformed officer, I believed sex sellers were acting of their own volition." *If you don't like it*," I thought," *get out and make better choices.*"

Unfortunately, a large segment of society still subscribes to that point of view, but they are uninformed and misguided. The paradigm shift I experienced truly made me a better cop, person, father, and husband.

I learned to be more thankful, as the line between being vulnerable and not is very thin. I learned to put things in perspective, and that maybe my kids not cleaning their rooms wasn't the worst thing in the world. I learned about the power of trust, how easily it is broken, and the incredible amount of work it takes to regain it. And I learned that long-lasting relationships can come from places you'd least expect.

I've attended more funerals than I care to recount, which means there is more work yet to do. The *Protection of Communities and Exploited*

Persons Act (2014), which criminalizes the purchase of sexual services, is a good start. It is bound to evolve, with case law, over the next several years.

In Alberta, Bill 8, the *Protecting Survivors of Human Trafficking Act* (2020), is a positive sign that the government is recognizing the issue of human trafficking. Only time will tell whether or not society has the intestinal fortitude to put its provisions into effect. The *Protection of Sexually Exploited Children Act*, based on conversations I've had with social workers and police officers from B.C. to Ontario, is the envy of those provinces that don't have similar legislation and the ability to intervene.

In the end, now retired from policing, I look back on my 11-plus years in Vice/Counter Exploitation as the most rewarding of over 34 years of public service. Perhaps it's because they came in the latter part of my career, or perhaps I realized we all have a story to tell. Our stories deserve to be heard, and sometimes the ugliest of stories can have a happy ending. As the saying goes, "There but for the grace of God go I."

6.

SLATZ, ANNA: CLASS CONFLICT

Anna Slatz is a writer and professional curmudgeon in Canada. She was a research student in her final year at the University of New Brunswick but was forced to leave her program before completing her dissertation after challenging a pro-commercial sex activist who spoke to her class. Later, she was threatened by the administration as a result of her stance on the subject. Anna now spends her time in community gardens and on the stock market and is much happier.

Class Conflict

I should start off by saying: my university isn't going to like me for this.

They didn't like me before, and this certainly isn't going to change anything for the better. But there isn't much I can do about that, considering I am not going to stay silent on the issue of women's rights simply because they've (repeatedly) asked me to.

In the past, they were *semi*-content with my opinions being relegated to an online platform and not puncturing the brick-and-mortar institution. But all of that changed in March of 2020, just before the pandemic shut everything down.

It all started in my first year as a graduate student in the vaguely-named-vaguely-organized Interdisciplinary Studies program. As a result of a lack of course selection due to a lack of graduate students at my small institution, I was forced to take levelled-up undergraduate courses for the few non-research credits required for my degree.

It was called Anti-Criminology, and while I wasn't necessarily *required* to attend the in-person classes, I did it anyway just to have a little bit of structure in my days.

That was a rather innocently-made mistake that ended up having tremendous consequences for me.

As much as the professor was as blatantly liberal as you'd expect a contemporary sociologist to be, he was kind and amusing, and his lectures were generally interesting. I would sit at the back of the room with my own computer and work away, focusing on other research-related matters unless called upon. I tried to keep my head to my desk, as they say, largely gritting my teeth through some of the more egregiously woke discussions that took place in the class.

But all of that changed the day a speaker was invited.

Her name was LW, and she was a graduate student at our university in her Ph.D. candidacy. The moment she was introduced as an advocate with Safe Harbour, a "sex work advocacy" organization, my attention became unceremoniously locked upon the projector screen through which she was being beamed in on.

In an instant, I knew I was in *trouble*.

As she spoke, my tongue began running across the back of my teeth, itching to flick out words that were practically *leaking* into my throat from my brain.

"No, Anna," I internally chastised myself, biting my lip in a physical attempt to keep myself at bay, *"You are a guest in this class. Don't turn it into a circus."*

But the more LW spoke, waxing poetic nothings about "de-stigmatization" and empowerment, the more I realized I wasn't at any risk of *turning* the class into a circus … it already was the proverbial big-top.

LW's thoughts were as disoriented as the majority of "sex work" activists are. Her arguments were largely premised on the less-than-logic that sex work was not an inherently dangerous or exploitative trade, but rather that it was made so by an intolerant environment and a lack of normalization.

My professor, bless his heart, then decided to contribute to LW's snide smarm, adding that he felt as though women who opposed the sex trade were almost "patriarchal," something with which LW vehemently agreed.

It was that moment I decided I was no longer going to bite my tongue. The moment my opportunity arose, my dainty little hand flew up into the air with all the gusto of a child wanting a bathroom break just before a test.

"How are women who oppose the sex trade *patriarchal*?" I asked, a bit of amusement in my voice.

"Well," he began, clearly perturbed by the fact he was being questioned on a point he had thought was a homerun, "They don't respect a woman's right to choose."

Ah. That old canard.

Nowadays, as women's access to sex-specific safe spaces, resources, and health care continues to melt away in the name of *tolerance* and *inclusivity*, it almost seems as though the trope of a "woman's right to choose" being the guiding factor behind policy is limited to a woman's "right" to commodify, debase, or politically disorient herself.

There is a phenomenal sort of DARVO (Deny, Attack, Reverse roles of Victim and Offender) in the liberal logic that a woman who opposes the sex trade is an agent of the patriarchy—one which I am still processing and unpacking to this day. The incredible suggestion that a woman who opposed the exploitation of her own sex was an agent of male supremacy inherently implied the exploited woman, and the men who use her were feminists by default. That exploitation itself was a feminist act, one which honoured and empowered women.

But, of course, within that DARVO is the assertion that prostitution is not inherently exploitative to begin with—rather, simply another *choice*. Another choice of employment, another choice of what to do with one's time. LW's presentation was centred around framing prostitution this way, her source-less argument being that prostitution was not inherently more or less exploitative or harmful than flipping burgers at McDonald's. That it was simply social *stigma* that made it so.

I didn't respond to my professor's nonsensical non-clarification on my supposed anti-woman male supremacy, instead cocking a brow and making my disdain known in silence. Instead, I turned my attention to LW's giant face, still looming on the bright projector screen like Big Brother beaming in over Skype.

"If stigmatization is what makes the sex trade dangerous and exploitative," I began, "why is it that even places like Amsterdam—arguably one of the most sex-friendly cities in the world—still have significant issues with violence against prostitutes?"

Unlike LW, I had sources to evidence my statement and provided them.

Amsterdam's red-light district is a known destination for buying sex. It is a fully regulated, taxed, decriminalized, and open arena for brothels to sell their wares. There is hardly a less-seedy, less-stigmatized place in the world to buy access to a woman's body. And yet despite this, prostitutes in Amsterdam face no less violence or abuse than anywhere else.

According to a 2018 study co-sponsored by Dutch "sex worker's interest group PROUD," most people who work in the Netherlands' sex industry faced some form of violence: 93% reported being victims of social-emotional violence, 78% experienced sexual violence, and 60% experienced physical violence.

I didn't anticipate LW to have a logical response to these statistics, nor did she. She simply continued to insist that "more de-stigmatization" was needed. But it is precisely this form of illogical goalpost-shifting that demonstrates people like LW, and the policies they advocate, are completely detached from reality—dangerously so.

To advance that point, I brought up yet another case—one that was far more specific. That of a young woman from Montreal who was murdered by a prisoner on day parole. The prisoner, Eustachio Gallese, had been serving a sentence for brutally slaughtering his wife with a hammer and had a history of violence against women. Yet despite this, he was reportedly encouraged by his parole board to seek out a prostitute during his day out as a "risk management strategy" in response to his "sexual needs."

The woman's tragic murder happened just one month before the very class LW was invited to and was a clear case of "de-stigmatization" to the point of state endorsement. Yet "de-stigmatization" did not save her, a

22-year-old woman whose life was cut tragically short as her function was reduced to an instrument of male relief.

Again, LW had no answer to this. She insisted such-and-such law or such-and-such law would have prevented her death, but it was simply one more goalpost-moving to avoid wrangling with the fact that women in the sex trade are in perpetual danger, no matter what policies exist or how destigmatized their trade is.

My professor stopped me from continuing shortly after, insisting others needed the opportunity to ask questions, but I know it was just a stopper on the mockery I was making of LW's entire poorly-thought-out presentation, one which was clearly intended for an audience she believed would be complacent and unquestioning. It had been nothing more than propaganda, that which she did not anticipate having to evidence in any way beyond her anecdotal handwringing and virtue-signaling buzzwords.

That such a biased perspective intending to frame "sex work" as an empowering, feminist act was shocking enough to me, but the final words LW offered the class left me nothing short of *enraged*.

In response to a final question from a young woman who asked how "sex workers" would reply to someone perceiving their work as pathetic or undignified, LW laughed and said: "Most of them would say that if you are hooking up on Friday night and you aren't getting paid, *you're* the pathetic one."

These words were spoken to a class of predominantly young, socio-economically vulnerable women who were expected to laugh and smile along.

Needless to say, I was not amused.

In that moment, I also felt exceptionally fortunate to have been record-ing the entire class, something I occasionally did for the purposes of taking notes. I almost felt like no one would ever believe me if I told them half the things LW asserted as fact when she had the floor.

I expressed my discontent with this experience in the class on my Twitter, going so far as to post some of the audio to evidence my claims of what I had been forced to endure with my own ears. Despite the fact that LW is a public figure whose identity is often revealed in news media as a source or expert on "sex work," I refrained from naming her publicly, deciding to let her words speak for themselves.

Months passed after that class. I finished my courses and entered the summer period, thinking nothing more of it. Little did I know an explosion had erupted in the back rooms of the university over my questioning of LW and subsequent discussion online, one I only became privy to almost a full six months later when I got a vaguely worded email from my professors asking if we could arrange a meeting to *talk*.

Now, I am a veteran of vaguely worded emails asking for meeting times. I have fought on the battlefields of, *"Are you free after class? There's a matter we need to discuss,"* and on the frontlines of, *"Can I see you in my office for a minute? This shouldn't take long."* So when I received that email, I knew precisely what crime I was being indicted for, but I far, far underestimated the extent of the explosivity that had erupted in the months following that fateful class.

A Zoom meeting was arranged for myself, my thesis supervisor, and the professor of that class. At the time, I was in the Dominican Republic recovering from surgeries, but despite my relatively fragile state, I logged in to the call.

While I had expected the talk to be about my questioning of LW, I could never have anticipated the degree of psychosis my challenge had apparently caused. Not only had LW been offended and horrified by my challenge, but she had also gone so far as to consider calling the *federal police* on me for having commented on the class on my Twitter. Apparently, she feared for her safety. The professor of the class "informed" me that had someone harmed LW as a result of my posts, I would have been legally responsible.

Hysterical. In fact, it was not only hysterical but a complete fabrication with no legal basis. I immediately understood it as nothing more than a way to scare me from speaking up.

Unfortunately for them, I don't scare easily. In fact, I responded to this suggestion with an encouragement that she do just that. If questioning an activist with an anti-woman agenda was a crime, I would happily turn myself in the moment I touched Canadian soil.

The professor also told me they had contacted Twitter and claimed the audio recording I had taken and posted was the university's intellectual property. Curiously (and I am sure not at all a coincidence) just a few months later I would be permanently banned from Twitter, where copyright infringements result in immediate suspensions.

After I challenged them on all the would-be threats they supplied, clearly unbothered by all of them, a major backtracking of intention was suddenly presented. The professors then claimed it wasn't about *any* of the things they had mentioned, but rather about me violating university policies on recording classes, policies I was unaware had existed.

I was told to simply supply a letter of apology to the School of Graduate Studies for my violations, as well as one to LW. Then, they insisted, all would be forgiven.

I told them I would most certainly be happy to supply *a letter*.

In my defence, I did not specify what kind.

Readers—believe me when I say a greater non-apology has never been penned. I attempted to slice through the space-time-continuum with just how unapologetic I was. I saturated every syllable with the complete lack of apology I was providing. I wanted the text to *drip* with the smug condescension of someone who had never even *considered* giving an apology, and so it did.

No apology. Only a firm doubling down of my position. To my letter, I affixed almost 40 pages of screenshots demonstrating how some of the rhetoric LW had used was not only anti-feminist but misogynistic.

I sent my non-apology letter to the Dean of Graduate Studies with a smiley face and a "namaste" and waited for the inevitable blowback.

Blowback, like meek threats from meeker professors, has never been something that has frightened me. It was a bridge I had mindfully chosen to set alight.

Perhaps 20 years ago, protesting the sexual exploitation of women would not have been an opinion I had to be mindful about regarding its impact in a university. Perhaps 20 years ago, we would not have even had someone like LW invited to our class, at least without any critical balance whatsoever.

But this isn't 20 years ago. This is the era of bourgeoise, liberal feminism and popular virtue signaling above all else, and a rejection of mainstream thought—especially on the mandated line that "sex work is work"—makes you radioactive, especially in academia.

Where the threats of police action and *firm-talkings-to* had failed, the next stage of punishment for my lack of lockstep was academic isolation.

I was given no teaching positions. I was offered no support. My emails often went unanswered. But most detrimentally, my supervisor informed me that no professors he spoke to wanted to take part in my committee. Without an organized committee to communicate with and defend a thesis against, a graduate student is effectively trapped in institutional limbo.

And that is where I remain to this day.

Am I deterred from my positions? Absolutely not. But I would be lying if I didn't admit that watching my academic career go up in flames didn't come with a poignant psychological toll. As one of the first women in my family to attend university, I mourned the loss of the excitement and bright-eyed eagerness to succeed that were part of my undergraduate years. The pride I'd accumulated in having a 4.0 GPA and two high-tag, distinguished scholarships is all but gone, and I look at the degree on my wall with nothing but disdain.

And why? I often interrogate my rapid descent into the pit of nihilism.

Over the months, I've come up with a good many reasons, none of which really satisfied me.

I originally thought it had strictly to do with the shadowy way the discussions about me and my opinions had taken place. *Months* had passed before I had become privy to the fact that police action against me had been considered, and naturally, that came with an *icky* feeling. But that explanation didn't seem to fit the bill, as the lingering doubt remained.

Then I thought it might have to do with the utter lack of support my university provided following the LW incident. The way my degree had been effectively halted after achieving excellent grades and meritorious scholarships that reflected positively on the university. My research had been a net benefit to the status of the university, yet I was being treated like dirt. *Surely*, I thought, *that* was the reason why. But again, the explanation didn't satisfy me.

It was only recently that I came to what I feel is the answer, that being the underlying realization that the modern university is a sham. A lie. A cesspit of liberal wannabe-intellectuals trading confirmation bias and virtue signals for social karma points.

While I had never considered myself an academic optimist, I realized that a part of me had apparently retained some hope for the university as an institution of higher thought and social progress. LW's visit to that fated March 2020 class had a greater impact on me than I had initially perceived. It wasn't even that someone like LW had been invited to spew the diatribe she had, but that we were all expected to uncritically clap along and screech *"You go, girl!"* while her unevidenced and illogical talking points were shoved down our throats. The critique was so fundamentally dangerous that it wasn't perceived just as disagreement but as a genuine threat to safety.

Because it wasn't a class. It wasn't a debate. It wasn't a discussion. It was a methodology—a process for indoctrination and the transmutation of liberal faux-feminist girl-boss talking points to be established as unquestionable doctrine. And I had interrupted that process with my pesky, *outdated* concerns about the humanity of women and the consequences of our commodification.

Well, readers, I did not pay tens of thousands of dollars in tuition to clap along. I did not fight for prestigious scholarships only to be told I was an agent of the patriarchy for having opinions that went against the liberal grain. And I most certainly did not spend nights cramming for exams and rubbing my fingers raw on keyboards to smile and giggle while being told how *totally, like, awesome* it would be if I sold my body on a Friday night.

I suppose by now it is quite obvious why my university doesn't like me. Unfortunately for them, I simply do not care anymore. If my degree is at risk because I stood up for my belief that a woman's body is not a workplace, then it was not much of a degree at all. If my future is at risk because I spoke out against an activist's opinion, then it was not much of a future at all.

If anything, this period of excommunication has strengthened my resolve, as I have spent my time realizing that this pit of nihilism isn't so bad. I can say whatever I want, and no one will call the police on me.

7.

WALKER, MEGAN: ALONG CAME A SPIDER...

Megan Walker is the former Executive Director of the London, Ontario, Abused Women's Centre, a position she held for 24 years. She identifies as an abolitionist, feminist, and advocate.

Along Came a Spider...

In September 2012, while working in my office at the Ontario London Abused Women's Centre (LAWC), a call came through for me. It was from a woman I didn't know named Sandra.[1] That's not unusual in my business.

In my 24 years as executive director of LAWC, telephone calls from people I didn't know, often in the middle of the night or on weekends, were not new to me. Sandra was like many other parents who contacted me. She was crying, desperate, and had no idea what to do next. She asked for my help. She was looking for anything that would give her hope, give her strength, and give her daughter back.

Sandra's 17-year-old daughter, Melissa, was away from home for the first time attending university and living in residence. She had moved a

---

1 The names have been changed and some circumstances slightly altered as a safety precaution.

long way from home to attend university. Melissa had always been a good student and cared about school. She loved meeting people and volunteering in her community. She was the kind of child parents dream of having.

But with one telephone call things changed. Sandra had no idea how much they'd changed, because everything Melissa told her was positive and wonderful. The call came from Melissa's roommate. The two had met on move-in day. Melissa's roommate called Sandra because she was worried about Melissa. She told Sandra that Melissa hadn't been attending classes or spending any time in residence. The roommate said she asked Melissa what was going on, why she wasn't attending classes, and why she was away from residence so often, many times overnight.

Melissa shook off the questions with, "I'm just working a lot," and claimed she was catching up with classes online. "No need to worry," Melissa told her roommate. "I know what I'm doing."

As I listened to the story from Sandra, alarm bells rang loud and long.

My gut told me Melissa was in trouble. I had heard similar scenarios over my career. I asked Sandra the same question I had asked many parents before.

"Does she have a boyfriend?" I asked. "Is he an old boyfriend or someone she's just met? Did the changes begin after she started going out with this man?"

The answer wasn't surprising. Yet again, it was something I'd heard over and over again.

"Yes," said Sandra. "Melissa had called home one night, excited that she had met 'the most amazing guy' at a bar. She said he had bought her the expensive leather bag she had always wanted and took her to an expensive restaurant for a wine tasting."

Sandra said all this was new. Melissa had never experienced these luxuries before. The attention the man was giving her was breathtaking. There was always another gift, another big night out, another new adventure on the arm of a handsome, experienced, and obviously well-off man.

Sandra and her husband, William, were hard-working middle-income earners. Their children had always been their priority. Like most parents, they wanted to make sure that, as they got older, their kids were prepared to take on the world and, if possible, have the benefit of what their parents had put aside for them.

Sandra and William invested in an educational fund for both Melissa and her sister and tried to tuck additional funds into a retirement fund. Like most middle-income earners raising children, there was rarely enough money left for extravagant and expensive purchases. Their priority was to invest in their daughters' education funds and extracurricular sports. Melissa played volleyball and basketball during high school, and her sister played hockey.

The hard work, strong family bond, and the right values the parents taught their daughters were paying off. They likely never expected any of them to wind up in a situation in which none of the family had any control. They would find out that you can do everything right in raising a child, but there's nothing you can do when evil comes knocking.

Sandra described both her daughters as well-liked and running with a 'good crowd.' They had lots of friends and did well at school.

During our hour-long conversation, Sandra spoke in detail about Melissa. She was olive-skinned, with brown eyes that at times took on a greenish tinge. She had flowing, long brown hair. She had been in an accident years earlier where she had slid down some rocks on a summer vacation resulting in stitches and a jagged scar down the outside of her right arm.

Melissa would be thought of as beautiful inside and out.

Melissa was a smart, funny, and mature 17-year-old. She cared about people. She was growing her natural brown hair out to eventually cut and donate it to help with wigs for kids with cancer.

She had never had a serious or long-term relationship. Like most young girls, she mentioned an attraction to certain boys on occasion. If there was one thing that Melissa vented to her mother about, it was the lack of attention from boys, that boys considered her to be only a friend. For a young woman, like most, Melissa considered that one of the worst things that could happen to her.

But that never caused Melissa to miss a beat at school, in her social life with friends or her extra-curricular activities in school. Melissa loved life.

She knew early on that she wanted to be a teacher. She had always respected the job of teaching and gone to her teachers for help as needed. The teachers were her role models. Melissa saw herself surrounded by young children, teaching in an elementary school. She loved learning. She also enjoyed everything else school provided, including the friendship, socializing, and the adventures that accompanied going to school.

It was incredibly gratifying when the letter arrived that gave her the news she had been hoping for. She was accepted to a top Canadian university to begin her post-secondary education. At the end of that journey, her 'dream job' as a teacher waited for her.

For someone who had never lived for any extended time away from home, Melissa was excited to be living in residence. It would be another step in her growth cycle. She would be taking care of herself and her living quarters. She would learn about managing money and solving whatever problems would come along. She was ready to take on more responsibility.

It's one reason Sandra was stunned when Melissa's roommate called her. This is not how her daughter acted. This is not what they had spent hours talking about.

Her mother couldn't understand why Melissa was telling friends she wasn't at school because she was working too much. Sandra didn't even know she had a job. Melissa and her parents talked about how her education would come first and a job certainly wasn't necessary because Melissa was accessing her education fund and had a scholarship. Money was not an issue.

The same question kept going around and around in Sandra's head: How could her daughter have stopped attending classes after only a month in school? Classes had barely begun. She didn't have time even to assess whether she liked her classes or not, yet Melissa was not attending.

All of this struck a chord of fear in Sandra. She called the university and was told Melissa's classes were not online. Students were actually provided with extra marks for attending and participating in class.

Sandra needed to get to the bottom of what was happening with Melissa, and she needed to find out quickly. She lived too far away to simply go to the university, so Sandra called ... and called ... and called, but Melissa wasn't answering the telephone. Melissa's roommate told Sandra that Melissa wasn't returning her calls either.

As I listened to the story, I was mentally checking off one box after the other. A young girl, first time away from home, excited about meeting new friends, maybe meeting a boy, having some freedom that might not have been available before, goes out and meets a mature, sophisticated individual.

He sweeps her off her feet by giving her all sorts of attention while buying her expensive gifts and taking her places she didn't think she'd ever be able to go while at university. He tells her how special she is and that he can't believe how lucky he is to have met her. If there is anything I can do, just ask me. Melissa doesn't see anything wrong. Why wouldn't she spend as much time as she could with this 'amazing guy?' What she doesn't see is that the trap is about to be sprung.

Suddenly, Melissa stops going to school. She is isolated from her friends and parents. She doesn't connect with her parents or her friends. Suddenly, this man is the centre of her universe. He is here, he is there, he is everywhere.

This box was checked. That box was checked. Most every box on the list was checked. Check. Check. Check. Check.

This is a story I've heard repeatedly. Every time I hear it, I hope that I'm wrong, that I don't have to speak the words out loud to a parent.

It was clear that the 'most amazing guy' Melissa had met was a trafficker.

For a parent or even the average person, believing that their daughter, their daughter's friend, the girl next door, or the one down the street is being 'trafficked' is completely foreign and unbelievable. It's often unbelievable to the supposedly most educated among us, including doctors, lawyers, clergy, teachers, and businesspeople. It's often most difficult to convince those who can do something about it, such as police officers, those in the justice system, and politicians.

Many people think trafficking isn't something that happens in their own back yard. "It certainly doesn't happen in my country, and it's completely unthinkable to believe it could happen to my daughter, my neighbour, or someone in my community."

Convincing these people that traffickers don't wear a sign or hand out business cards that say 'trafficker' is the first step. Understanding the standard operating procedure of a human trafficker is the next.

Traffickers hang out where young girls go. They are predators. They prey on girls who look out of place in a new environment, like at a bar. During one of the numerous conversations I had with Sandra, she said she didn't think Melissa had ever been to a bar before. Melissa had never come home intoxicated.

Sandra wasn't naive and knew that just because she hadn't been aware of Melissa drinking didn't mean she hadn't been. However, it wasn't a regular occurrence.

But moving away from home wasn't a regular occurrence either. Like almost everything happening in Melissa's life away from home, going to a bar would be a new and exciting experience.

It was time. Sandra and William needed to be told one of the most difficult truths that I had to speak. It's heart wrenching to tell parents that everything Melissa was doing, everything they had told me, was consistent with Melissa falling into the hands of a trafficker.

There is no immediate concrete evidence. That usually comes much later. But I had experience working with far too many other families who came to me living the same nightmare Sandra and William were living with Melissa. There was a parade of red flags waving in front of me, and I had a responsibility to tell them what Melissa could be facing.

I went through a painful step-by-step of a trafficker's manual to 'turning out girls' into the sex trade.

Traffickers utilize several strategies to lure girls into their web, like a spider immobilizing an insect. The spider carefully builds its web in a location where it knows insects will be. The web looks beautiful, almost alluring. Strand by strand the spider builds its trap until the time comes when an unsuspecting victim is entangled in a web that is almost impossible to escape. The insect is now under the spider's control to do with it what it wants.

Sandra and William were stunned to hear the words that are foreign to most people, that they'd only previously heard on television or read in a newspaper or a book.

"My daughter met a trafficker? How is that even possible?" they wondered.

They needed to know more. They somehow needed to make sense of how things could go so wrong for a daughter they thought they had raised to do everything so right.

Even the greatest parents with the best of intentions, whether they are rich or poor, whether they have influence or not in society, are most times no match for a trafficker.

Traffickers are professionals at what they do. They are as adept at selling as any successful salesperson. They are as knowledgeable in what impresses someone as any businessman taking a client out to lunch. The most successful traffickers have learned how to read people as well as some psychologists. They are expert manipulators and liars. They find the vulnerabilities of girls and feed into them. Traffickers are understanding of a girl's problems, their fears, and their weaknesses. They meet them and talk to them often, becoming their confidant. They are there to help her with her problems. They lure girls from fast food restaurants, buses, universities or colleges, parties, and bars.

Less experienced traffickers sometimes work the bar scene in tandem. It's the good-guy, bad-guy routine. One of the traffickers would harass a girl while the other watched and waited until it became obvious the girl was fed up and didn't know what to do. Then he would come to her rescue, confronting the first trafficker, getting him out of the bar, saving the girl from the situation. The 'rescuer' would apologize to the girl on behalf of all men and sympathize with her about how difficult it must be for a girl always to be put in those horrible situations. They talk. He buys her a drink and continues to spend the evening with her. The trafficker always finds opportunities to tell her she is beautiful and should have a future where she is given the best of everything. He would say he was a high-profile lawyer or accountant or businessman. It would always be a prestigious job. He'd let her know he had the means to take care of her. They might arrange for another date, but in many cases, the girl would go back to his place to hook up that very night.

Sandra and William were shocked that it could happen so quickly. Most people are surprised that it could happen so easily and so quickly.

It's difficult to understand because many people fail to recognize that women and girls are groomed to satisfy men from an early age. Their daughters, like all our daughters, are growing up in a pornified culture where misogyny is blatant, subtle, and accepted. It's the pornified culture that normalizes prostitution, pornography, and sexual exploitation and, no matter how vile, accepts it as entertainment.

Women and girls are groomed to believe their value comes from the attention boys and men give them. This is reinforced by the media and advertisers who know sex sells. They sell their products by sexualizing women and girls. It's reinforced on the playground at school, in bars, and on the streets when boys pay attention to the girls wearing skimpy clothes while ignoring those dressed more conservatively. Most girls want to be popular and even at a young age are taught to please men. They don't want to be ignored, left out, or thought of as no-fun, so they change their behaviour to grab the attention of boys and men. Traffickers rely on misogyny to make luring easy and seamless. They recognize the desires, hopes, and dreams of many girls and women. They feed those dreams before destroying them.

It's never an easy discussion to have with parents, but once parents begin to understand the situation their daughter is in, they want to take action. Sandra called the police, who eventually found Melissa. They asked her if she was okay, if she was being held against her will. The answer wasn't surprising. Of course not, she wasn't being held against her will. She was spending a lovely evening with her boyfriend. He loved her and cared for her and would never hurt her.

The web was complete, control was established, and the prey wasn't going anywhere.

Only weeks after that visit from police, Sandra found an ad online with a picture of her daughter from the waist down. She recognized the scar down Melissa's right arm from the accident she had when she slipped down the rocks all those years ago.

Melissa was being advertised as a 'horny bad girl available to fulfill your fantasies.' It was all about fulfilling the fantasies of men, fantasies that come from viewing pornography often so violent that if there were non-state torture legislation in Canada, most pornography would meet the criteria.

It was about domination, control, and ownership of a woman's body. The fantasies were all about men doing what they wanted, as often as they wanted, regardless of what the woman wanted. It should have been advertised as *'bad, horny man looking to fulfill a fantasy any way he can.'*

Sandra called the police again, this time to report her daughter was advertised on a website. She wanted them to intervene, to somehow find her, and bring her home. Surely this was proof that Melissa was being forced to do things she didn't want to do, that she was being held against her will.

The police repeated what they had told her before: there was nothing they could do.

There was nothing LAWC or I could do except support Sandra and hope that Melissa would come into LAWC if she were in London. We could then help her or at the least tell Melissa that if she wanted out, we could help her get out.

It is the frustration faced by anti-trafficking agencies around the globe. It's a constant battle with legislation, the judiciary, traffickers, brothel-owners, gangs, and the often-vicious supporters of a full-blown sex trade. It's easy to say the words that the sex trade is a choice, especially when it often comes from the criminal element, the porn industry, traffickers, and brothel owners. Melissa's trafficker made the choice for her. Her choice was to obey or face the consequences: beatings, threats made to harm family and friends, and the constant threat of death. After all, she was now owned and was nothing more than a piece of meat. You could always replace one piece of meat with another.

So began the nightmare for Sandra and her family. But this nightmare was not limited to the dark of night when sleep finally came to Sandra and William. This was a nightmare that screamed at Sandra and William 24 hours a day, that lived with them with every picture of Melissa they had, with every possession that Melissa had left at their home, with every friend of Melissa they heard from and saw.

In March 2013 I heard from Sandra again. Although she hadn't spoken to Melissa, she knew her daughter was alive, not because she talked to her or saw her personally, but because she followed her daughter's life daily by reading the advertisements about the availability of a 'hot, horny woman.' If Sandra went a couple of days without seeing an ad with Melissa in it, she would wait for the telephone to ring. She expected the call would be from police telling her Melissa was dead.

The spider has many legs, and they sink into the victims and those around them. Sandra was on sick leave away from work. Her relationship with her husband was strained. He wanted her to stop reading about the horrendous sex acts that Melissa was providing to men.

As hard as Sandra tried, she couldn't stop. It was the only connection she had left with Melissa. Severing that connection would be like cutting the tether that kept her connected to her daughter and watching Melissa float away.

Melissa's face was shown in some of the ads. Sandra sent me before and after pictures of her daughter. The Melissa everyone remembered was seen as a vibrant, healthy woman caught in the middle of laughter. She was so full of joy and life. I was struck by the confidence she exuded.

The picture from the sex advertisement looked nothing like Melissa. It was a human shell, a gaunt woman of indeterminant age with a 1,000-yard stare and black circles under her eyes. She looked nothing like the Melissa who'd left home only months earlier to begin her new adventure, her new life at university.

The act of prostitution itself (trading of sex for resources) has never been an offence in Canada's *Criminal Code*, although women were often singled out and charged with related offences such as vagrancy, loitering, and solicitation. Prior to 2014, there was no legislation criminalizing the purchase of sexual services. Pimps, traffickers, and sex purchasers went about their business of violating women, while the police staged sting operations that netted them women; those most victimized and violated became the easy catch for police. Those women still have criminal records preventing them from exiting the sex industry into the jobs they always dreamt of having.

Supporters of a free and open sex industry mounted a challenge that made its way before the Supreme Court of Canada. Behind this movement was organized crime, pornographers, traffickers, and brothel-owners who wanted to decriminalize the entire sex industry. Their concern was never for the women and girls forced into prostitution. Those women are their products to be bought, sold, and when used up, thrown out. The sex industry's concern was more control without any legal oversight. Decriminalizing the sexual exploitation of women would be a gold mine. The sex industry salivated at the idea of being allowed uncontrolled exploitation of women and girls. Lobbyists were aggressively campaigning to decriminalize the entire industry, which would also include the decriminalization of traffickers, sex purchasers, and brothel owners.

The Big Sell by the lobbyists was convincing the public, courts, and politicians that the sexual abuse, rape, torture, and beatings women experience regularly in the sex and porn industry was a job. It was also the Big Lie. No one with the power to change the legislation would encourage their own daughters to work in the commercial sex industry.

It's inconceivable that anyone could think sexual exploitation was the glass ceiling women strived to break. LAWC vowed to do all it could to fight any normalization of sexual exploitation. LAWC joined agencies across Canada doing front-line work with prostituted, trafficked, and sexually exploited women and girls. Collectively we advocated for what was first known as the Nordic Model and is now known as the Equality Model.

The Equality Model recognizes prostitution as incompatible with women's equality and human rights. It criminalizes sex purchasers, traffickers, and brothel-owners while providing women and girls with immunity from prosecution. Sexually exploited women and girls are provided access to long-term advocacy and counselling services to help them escape the sex industry.

Canada's *Protection of Communities and Exploited Persons Act (PCEPA)* came into effect on Dec. 6, 2014. It recognizes prostitution as inherently violent, which disproportionately impacts women and girls, and in particular Indigenous women and children. This is the first time in Canada that its prostitution legislation does not criminalize women but criminalizes those who use and provide the merchandise: sex purchasers and traffickers. The legislation is based on the economics of supply and demand. If the demand by sex purchasers for women and girls decreases because of legislation, so will the supply of women and girls by traffickers.

Ending demand is the most effective tool police and society have to end prostitution, trafficking, and sexual exploitation.

No matter the Big Lie, prostitution is not a job like all others. In no other job would women and girls be exposed to the extreme physical, psychological, emotional violence and torture that prostituted and sexually exploited women and girls are subjected to daily.

In no other job are women expected to act out the fetish and porn-fuelled fantasies of men. In no other job do employers ask staff to engage in knife play, rape scenes, and unprotected sex.

Prostitution is not a job. It's a physical and mental assault on women and girls who have no other options for survival. It must never be normalized. In truth, stronger legislation is needed to protect women and girls, along with more severe punishment for traffickers and those who live off the avails of prostitution.

The Public Health Agency of Canada has recommended *Routine Practices and Additional Precautions for Preventing the Transmission of Infection in Health Care* for those dealing with bodily fluids. This includes the use of personal protective equipment like gloves, gowns, masks, and face shields.[2] If prostitution is a job like others, then prostitution too would have to comply with public health agency policies. However, notwithstanding their claims that prostitution is a job like all others, the prostitution decriminalization lobby believes it should be exempt from these routine practices.

While there are recommended routine practices to prevent the transmission of infection, there are no occupation and safety standards to eliminate the violence in prostitution. Prostitution at its core is about men violating women. The best way of ending the violence in prostitution is to end prostitution.

As we fought for women and girls against the well-funded decriminalization lobby, my thoughts were with Sandra, William, Melissa, and every family I had met over two decades who had lost their daughters to traffickers. This can't be said enough: no family should ever have to go

---

2   Public Health Agency of Canada. 2016. *Routine Practices and Additional Precautions for Preventing the Transmission of Infection in Health Care.* Government of Canada.

through the trauma of watching their daughters destroyed by traffickers and the sex industry.

As the Equality Model legislation was making its way through parliament and its various committees, we heard a lot of claims that entering prostitution is a personal 'choice' for women. This was another lie repeated until it became the truth for some members of parliament, especially male members of the New Democratic Party. They were so quick to spew the tripe that one could only assume some men in parliament might have been users of the service. Either that or they simply wanted to keep women in subordinate positions to do as they were told, including meeting the porn- and fetish-fuelled fantasies of men on demand.

Lies and personal attacks, of course no facts, were the ammunition used by some decriminalization lobbyists. They lied. They lied about the agencies advocating for the Equality Model. They lied about the advocates fighting for the Equality Model, hoping to get them fired. They lied about the number of women charged with offences after the passage of *PCEPA*.

They claimed hundreds of women were charged with prostitution-related offences.

A Lie. Only five women in Canada were charged. Rather than advocating for the Equality Model, abolitionists had to defend themselves against the lies.

Yes, there is a group of women who support decriminalizing prostitution. Many in that group are deeply rooted in prostitution and the porn industry. They are the overseers for their masters, who are high up the food chain. These overseers also thrive off the suffering and degradation of their sisters lower down the chain.

As for those who aren't in the business and support decriminalization, they are swept away by the loud, aggressive, and unrelenting pressure of the masters and overseers.

Decision-makers and legislators must recognize that the loud, rich, aggressive lobby that supports decriminalization does not represent all people. The most vulnerable and oppressed often don't know their lives are being discussed and decided by the loud, aggressive voices of only a few.

The decriminalization lobby does not represent the most vulnerable women and girls, which include Indigenous peoples; trafficking victims; survivors; street-involved women in prostitution; women suffering from trauma, mental illness, and substance abuse; and girls like Melissa and her parents.

When I heard from Sandra again it was in late 2015, a year after *PCEPA* had passed and three years after she first called. She said Melissa was still under the control of a trafficker, although it appeared it was a new trafficker.

Trafficking is a complex issue. Girls can be sold from trafficker to trafficker or simply taken from one trafficker by another.

Sandra had all but given up looking for Melissa and had been in counselling with William to help them address the loss of their daughter. They had come to understand that Melissa would never come home.

Sandra sent me a recent ad for Melissa that she had found before calling me. Melissa was advertised as being in a London hotel, off Highway 401, a hotel known on the trafficking circuit. She looked nothing like that young girl headed to university.

Sandra asked me to reach out to Melissa.

I have been asked to do this by many parents. I can't commit to finding their daughters or talking to them. It's too risky for the women and girls. Their traffickers are never far away. However, I have watched trafficking activity outside of hotels and sometimes approached sex purchasers to tell them their activity is illegal. It was dangerous, but I went to see if I could spot Melissa.

After some time, I saw her. She was alone, walking toward the hotel. I walked a little behind her as if I were a hotel guest.

"Hi, Melissa, I'm a friend of your mom's," I said. "Your family loves you. Can I help you with anything?"

She stopped at the door into the hotel. I moved in front and held the door open. She looked at me, her eyes blank. Her long brown hair was now short and dyed red. She was alive but there was no life left in her. I had seen that look so many times. Her soul had been taken.

The decriminalization lobby doesn't care about Melissa or the hundreds of thousands of Melissas across the country.

One day, the spider will be done with Melissa when he senses she is no longer useful. He will set an empty husk free to soon become one of the many dead found in some alley, a flophouse, or under a bridge.

Her family may never even know.

Image credit: Nordic Model Now! (Facebook Oct. 8, 2018)

PART SEVEN:

REVIEW OF NON-STATE TORTURE

with Jeanne Sarson & Linda MacDonald

357

PROLOGUE

THE TORTURE INVOLVED in grooming, trafficking, and delivery of human beings for sexual exploitation is seldom mentioned, nor is the torture that is part of gratification for sadistic buyers. The concept of "non-State" torture (NST) has been largely absent in this book as it was not named by the experiential contributors who shared histories, nor was it part of the authors' awareness prior to 2020. However, in retrospect, much of the suffering discussed can be judged as torture. The intentional insidious infliction of pain is shrouded in silence just as the brutality of commercial sexual exploitation is largely discounted by social indifference.

When Men Buy Sex: Who Really Pays? explores multiple harms to individuals, communities, and social institutions from the perspective of victimized participants. Buying sex occurs because of social vulnerability and marginalization. This contributes to a hidden world of coercion and exploitation as unscrupulous vendors and traffickers capitalize on the obsessions of the monied class. Those being sold run the risk of trauma from continual demoralization, commodification, and objectification; those who purchase sexual "services" wallow in their own gratification. Those who support the legal right of men to sexual entitlement blindly overlook the predominate principles of common good.

The buying of sex is driven by economic oppression from those in positions of status and privilege while selling often entraps social and ethnic minorities who are already disadvantaged. The myth of "consensual" involvement is propagated to boost the rationalization of

358

entitled buyers and their political supporters. Pornography becomes part of the vicious circle of denial and justification. As increasingly violent and disturbing images are created, expectations of healthy relationships become distorted and more bizarre markets develop.

Gaslighting of society happens on many levels. A carefully constructed myth exists that commercial sexual exploitation can be consensual and empowering for those "choosing" to participate. As more and more politicians join forces to "fight trafficking," the vast middle ground of economic desperation and victimization between the polarities of "consent" and coercion is obliterated. This enables the average citizen to accept an ambiguous status quo. What many fail to realize is that unless consumer demand is directly addressed, the inevitable political option is decriminalized buying. The tragic irony is that focus on recruitment of "voluntary" sellers ultimately leads to increased trafficking to meet market demands.

The silencing of torture victims within commercial sexual exploitation requires deeper examination as they are seldom heard. Common associations of torture are military or gang related. We hear horrible stories of interrogation involving prisoners as acts of war. That would be "State" torture, still practiced in some countries although prohibited by international law. Survivors, usually men, are honoured as military heroes and provided with healing services.

Jeanne Sarson and Linda MacDonald were the first advocates to name the torture suffered by women and children within patriarchal circumstances. They began their work in 1993 after meeting a young woman who had been systematically tortured and trafficked from childhood by her own family. Their ground-breaking book, *Women Unsilenced: Our Refusal to Let Torturer-Traffickers Win* (2021), tells the stories of women who remained silent for years. The women speak of extreme ongoing violence, torture parties, and horrific conditioning by their perpetrators, often family members and respected community members hidden in plain sight.

Sarson and MacDonald were among those who testified on behalf of victims at the Canadian government's Standing Committee on Justice and Human Rights regarding a legislative response to commercial sex following the *Bedford (AG)* decision in 2013. They presented one woman's story as evidence that acts of torture are committed against women in prostitution. The Committee's legislative response to commercial sex resulted in the *Protection of Communities and Exploited Persons Act (PCEPA)*, which passed in 2014.

As part of their life work, spanning 30 years, Sarson and MacDonald call for the specific naming of non-State torture, increased awareness, prevention, recognition within the *Criminal Code*, and improved legal recourse and therapeutic options for those who escape. They present a review of their research in the following article written for inclusion in this book.

FELLING THE BASTION OF PATRIARCHAL PROSTITUTION: CRIMINALIZING NON-STATE TORTURE TO DESTROY SELLERS' AND BUYERS' IMPUNITY

Jeanne Sarson and Linda MacDonald

In this chapter we explain that: (1) women[3] exploited in prostitution are subjected to torture, specifically sharing Lynn's story, (2) the universal questionnaire we developed provides evidence of the acts of torture sellers and buyers inflict against women exploited[4] in prostitution, (3) it is essential to challenge the normalization of exploitation, and (4) a complaint under article 6 of the United Nations *Convention of the Elimination of All Forms of Discrimination against Women* (1979) could fell the bastion of patriarchal prostitution.

Torture of Women Prostituted: Lynn's Story

When torture is inflicted by private individuals or groups such as sellers or pimps, buyers or johns, and other exploiters such as traffickers and pornographers, they are referred to as *non-State actors* and the torture they commit we named *non-State torture (NST)* (Sarson & MacDonald,

---

3 We are limiting our discussion of prostitution to women; however, the reality is that girls, as children under the age of 18, are also exploited and their vulnerability is recognized and addressed in the *Protection of Communities and Exploited Persons Act (PCEPA)*.

4 See UNDOC. (2013). *Abuse of a position of vulnerability and other "means" within the definition of trafficking in persons.* https://www.unodc.org/documents/human-trafficking/2012/UNODC 2012 Issue Paper - Abuse of a Position of Vulnerability.pdf This issue paper discusses the integration of the abuse of a position of vulnerability as a way of understanding the meaning of the term "exploitation"; vulnerabilities include, for example, women's inequality and sexualized victimization referring to the prostitution and trafficking of women and girls.

2009; 2014; 2019a; 2021). These terms distinguish non-State torturers from State torturers, for example government police and military personnel. Globally it is understood that State torturers' aim to dehumanize those they torture (Kooijmans, 1986), as do informal militia groups as verbalized by one woman they tortured who said, "I don't know if they realized I was a person" (Amnesty International, 2021, p. 13). Similarly, sellers and buyers, or pimps and johns, torture and dehumanize women prostituted as "non-human."

For years Lynn tried to tell her story but society did not believe her; the Canadian Government's Standing Committee on Justice and Human Rights (JUST) rejected criminalizing acts of torture committed by private individuals such as sellers and buyers of women prostituted as a non-State torture crime (2016). Lynn wanted it understood that the man she married had intentionally groomed her, in partnership with three male friends who organized their plan to hold her captive and make "their living" by exploiting or trafficking her into prostitution. Lynn described that torturing her was their pleasure, just as it was the pleasure for those they repeatedly sold her to for profit (Sarson & MacDonald, 2009; 2019a; 2019b). Condensing her four and a half years of torture-horror captivity Lynn said:

> I was called bitch, slut, whore, and "piece of meat." Stripped naked and raped—"broken in"—by three goons who, along with my husband Ben, held me captive in a windowless room handcuffed to a radiator. Their laughter humiliated me as they tied me down spread eagled for the men they sold my body to. Raped and tortured, their penises and semen suffocated me; I was choked or almost drowned when they held me underwater, threatening to electrocute me in the tub. Pliers were used to twist my nipples, I was whipped with the looped wires of clothes hangers, ropes, and electric cords; I was drugged, pulled around by my hair, and forced to cut myself with razor blades for men's sadistic pleasure. Guns threatened my life as they played Russian roulette with me. Starved, beaten with a baseball bat, kicked, and left cold and dirty, I suffered five pregnancies and violent beatings forced abortions. They beat the soles of my feet and

when I tried to rub the pain away they beat me more. Ben enjoyed sodomizing me with a Hermit 827 wine bottle, causing me to hemorrhage, and I saw my blood everywhere when I was ganged raped with a knife. Every time his torturing created terror in my eyes he'd say, "Look at me bitch; I like to see the terror in your eyes." I never stopped fearing I was going to die. I escaped or maybe they let me escape, thinking I'd die a Jane Doe on that cold November night (Standing Committee on Justice and Human Rights, 2014).

Stepping back into 2014, JUST was studying Bill C-36 from the perspective that prostitution was/is a form of sexualized exploitation that disproportionately harms women. The Bill passed. It became the *Protection of Communities and Exploited Persons Act* (*PCEPA*) (Department of Justice, 2018). We presented Lynn's story to the JUST Committee to make it absolutely real that acts of torture are committed by sellers and buyers against women exploited into prostitution.

We ended our evidentiary support of Bill C-36, recommending that section 269.1 on torture in the *Criminal Code of Canada* must be amended by naming NST as a torture crime. This has not happened. Dismissing this brutal truth is political cruelty in our opinion (Sarson & MacDonald, 2021).

Prior to providing this evidence to the JUST, we had become professionally focused, in 1993, on developing theoretical and practice models that revealed and explained the NST victimization of women and girls. This was the year the first woman, Sara, asked us for support to exit and recover from being conditionally trapped since birth, in a non-State torturing and exploiting family system. Back then NST victimization was not identified in the literature as a distinct form of violence inflicted against women (Sarson & MacDonald, 2016; 2018a; 2018b; 2021).

NAMING HUMAN RIGHTS LEGAL DISCRIMINATION REGARDING THE APPLICATION OF THE LAW ON TORTURE

STATE TORTURE	LEGAL DISCRIMINATION	NON-STATE TORTURE
• Electric shocking		• Electric shocking
• Beaten, burned, cut, whipped		• Beaten, burned, cut, whipped
• Immobilization tortures, tied, hung, caged		• Immobilization tortures, tied, hung, caged
• Water tortures		• Water tortures
• Suffocation/strangulation/choking tortures		• Suffocation/strangulation/choking tortures
• Sexualized tortures: Rapes, gang rapes, repetitive raping, gun, hand/object rapes		• Sexualized tortures: Rapes, gang rapes, repetitive raping, gun, hand/object rapes
• Forced drugging		• Forced drugging
• Nutritional deprivation		• Nutritional deprivation
• Psychological tortures: Humiliation, degradation, dehumanization, animalization, terrorization, horrification		• Psychological tortures: Humiliation, degradation, dehumanization, animalization, terrorization, horrification
• Forced nakedness		• Forced nakedness
• Sleep deprivation		• Sleep deprivation
• Witnessing torture of others		• Witnessing torture of others
• Powerlessness		• Powerlessness

Canada defines torture as severe pain or suffering, whether physical or mental intentionally inflicted and legally only applicable if inflicted by State actors.

L. Sarson & J. MacDonald © 2020

Fig. 1: Model of Legal Discrimination Relating to Non-State Torture

To address Sara's needs we researched State torture publications, comparing this knowledge to the NST details Sara shared. This reality emerged: Regardless of who the torturers were/are—non-State or State—they inflict similar acts of torture as illustrated in the model of legal discrimination relating to NST, figure 1 (Sarson & MacDonald, 2018b; 2018c; 2021).

Evidence: The Universal Questionnaire

To gather truth-telling evidence that women exploited in prostitution suffer NST victimizations, we placed a participatory questionnaire about the NST inflicted in prostitution on our website (Persons Against Non-State Torture, n.d., a). The questionnaire breaks down the major forms of NST listed in figure 1, into 48 acts of torture, leaving room for respondents to add additional information. Respondents are asked to indicate what acts of NST they suffered as illustrated in figure 2 which is Lynn's NST questionnaire response. Marking with a "x" the many acts of NST intentionally committed against her by her husband, his three criminal male friends Lynn called "goons," the men who gang torture-raped her with a knife, and by other male buyers.

EXPLOITED in PROSTITUTION: LYNN 'S REPORT of NST VICTIMIZATION

1. food/drink withheld _X_
2. chained or handcuffed to a stationary object _X_
3. savagely and repeatedly beaten _X_
4. savagely and repeatedly kicked _X_
5. hung by your limbs _____
6. burnt _____
7. cut _X_
8. whipped _X_
9. soles of feet beaten (falanga) _X_
10. fingers, toes, and limbs twisted _____
11. fingers, toes, and limbs broken _____
12. fingers, toes, and limbs dislocated_____
13. tied down naked for prolonged periods of time _X_
14. sat on making breathing difficult _X_
15. forced to lie naked on the floor/ground without bedding/warmth _X_
16. confined to a dark enclosed space _X_
17. placed in crate/box _____
18. caged _____
19. electric shocked _____
20. forcibly impregnated _X_
21. forcibly aborted _X_
22. forced to eat one's vomitus (throw-up) _____
23. forced to eat one's bowel movements _____
24. raped by one person _X_
25. raped by a family/group _X_
26. raped with a weapon (gun or knife)/other objects X

27. raped with animals _____
28. prevented from using toilet _X_
29. smeared with urine, feces, or blood _X_
30. forced under cold or burning hot water _X_
31. placed in a freezer _____
32. near drowned when held under water in the tub, toilet, bucket, stream _X_
33. drugged with alcohol _____
34. drugged with pills _X_
35. drugged with injections _X_
36. drugged with by mask _____
37. choked _X_
38. suffocated by object placed over one's face _____
39. pornography pictures taken _X_
40. pornography or snuff films made/used _____
41. forced to harm others _____
42. forced to watch others being harmed _____
43. forced to watch pets being harmed or killed _____
44. forced to harm or kill pets or animals _____
45. threatened to be killed _X_
46. called derogatory names _X_
47. put down _X_
48. treated as non-human _X_
49. Comment on other non-State torture harms you suffered that are not included on this list or share other comments other harms that you are aware of _____

J. Sarson & L. MacDonald © 2021

Fig. 2: Lynn's NST questionnaire response

Thirty respondents to this questionnaire are shown in the bar graph figure 3. The respondents were from Canada (11), USA (8), Philippines (7), Australia (2), Ireland (1), and the UK (1) and 97 percent were women (Sarson & MacDonald, 2021). One respondent did not complete the questionnaire; this response is identified as "0." Each vertical column in the bar graph is a layer of "torture bricks" with each brick representing a different NST act. Although the responses to this questionnaire do not tell whether the acts of NST were inflicted once or repeatedly over a period of time, or, by the same or different non-State torturers, it does expose non-State torturers'—the sellers and buyers—intentional infliction of severe physical and mental pain and suffering. Some of the women who responded shared herstorical ordeals such as this Canadian woman who said:

> A very close family friend started sexually abusing me at a young age. He introduced me to a child porn/prostitution ring when I was 10. The three main people in this

child porn/prostitution ring inflicted multiple tortures on me and found clients and groups of clients who also added to the tortures (received June 23, 2017).

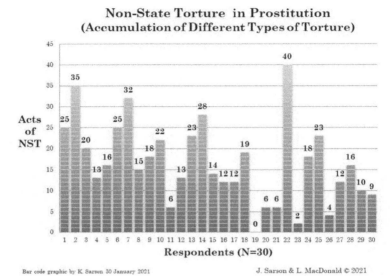

Fig. 3: Non-State torture in prostitution

In this questionnaire on NST inflicted against women prostituted, we listed three acts of mental torture sellers and buyers inflict, as they commit acts of physical and sexualized tortures. These are: (1) being called derogatory names, (2) put down, and (3) treated as non-human. These three acts of mental torture were also listed in another of our NST questionnaires centered on individuals who identified being subjected to NST within family relationships, such as Sara was (Persons Against Non-State Torture, n.d., b). Women's responses from both groups are shown in figure 4. Non-State torturers' misogynistic dehumanization of women becomes striking given the percentage of women from both groups who identified being called derogatory names, put down, and severely *"treated as non-human."*

Three acts of mental non-State torture that contribute to dehumanization	Questionnaire 3: Torture Inflicted in Prostitution N=29	Questionnaire 2: Family-based inflicted NST N=87
(1) called derogatory names	28 responses = 96%	80 responses = 92%
(2) put down	27 responses = 93%	81 responses = 93%
(3) treated as non-human	3 responses = 79%	79 responses = 91%

Fig. 3: Women's responses to acts of mental non-State torture

Fig. 4: Acts indicting mental NST victimization

We do not know the childhood herstories of the women responding to the questionnaire on NST and prostitution; whereas women responding to questionnaire 2 identified being tortured and exploited in childhood by family members and/or like-minded others, such as "a very close family friend" as previously described by the Canadian woman. When women escape such families, some said their involvement in prostitution was a consequence of never knowing any relationships other than NST relationships, that is, until they learned of non-violent relationships.

Further examination of the 48 different NST acts shared on the questionnaire on prostitution, the most common reported victimizations were:

- Raped by one person - 77%
- Raped by gun/knife, other objects - 77%
- Threatened to be killed - 73%
- Choked - 70%
- Savagely and repeatedly beaten - 63%

- Raped by family or group - 77%
- Pornographic pictures taken - 57%
- Drugged with alcohol - 50%
- Drugged with pills - 50%
- Soles of the feet beaten - 50%

"Treated as non-human" can critically wound a woman's perception of her relationship with/to/for Self.[5] For instance, Lynn described that she conceptualized her-Self only as "a head." Likewise, Sara and other women NST exploited often stated perceiving they were an "it," or "a thing" (Sarson & MacDonald, 2014; 2018a; 2018b; 2018c; 2021). Women's statements that they were treated as non-human reflects the misogynistic destruction caused by the physical, sexualized, and mental and emotional tortures committed against them by sellers and buyers, whose domination, power, and control pleasure is torturing. Experiencing her-Self as non-human exemplifies the "objectification of the human

---

5   We spell "Self" with a capital "S" because developing a relationship with/to/ for Self is as intimate as having a name.

body" and "commodification" statements written in the preamble of *PCEPA* (Department of Justice, 2018).

Over the years, prior to our presentations, we collected 734 responses from audiences who responded to another of our questionnaires (Persons Against Non-State Torture, n.d., c). It asked respondents if they categorized NST victimization as distinct from assault or abuse. Over 90 percent differentiated NST crimes as distinct from abuse or assault crimes. Respondents said NST was more destructive, severe, sadistic, caused more pain and suffering, and was dehumanizing and deadly. These everyday persons' opinions show that the *Criminal Code of Canada* needs to be amended to strengthen enacting *PCEPA*. Legally admitting that NST crimes are committed reveals why *PCEPA* aims to prevent the "institutionalization of prostitution" as an everyday business within Canadian society (Department of Justice, 2018).

Challenging Patriarchal Misogyny

Back to Lynn

During the four and a half years of prostituted NST victimizations and captivity, Lynn said policemen were repetitive buyer-torturers who protected her husband and his three male criminal partners. Lynn described her devastation caused by the policemen's betrayal and brutality, saying (Sarson & MacDonald, 2021):

> One day I saw policemen in the hallway—my heart raced—I was being rescued. The cops weren't there to rescue me...they were my next perpetrator-clients. In one fell swoop...an over-whelming sense of hopeless-ness, helplessness, powerlessness, and despair.

> The policemen became regulars. Coming in pairs, six plus four—ten in total—from two different police forces, young, good-looking, dark haired, moustached, married... Policemen raping me with their police shirts on, numbers on badges with sharp points that stuck into the cold flesh of my chest...Violent oral rapes followed by cold, hard... guns stuck deep into my throat. Three clicks: click...click...

click...pierced my left ear...More terror as their ice-cold voices punctured me with, "Stay still bitch or I'll kill you!"

When the policemen used their guns, the terror I felt for my life flew off the scale—this I do know...I was just a disposable "it" to Ben, the goons, and the policemen with their guns...I was just a piece of meat.

But what of the ten policemen—would the present Canadian legal system consider them to be State torturers and charged under section 269.1 of the *Criminal Code of Canada*? To answer this question we refer to the legal case of *Bedford v. Canada, 2010,* paragraph 531. It says police can charge pimps and johns under various sections of the *Criminal Code,* including with torture. If paragraph 531 was operationalized non-discriminately, then the answer would appear to be "yes." These ten policemen were "State-johns" and if investigated today ought to be charged as torturers and the legal system open to listening to Lynn denounce them as torturers.

But wait! Torture, section 269.1 reads that "every official—[specifically a peace officer, public officer, or a Canadian military member]—or every person acting at the instigation of or with the consent or acquiescence of an official, who inflicts torture...is guilty of an indictable offence" (Justice Law Website, 2021). This is a legally limiting definition. It will excuse the policemen—State-johns—from being identified as criminal State torturers of Lynn. Why? Because it is reasonable to say the ten policemen who tortured Lynn were not instigated or told to torture Lynn by an official such as their police chief. Therefore, it is sensible to presume the policemen would escape being charged with the crime of torture of Lynn.

This discriminatory legal definition of who a torturer can be, contributes to Canadians misunderstanding that the NST acts committed against women prostituted is never "sex" or "work." This is how political cruelty contributes to social ignorance, especially when politicians use the euphemism "sex work" when referring to women prostituted. Intentionally being dismissive of the preamble of *PCEPA* that speaks of "the objectification of the human body" (Justice Laws Website, 2020a), is similar to exploited women's expression of being "treated as non-human." Political cruelty adds another layer of pain and harm. What other phrase but political cruelty can capture such misogynistic injustice and human rights inequality directed at women prostituted and tortured?

Herstorical Reclaimed

Political cruelty ignores herstorical truths. We therefore retrieve herstories to reveal women's truth that sellers and buyers and other exploiters torture Canadian women prostituted. For instance in:

1) **1979**, Reverend Brad Massman of Toronto testified before the House of Commons Justice Committee, saying johns want "to burn, torture and beat..." women prostituted (Robertson, p. 13);

2) **2010**, Doug Lepard's *Missing Women Investigation Review* referred to the johns who tortured several women prostituted;

3) **2010**, Terri Jean Bedford, in her appearance in the Ontario Superior Court of Justice, identified her-Self as a woman engaged in prostitution, describing the "physical and psychological torture" she suffered, being "raped and gang-raped too many times to talk about," and "beaten on the head with a baseball bat" (*Bedford v. Canada,* para. 26). This patriarchal political-legal-court structure ignored the violent truth that sellers and buyers torture women prostituted;

4) **2013**, a federal RCMP report addressing sexualized exploitation of Canadian Indigenous and non-Indigenous youth and women, aged 14 to 22, described acts of "torture" inflicted by traffickers who exploited them (Human Trafficking National Coordination Centre, p. 22); and

5) **2014**, one Indigenous woman's voice included in the Native Women's Association of Canada report said, "Torture is torture. I survived it. I'm an expert of it" (p. 51).

Discriminatory Practices and Lawlessness

The *Criminal Code of Canada* explains to Canadians that acts of torture occur when severe physical or mental pain and suffering are intentionally inflicted on another person including "for any reason based on discrimination of any kind" (Justice Laws Website, 2021). The *Canadian Human Rights Act* says discrimination occurs when discriminatory practices are applied against a person because, for example, of their "sex" (Justice Laws Website, 2020b). We argue that the sexualized exploitation of women prostituted is a discriminatory practice because women are disproportionally affected. And that political-legal discrimination exists by failing to uphold NST victimizations as a distinct crime of torture that causes severe physical or mental pain and suffering to the extent, women say, they are *"treated as non-human."*

Furthermore, in 1981, Canada ratified the United Nations Convention on the Elimination of All Forms of Discrimination against Women (CEDAW). It legally binds Canada to condemn and prohibit discrimination against women "by any person, organization or enterprise...[and] introduce legislation...or abolish laws...which constitute discrimination against women" (Article 2) (United Nations General Assembly, 1979). *PCEPA* upholds Canada's legal treaty obligations because prostitution discriminatorily impacts women. Recommending that Canada criminalize NST crimes as torture would eliminate legal discrimination and endorse *PCEPA*.

Moreover, CEDAW Committee's General Recommendations (GR) 19 (1992) and 35 (2017) on violence against women clearly state that women have the human right not to be subjected to torture. Furthermore, GR 35 expands women's human right not to be subjected to torture by non-State actors. However, if the CEDAW Committee recommended Canada create a national law to specifically name NST as a torture crime, based on GRs 19 and 35, Canada can and has legally rejected such recommendations. This happens because these two GRs are outside the wording of the legally binding CEDAW treaty, so are considered "soft laws," which are not legally binding on Canada (Jones, et al., 2018). Explaining Canada's position to us, a government lawyer said:

> General comments and concluding observations of the treaty bodies...are given serious consideration by governments in Canada, but Canada's view is that States Parties are not legally bound to implement them (E. Brady, Senior Council, Justice Canada, Human Rights Section, personal communication, May 26, 2013).

CEDAW Committee experts have verbally asked Canada twice to create a NST law but Canada can and does legally reject such a recommendation or general comment (CEDAW 2009; Sarson & MacDonald, 2018a). Subsequently non-State actors—the sellers and buyers—are not held legally accountable for the torture acts they inflict. This discrimination is coated in the lawlessness of impunity granted the sellers and buyers for the NST crimes they commit against women prostituted. Our 2014 ask of JUST to amend the *Criminal Code of Canada* by criminalizing NST as a crime of torture would strengthen the intent of *PCEPA*, which seeks to protect women prostituted, as well as children and communities from harms by reducing the demand for the socio-cultural and legal institutionalization of the prostitution of women (Department of Justice, 2018).

Banishing State-Centric Misogyny

The patriarchal misogynistic mind-set is that the prostitution of women is "sex work." This was revealed in a JUST meeting when Randall Garrison, Member of Parliament (MP), asked David Lametti, Minister of Justice, "When...can [we] expect some initiative on the review of sex work. I believe...that the current legislation is very damaging and dangerous for those in sex work." To which Minister Lametti replied, "Sex work is legal.... A bunch of things around it were criminalized by the previous government. That's what we have to review" (Standing Committee on Justice and Human Rights, 2020).

This patriarchal misogynistic mind-set intentionally invisibilizes the sellers and the buyers—the married men with families and the single men—who torture and dehumanize women prostituted. This mind-set continues because the Canadian political position on torture victimization refuses to acknowledge the evidence that all women, including women prostituted, have the human right not to be subjected to torture regardless of who the torturers are—non-State or State actors. Author Andrew Clapham explains that when patriarchy thinks an extension of human rights to non-State actors will somehow end up disintegrating human rights ignores that the human rights system has the ability to adapt, to equally provide individuals human rights protection from non-State actors (2006). Reinforcing his position Clapham quotes Christine Chinkin who says, "Women argue that the system has excluded harms most frequently inflicted upon them...[and] never held out the same... fulfilment of human dignity to them as to men" (p. 32). How true. Canada must banish its State-centric discriminatory law on torture crimes as it invisibilizes the dangers inherent in the exploitative prostitution industry.

Felling the Bastion of Patriarchy Exposes
the Exploitative Prostitution Industry

The human and legal right to be protected from torture victimization has historically been operationalized as belonging only to men (Jones, et al., 2018; Méndez, 2018; Sarson and MacDonald, 2016, 2021). It must threaten patriarchal dominance when we argue that women have an equal human and legal right not to be subjected to torture regardless of who the torturers are—non-State or State actors. To admit that sellers and buyers, predominately men, inflict non-State torture on women prostituted and girls exploited, supports that maintaining *PCEPA* is vital.

Felling the bastion of patriarchal misogyny exposes the exploitation innate to the prostitution industry. It would no longer permit dismissing sellers and buyers—whether non-State or State torturers—from being criminalized as torturers of women prostituted. Is Canada's political culture so great a hypocrisy as to intentionally disregard that it is a human right of all women—of women prostituted—not to be subjected to torture? If so, then women so harmed and all of us who resist patriarchal inequality have power to claim that non-State torture must be recognized as a torture crime in Canada, so this bastion of patriarchal human rights domination and misogynistic discrimination falls and no longer threatens maintaining PCEPA.

How to achieve this? It may come as a complaint to the CEDAW Committee, under article 6 of the treaty (United Nations General Assembly, 1979) which says:

> Traffic in women and exploitation of prostitution... requires States parties to take appropriate measures, including legislation, to suppress traffic in women and the exploitation of prostitution in women.

A complaint under article 6 could argue that Canada knows that torture by non-State actors is committed against women prostituted and knowingly rejects to amend its *Criminal Code* to eliminate this legal discrimination by specifically criminalizing non-State torture. This is the advice we have been given when repeatedly speaking to CEDAW Committee experts. They say, *"Bring us a case!"*

REFERENCES

Amnesty International. (2021). *"I don't know if they realized I was a person" rape and other sexual violence in the conflict in Tigray, Ethiopia.* https://www.amnesty.org/download/Documents/AFR2545692021ENGLISH.PDF

Bedford v Canada, 2010 ONSC 4264 (CanLII). http://canlii.ca/t/2cr62

CEDAW. (1992). *General recommendation no. 19: Violence against women.* https://tbinternet.ohchr.org/Treaties/CEDAW/Shared%20Documents/1_Global/INT_CEDAW_GEC_3731_E.pdf

CEDAW. (2009). *Summary record of the 854th meeting (chamber A).* (CEDAW/C/SR.854 (A)). United Nations, Geneva.

CEDAW. (2017). *General recommendation no. 35 on gender-based violence against women, updating general recommendation no. 19.* https://tbinternet.ohchr.org/Treaties/CEDAW/Shared%20Documents/1_Global/CEDAW_C_GC_35_8267_E.pdf

Clapham, A. (2006). *Human rights obligations on non-state actors* (Vol. XV/1). Oxford University Press.

Criminal Code, RSC (1985) c C-46. https://laws-lois.justice.gc.ca/eng/acts/c-46/

Department of Justice. (2018). *Prostitution criminal law reform: Bill C-36, the protection of communities and exploited persons act.* Government of Canada. https://www.justice.gc.ca/eng/rp-pr/other-autre/c36fs_fi/

Human Trafficking National Coordination Centre. (2013). *Domestic human trafficking for sexual exploitation in Canada.* Ottawa: Royal Canadian Mounted Police. http://www.cathii.org/sites/www.cathii.org/files/Project-SAFEKEEPING-EN-Unclassified-FINAL.pdf

Jones, J., Sarson, J., & MacDonald, L. (2018). How non-state torture is gendered and invisibilized: Canada's non-compliance with the committee against torture' recommendations. In Center for Human Rights & Humanitarian Law Anti-Torture Initiative (Ed.), *Gender perspectives on torture: Law and practice* (pp. 33–56). https://www.

wcl.american.edu/impact/initiatives-programs/center/documents/
gender-perspectives-on-torture/

Justice Laws Website. (2020a). *Protection of communities and exploited persons act.* https://laws-lois.justice.gc.ca/eng/annualstatutes/2014_25/page-1.html

Justice Laws Website. (2020b). *Canadian human rights act.* https://laws-lois.justice.gc.ca/eng/acts/h-6/page-1.html?wbdisable=true

Justice Laws Website. (2021). *Torture.* https://laws-lois.justice.gc.ca/eng/acts/C-46/section-269.1.html

Kooijmans, P. (1986). *Torture and other cruel, inhuman or degrading treatment or punishment* (E/CN.4/1986/15). UN Commission on Human Rights.

Lepard, D. (2010). *Missing women investigation review.* Vancouver Police Department. https://www.bwss.org/wp-content/uploads/2010/08/36185748-VPD-Missing-Women-Report.pdf

Méndez, J. E. (2018). Introduction. In Center for Human Rights & Humanitarian Law Anti-Torture Initiative (Ed.), *Gender perspective on torture: Law and practice* (pp. xi–xiv). https://www.wcl.american.edu/impact/initiatives-programs/center/documents/gender-perspectives-on-torture/

Native Women's Association of Canada. (2014). *Sexual exploitation and trafficking of Aboriginal women and girls: Literature review and key informant interviews.* http://drc.usask.ca/projects/legal_aid/file/resource336-2d37041a.pdf

Persons Against Non-State Torture. (n.d., a). *Questionnaire 3 torture inflicted in prostitution.* https://www.nonstatetorture.org/~nonstate/research/participate/questionnaire-3

Persons Against Non-State Torture. (n.d., b). *Questionnaire 2 for persons who may have survived NST.* https://www.nonstatetorture.org/~nonstate/research/participate/questionnaire-2

Persons Against Non-State Torture. (n.d., c). *Questionnaire 1 abuse/assault vs. non-state torture.* https://nonstatetorture.org/research/participate/questionnaire-1

Robertson, J. (1979). *Pornography and its effects A survey of recent literature.* Toronto: Ontario Status of Women Council.

Sarson, J., & MacDonald, L. (2009). Defining torture by non-state actors in the Canadian private sphere. *First Light*, 29-33. http://ccvt.org/assets/ccvt-first-light-2009.pdf

Sarson, J., & MacDonald, L. (2014). Torture victimization—Child to adult: Flashbacks and connection with first responders. *Family & Intimate Partner Violence Quarterly*, 6(3):47–56.

Sarson, J., & MacDonald, L. (2016). Seeking equality—Justice and women's and girls' human right not to be subjected to non-state torture. In J. A. Scutt. (Ed.), *Women, law and culture Conformity, contradiction and conflict* (pp. 263-281). Springer. https://link.springer.com/chapter/10.1007/978-3-319-44938-8_15

Sarson, J., & MacDonald, L. (2018a). Having non-state torture recognized by the UN and member states as an infringement of woman's human rights is imperative. *Canadian Woman Studies/Les Cahiers de la Femme, 33*(1. 2):143–155. https://cws.journals.yorku.ca/index.php/cws/article/view/37766/34313

Sarson, J., & MacDonald, L. (2018b). No longer invisible: Families that torture, traffic, and exploit their girl child. In J. Jones, & J. Winterdyk (Eds.), *Human trafficking: Challenges for the 21st century* (pp. 112-137). Lambert Academic Publishing. https://www.amazon.ca/Human-Trafficking-Challenges-Opportunities-Century/dp/6139852404

Sarson, J., & MacDonald, L. (2018c). No longer invisible: Families that torture, traffic, and exploit their girl child. *Oñati Socio-legal Series, 8*(1), 85–105. http://opo.iisj.net/index.php/osls/article/viewFile/908/1078

Sarson, J., & MacDonald, L. (2019a). Non-state torture human trafficking family systems: Coming out alive—normalizing women's survival responses. *Justice Report, 34*(3), 11–15.

Sarson, J., & MacDonald, L. (2019b). "A difficult client": Lynn's story of captivity, non-state torture, and human trafficking by her husband. *International Journal of Advanced Nursing Education and Research, 4*(3), 107-124.

Sarson, J., & MacDonald, L. (2021). *Non-state torture and sexualized exploitation: Lynn's story—Challenging sellers and buyers' impunity* [Presentation educational handout]. Canadian Sexual Exploitation Summit 2021 Online. https://nonstatetorture.org/application/files/9816/2048/7355/NSTPAPERSEXUALIZEDEXPLOITATIONSUMMIT.pdf?fbclid=IwAR1nHkAzqU_q47PHRa9aSCmJ00yXO9k7peJXItE53yCOcBCf5uzEMk6cXZE

Sarson, J., & MacDonald, L. (2021). *Women unsilenced: Our refusal to let non-state torturer-traffickers win.* FriesenPress.

Standing Committee on Justice and Human Rights. (2014, July 9). *Evidence.* House of Commons, Number 040 2nd Session, 41st Parliament. https://www.ourcommons.ca/DocumentViewer/en/41-2/JUST/meeting-40/evidence#Int-8431536

Standing Committee on Justice and Human Rights. (2016, October 6). *Fifth report*. House of Commons, 42nd Parliament, 1st Session. https://www.ourcommons.ca/DocumentViewer/en/42-1/JUST/report-5/

Standing Committee on Justice and Human Rights. (2020, October 29). *JUST meeting no. 3* [Parl VU]. https://parlvu.parl.gc.ca/Harmony/en/PowerBrowser/PowerBrowserV2/20201029/-1/34125?Language=English&Stream=Video

United Nations General Assembly. (1979). *Convention of the elimination of all forms of discrimination against women* (entered into force 3 September 1981). https://www.ohchr.org/en/professionalinterest/pages/cedaw.aspx

EPILOGUE

Personal reflection, Andrea:

"Torture." If someone had used that word to describe my experience in prostitution while I was actively involved, I would have thought they had lost their mind. I probably would have thought the same had someone suggested it a couple years after I exited, maybe even five or six years later. Why? There are two reasons:

Firstly, choice feminism reinforces the dominant narrative that women who end up in prostitution are there on account of personal choice, even if their choices are of a constrained nature. It was not until I had many years of repeated exposure to radical, counter ideologies on materially-coerced sex that I began to discern what exactly constitutes a genuine choice. Can a constrained choice truly be considered a choice? My friend and fellow exited Canadian advocate Casandra Diamond once said, as an example, "Do I want to get punched or do I want to get slapped?"

Since I have exited, more than any other comment, I have been told that sexually exploited women "choose" the sex industry. The reality, however, is that countless women I know entered because of socioeconomic marginalization and the perception of no choice at all. A wise advocate reframed it well to me in saying, "You didn't choose to enter the sex trade, you decided to enter." It took me a while to wrap my head around that statement, but she was right. Choices and decisions are two completely different things. I can choose between coffee or tea, but did I ever choose to have strange and violent men enter my body just so I could survive? I can assure you that was never something I had any desire for whatsoever. I "decided" to sacrifice myself because it was either that or homelessness, hardly a choice now when I reflect on it.

Too often we accept statements as they are with no critical analysis or dissection. When mainstream society insists that "sex work is work," how do we stop to look at women's situations through anything other than the generic presentation of labour? It is difficult for some people to consider that coercive paid sex could be anything other than "a job."

This ties in closely to the second reason why I could not see my prostitution experience as involving torture. There was a complete lack of exposure to torture as something that could exist outside of the military or government. When I heard the term, I immediately thought of a top-secret military bunker where spies and terrorists were taken to be physically and mentally anguished as a means of getting them to disclose hidden information. Hollywood sensationalism certainly has a role in contributing to this narrative, just as it tends to romanticize commercial sexual exploitation. I certainly did not know of a single person who had been tortured by the state, nor did I know of any "unhappy hookers" during my time in prostitution.

Despite knowing several women who have been subjected to assault and/or intimate partner violence, their experiences did not constitute torture in my mind. The terms "assault" or "aggravated assault" seemed to adequately encapsulate their victimization. It was not until 2020 that I came across the work of Jeanne Sarson and Linda MacDonald, two nurses from Nova Scotia, Canada, who coined the term and concept of "non-State Torture" (NST). As I read through their work, which spans nearly three decades, I was astonished at how much it suddenly made sense, how the description and characteristics of torture were applicable not only to several of my experiences, but to the inhumane cruelty I witnessed other women be subjected to as well.

Although it is difficult to dissolve the embedded narrative that we are, or were, responsible for our "choice" to enter the sex industry, and therefore responsible for whatever happens to us, it is made a bit easier when others come forth with clarity and language that helps us unpack and make sense of our trauma and victimization. All the times that men choked me, raped me without condoms, filmed and photographed me without my knowledge, called me derogatory names, and treated me as non-human, now suddenly had a name: "non-State Torture." It was no longer "sex work"; it was no longer "assault." It was non-State torture.

That word consistently acknowledged the excruciating experiences I endured, tortures that continue to frequent my dreams at night, or during the day when my mind falls still in quiet moments. It was proof of the power of language, and how important it is that we name things for what they are, rather than using palatable euphemisms or words that are "kind of/sort of" applicable. Having my torture named gave me an instant feeling of having been seen and heard. Sarson and MacDonald gave me a healing gift that I never knew I needed, and one for which I am incredibly thankful.

On November 15th, 2022, Sarson and MacDonald gifted me further by inviting me to share my experiences of NST in an exhibition they organized at the United Nations Headquarters in Vienna, Austria. Alongside six other women healing from NST and eight supporters, we called on the United Nations to officially declare non-State torture a global human rights violation.

Sarson and MacDonald, powerhouse activists, are two individuals in a sea of people who have not personally experienced commercial sexual exploitation and come instead from a place of listening and allyship. The tireless advocacy of these two remarkable and compassionate women has also given me an extra tool in my toolkit, the ability to provide the gift of truth and acknowledgment to other women who, like me, have experienced non-State torture in prostitution.

While it is impossible to name everyone who listens to the stories of experiential women and walks alongside us in fighting for change, it is important to recognize the colossal impact of those who join us on the movement for equality. These earth angels selflessly create space in which the harmed can be heard and, in turn, help raise the voices of those who are all too often silenced through fear, blame, and shame. They provide support and encouragement for those simply trying to find some sense of normalcy after experiences which were anything but.

It is very common to hear the masses say, "listen to sex workers," but what that phrase often means is, "listen to the vocal minority of sex sellers who want to see commercial sex buying normalized." I know firsthand through belittling, mocking, and threats that it does not mean listen to women like me, women who have defected from "sex work" ideology and now, through years of healing and support, see the sex industry as something incredibly destructive to individuals and societies.

Even more incomprehensible are the horrible situations of young people coerced, kidnapped, pimped, and trafficked into sexual exploitation. These are voices even more likely to be silenced.

Some of the most powerful voices are those who have never set foot in a brothel, never had to give oral sex to buy bread at Walmart. They are simply people who carry within themselves a bottomless well of love for their fellow humans and want to heal the world from the destruction of toxic individualism and self-serving interests. I want to honor all the allies of the world. Their work is not easy; many of them incur a great deal of vicarious trauma, and some have taken their own lives as a result. Through love and through oneness, I have no doubt that the world can one day reach a state of total unity consciousness. Until then, we all carry on.

AUTHOR ACKNOWLEDGEMENTS

Andrea:

We are all a perfectly messy mash-up of every interaction and experience in our lives, so it's nearly impossible to thank everyone who has brought me here. Nevertheless, some people certainly stand out in my mind.

There is no better gift the Universe can give you than loving, involved parents. My mom and dad succeeded at being the best possible parents they could be to me and my older sister. Although we rode the boom-bust life in the Alberta oil patch, they always made sure we never wanted for anything, and love was always at the top of the list.

My dojo family from the Fort McMurray Renshikan Karate Club spent nearly a decade as my close friends and training partners, prepping me for competitions and ultimately journeying with me to achieve my black belt. To Sensei David Akutagawa, Sensei Greg Davis, Sensei Brad Hemstock, and my brothers Mark, Cody, Garett, and Chris, "*Domo arigato gozaimasu.*" With every fight I take on, I'm ready for it, thanks to all of you.

Much appreciation to all the brilliant educators and academics who have shaped my mind and my perspective as a lifelong student. Most notably, my high school English teacher, Garth Miller, who instilled an early love of writing in me, and Dr. Donna M. Hughes, editor-in-chief of *Dignity*, for recognizing me as a scholar in 2020. Also, many thanks to the incredible women at *Nordic Model Now!* for readily publishing my works and affording me regular opportunities to share my insights on the international stage.

My mentor and dear friend, Kate Quinn: I'm not sure enough thanks exist in the world for me to give to you. My life is where it is today only because you saw me for who I am, not as the brothel owner and escort I was when we first met. Every day I wonder where I'd be today if you had not offered me employment at CEASE and taken that crazy, brave chance on me. It has been an absolute honour to walk alongside you all these years in our shared arduous battle to better the lives of exploited women in Edmonton. You are what they speak of when referencing "giants," an impeccable woman's woman.

Kathy King, my co-author and very close friend: Your ability to raise your compassion despite all you have endured continues to inspire me and reinforces how big your heart is. I always enjoy our writing sessions and am grateful for your ongoing editorial assistance. Above all else, I love your sarcasm and the laughs we share. Time with you is a balm to my soul, as is the case with others in our little feminist circle—Juanita, Sue, and Kylee included.

Everything I do has been bettered by the encouragement and support of my husband and our three totally rad children. No matter what the world throws at me, I know I am unconditionally loved within our exclusive party of five. From the hours upon hours I spend on my projects to the early morning runs when I sneak out the door, I am fortunate to have a husband who is truly an equal partner and constantly picks up my slack. Our children provide me a constant source of humour and hugs. I am rich in love.

To the good men of the world: I stand for you all. Whether you are writing, speaking, creating, or just being an example of healthy masculinity, I see you and appreciate you for your efforts. Special thanks to "B," a reformed sex buyer of 15 years who has generously contributed to many of my recent abolitionist projects, and "J," a reformed buyer of 35 years who courageously shares his journey and reflections with the men at the STOP. Men leading the way IS the way.

My fellow women, the reason for it all: From every remarkable woman I suffered alongside in the sex industry, to the exited women, to those who still struggle to find their way - beauty, strength, resiliency, and perseverance are gross understatements of all that you embody. To the women who center women in their lives and careers, advocating tirelessly for our safety, equality, and well-being: you are sturdy pillars of strength and hope. To the feminists online from whom I learn so much. Thank you. You are the warriors fighting the good fight in the weeds. I can't even begin to encapsulate just how intelligent, assured, and determined you all are. To all the women organizing, speaking out, and doing any act of feminism for the collective good: You are needed and making a difference.

And finally, you, the reader: Time is precious, and to be granted some of yours is humbling. I hope this book has served you well in some ways. I appreciate all you will do for the advancement of women and girls going forward.

* * * *

Kathy:

To say I don't know where to start is an understatement. For the most part, I will not list names, as I have advocated for over three decades, and there are far too many influences to remember.

Of course, I thank my daughter, Cara, without whom I might have had a more ordinary life but perhaps would not have been inspired to dig deeper to understand the shades of vulnerability that trouble our world. I am grateful that her indomitable spirit continues to guide me. I thank her former friends for adding joy to her life and am grateful to those who keep her memory alive.

Special thanks to Kate Quinn, executive director of CEASE: Centre to End All Sexual Exploitation in Edmonton. In the early years after Cara's disappearance and death, the people of CEASE seemed to be the only ones who understood and were trying to help victimized young women like my daughter, much less parents like myself who faced stigmatizing headlines and societal scorn over and above the loss of our loved ones. I met Kate in 1998, and we have worked together since, with her providing many opportunities for me to develop and share my voice. That included about 150 STOPS with about 3,000 participants.

I was also fortunate to find the Edmonton Victims of Homicide Support Society around the same time. This group gathers families whose loved ones were murdered and provides a safe place to remember and begin to process our grief. The murder of one's child is simply not coffee talk, no matter how supportive one's workplace is. The "VoH" has been an important part of my journey. Unfortunately, many cities still lack such a service.

I would like to thank friends, family, and colleagues over the years who remained steadfast in their support, the many survivors I met through my paid and volunteer work who taught me about trauma and resilience, and numerous educators and authors who provided inspiration.

I would like to thank my co-author, Andrea, who has been a constant source of inspiration since we met as educators at STOP in 2013. I have learned so much from her and honour her voice as an exceptional survivor. I hope to channel her passion, as our subject of the sex trade is outside of my direct experience. Thank you to our many friends and supporters who read and commented on countless drafts, and to members of my writing and other groups for camaraderie, feedback, and encouragement.

Although the sex trade is largely a gendered issue, it is reassuring to remember a large contingent of men exists who are true allies. I am truly grateful for the many men in my life who demonstrate decency, respect, and integrity. I hope they never feel taken for granted. Thank you to the many STOP men who appreciated their new learning and welcomed the challenge to change their behaviour.

Last but not least, I thank my husband, who has been a steady source of love and support through my ambitious and sometimes challenging times. He was extremely patient through the COVID years as my world shrank to computer, research, and a virtual life, albeit what made this book possible. We were fortunate to have found each other in 1993 when we were both experiencing life transitions and ready for a new beginning.

Without readers, a book is simply words on a page. My heart is full of gratitude for the opportunity to be a voice for the voiceless and to help promote others brave enough to share their stories. Thank you for hearing them. I hope our words help shed light on a dark and difficult subject and that you, our readers, will be motivated to move from awareness to action in ending the horrors of sexual exploitation and human trafficking.

There's a story about people
on a boat. A guy decides to dig
through the floor of his cabin.
Water flows in.
Other passengers are pissed.
But it's his own cabin,
the guy argues, so why
should it matter?

Personal choice only goes so far
when we're all on the same boat.

ANNOTATED BIBLIOGRAPHIES

Bindel, Julie (2017). *The Pimping of Prostitution: Abolishing the Sex Work Myth* provides a study of 250 interviews in almost 40 countries worldwide. She uncovers the lies, mythology, and criminal activity that shroud the global sex trade and suggests there is a way forward for women seeking to abolish it.

Boge, Paul H. (2018). *The True Story of Canadian Human Trafficking* is fascinating, creative non-fiction. It tells parallel stories of a young trafficking victim, as well as the politician Joy Smith who works tirelessly to change criminal legislation. The young teen is a composite of many survivors, with her harrowing journey of being groomed, lured by false promises, enslaved by drugs and fear, and trafficked across Canada.

Dines, Gail (2010). *Pornland: How Porn has Hijacked our Sexuality* is a provocative analysis of how pornography has infiltrated American society. As more and younger people are exposed than ever before, and as the material has become more hard-core, violent, sexist, and racist, pornography has become a major public health concern. It distorts social norms and desensitizes people away from healthy relationship expectations, thereby actually limiting our sexual freedom. Dines is a professor of sociology and women's studies.

Doring, Mia (2022). *Any Girl: A Memoir of Sexual Exploration and Recovery* is the provocative reflection of a psychotherapist about her own trauma as a teen sexually exploited by an older man and her subsequent years in the Irish sex trade. As part of her recovery, she refutes the culture that affirms sexual violation and calls for everyone, both men and women, to access their full humanity, hold themselves accountable, and learn to love in authentic connection.

Gates, Melinda (2019). *The Moment of Lift: How Empowering Women Changes the World* is a wide-reaching narrative about how gender inequality impacts women worldwide, from maternal and newborn health, family planning, opportunities for education, child marriage, unpaid labour, and agriculture. Yet even laudable goals and substantial resources require learning to work within local cultures to understand ingrained values and the underlying needs of families.

Häggström, Simon (2016). *Shadow's Law: The True Story of a Swedish Detective Inspector Fighting Prostitution* describes his work in Sweden, the first country in the world to criminalize the purchase of sex. Although some women work to finance drug addiction and others are still trafficked, the legislation has effectively shifted social attitudes.

Kristof, Nicolas D & WuDunn, Sheryl (2010). *Half the Sky: Turning Oppression into Opportunity for Women Worldwide* is a disturbing and compelling exposé of injustices faced by women around the world. At the time of writing, India was believed to have up to three million women forced into brothels, with China having 10 million or more "freelancers" existing in a grey zone between freedom and slavery. The authors claim these global numbers are higher than Africans shipped during the Atlantic slave trade.

Malarek, Victor (2010). *The Johns: Sex for Sale and the Men Who Buy It* provides one of the first, but long overdue, exposés of the international sexual enslavement of women, emphasizing the men who fuel the demand. He calls for extensive changes, from the education of men and boys to addressing the inequalities that force women into positions of vulnerability. He presents unequivocally the bottom line that we cannot protect women from human trafficking unless we stop men from buying sex from trafficked victims.

Michelle, Tanya (2018). *Out of the Shadows: a Memoir of a Childhood Lost, Modern-day Slavery, and a Life Reborn* is the true story of a girl who spent 10 years as a victim in the underground world of child sex trafficking. She was groomed at age 13 and lived on the streets of Vancouver and Edmonton. The author wrote and published her own book to help raise money for her Made for More Project, an organization shining light on the darkness of human trafficking and helping bring freedom to the exploited.

Moran, Rachel (2013). *Paid For: My Journey through Prostitution* is the true story of a remarkable woman who survived seven years, from age 15 to 22, of being bought on the streets and brothels of Dublin. Her book has been aptly described as a paradigm-shifter. She provides insightful and empathic reflections on her vulnerability, fears, psychological damage, and manipulations required to survive.

Nagy, Timea E. & Moroney, Shannon (2019). *Out of the Shadows: A Memoir* is the true story of 20-year-old Nagy coming to Canada in 1998 for what she thought was a babysitting job. Instead, she was lured by a ring of international human traffickers. She was forced into the sex trade in Toronto and brainwashed to believe she needed to repay accumulated debts to gain her freedom.

Norma, Caroline & Tankard Reist, Melinda (Eds.) (2015). *Prostitution Narratives: Stories of Survival in the Sex Trade* shares powerful testimonies from 20 women worldwide who have survived their time in the so-called prostitution industry. These women bravely share their experiences of harm and humiliation at the hands of sex buyers, pimps, and traffickers. Along with the editors, they argue passionately for abolition and an end to modern-day slavery.

Perrin, Benjamin (2011). *Invisible Chains: Canada's Underground World of Human Trafficking* is a solid and well-documented exposé of the insidious crime of sex trafficking. Perrin covers child sex tourism, the complexities of cross-border transporting, and "grooming" used by traffickers on vulnerable young women. At the time of his research, Canada was still developing relevant legislation.

Sarson, Jeanne & MacDonald, Linda (2021). *Women Unsilenced: Our Refusal to Let Torturer-Traffickers Win* captures the insights of two public health nurses who, in 1993, first dared to hear and support women who disclosed ordeals of torture, often perpetrated by family members who were otherwise respected community members. Their 28 years of research led them to women world-wide who had been trafficked and tortured for sexualized violence in prostitution and pornography.

RESOURCES / AGENCIES ACROSS CANADA

Aboriginal Alert is a grassroots website developed in 2021 to share information about missing Aboriginal people across Canada. Posts are removed when people are found. https://aboriginalalert.ca

Act Alberta: The Action Coalition on Human Trafficking Alberta developed from an environmental scan conducted in 2007 by Changing Together, A Centre of Immigrant Women. Respondents indicated a need for training to identify and respond to victims. ACT was formed in 2010 to advocate for the rights of human trafficking victims and to help create a network of services. They provide training, research, and victim referrals. https://actalberta.org

Aura Freedom International is a grassroots feminist organization founded by Marissa Kokkoros in 2013. Based in Toronto, they work with a diverse group of partners in Canada and internationally to end gender-based violence through advocacy and education. https://aurafreedom.org

Buyer Resist is a Canadian-based confidential web support for men. Their mission is based on the belief that the purchasing of sex is destroying the lives of men all over the world. They want to help men discover the truth and provide resources to overcome sexual addiction. https://buyerresist.ca

The Canadian Centre to End Human Trafficking is a national charity dedicated to ending all types of human trafficking in Canada. The centre works with all levels of government, private sector business, and front-line service providers to advance best practices and eliminate duplicate efforts across Canada. Their goal is to mobilize collective action and system change. Regular information blogs are posted on their website. https://canadiancentretoendhuman-trafficking.ca

Canadian Human Trafficking Hotline: 1-833-900-1010 is a multilingual service operating 24/7 to connect victims and survivors with social services, law enforcement, and emergency services. It is operated by the Canadian Centre to End Human Trafficking, a non-government organization and registered charity. Referral to law enforcement is done on a case-by-case basis.

Defend Dignity is an initiative of the Christian and Missionary Alliance in Canada, a group of approximately 440 local churches, to end all forms of sexual exploitation. Based in Mississauga, their work is focused on education and awareness, advocacy for social and legal deterrents, and providing assistance to survivors. https://defenddignity.ca

Feministas of Canada is a Facebook group founded in 2013 to provide news about women's issues worldwide, especially in Canada. Feministas are abolitionists who wish to end the global sex trade and support the Nordic/Equality Model, which criminalizes buyers and decriminalizes sellers while offering programs to facilitate exit from the sex trade.

The **Joy Smith Foundation** was established in 2012 as a registered non-profit charity to fund NGOs (non-government organizations) caring for victims. Women are provided with food, clothing, shelter, counselling, and support to begin their lives anew. https://joysmithfoundation.com

#NotInMyCity is a facilitative organization launched in 2017 by country music star Paul Brandt with his wife, Liz, to raise awareness and bring together people to end human trafficking and sexual exploitation. They build alliances to support, facilitate, and advocate for a strategic plan to bring about transformational change at the grassroots, practice, policy, and legislative levels. https://notinmycity.ca

Vancouver Collective Against Sexual Exploitation (VCASE) is a diverse, non-partisan group of individuals who come together as a single voice to end all forms of sexual exploitation. There are several educational videos on their website. https://vcase.ca

Victims of Homicide Edmonton is a self-help group founded in 1995 to offer emotional support and information about surviving the loss of a loved one to murder. Because of the high risk to people caught in sexual exploitation, such groups offer an important service to surviving family members. https://victimsofhomicide.org

LINKS TO AMERICAN & INTERNATIONAL VOICES

CAP International (Coalition for the Abolition of Prostitution) is a coalition of 35 grassroots and survivors-led organizations in 27 countries with a common goal of abolition of the systems of prostitution and human trafficking for the purpose of sexual exploitation. https://cap-international.org

Coalition Against Trafficking in Women (CATW) is an international non-government organization established in New York in 1988, working to end human trafficking and sexual exploitation worldwide, including commercial sex, pornography, sex tourism, and mail-order brides. https://catwinternatonal.org

Coalition to End Sexual Exploitation (CESE) Global Summits to end sexual exploitation are hosted annually by NCOSE: National Centre on Sexual Exploitation.

Culture Reframed was founded as a health promotion project by Dr. Gail Dines in 2015 to build resilience and resistance to hypersexualized media and porn. Dines has researched and written about the porn industry for more than 30 years and is internationally recognized as a leading expert. The crisis of a porn culture is identified; free programs are offered for parents; a blog, resource library, and Facebook page are maintained to promote awareness. https://culturereframed.org

Equality Now was founded in 1992 in New York by three lawyers who believed acts of violence again women were violations of fundamental human rights. They helped raise awareness of domestic violence, rape, female genital cutting, child marriage, trafficking, and reproductive rights. An African office was opened in 2000, London in 2004, and Beirut in 2019, with additional outposts in the U.S. and several other countries. https://equalitynow.org

Exodus Cry is a non-profit Christian advocacy organization founded in Sacramento, California in 2007 to fight sex trafficking and break the cycle of exploitation. https://exoduscry.com

Living in Freedom Together (LIFT) was founded by Nikki Bell in 2014 in Worcester, Massachusetts. LIFT is a survivor-led and survivor-focused organization comprised of those who have overcome commercial sexual exploitation. Bell has grown her one-woman operation into a multi-million-dollar abolitionist organization with numerous programs and a team of almost 30 survivors and allies. They raise community awareness through advocacy and provide a range of direct services. https://liftworcester.org

National Center on Sexual Exploitation (NCOSE) is an American non-profit founded in 2015, evolving from work dating back to 1962 to advocate for a world free from sexual abuse and exploitation. **NCOSE** is based on defending human dignity, exposes the links between all forms of sexual exploitation, and advances the public-health crisis of pornography as one of the links often overlooked by society. **NCOSE** conducts political activism, provides educational resources, maintains a research website, and leads a coalition that unites advocates from various fields. Activities include the annual CESE Summit, corporate advocacy, international collaboration, legal strategies, and research. https://endsexualexploitation.org

National Survivor Network (NSN) is a survivor-led program of CAST (Coalition to Abolish Slavery and Human Trafficking). It was launched in 2011 to foster connection between survivors to build a national anti-trafficking movement in which survivors are recognized as leaders. Members of NSN span 40 states and 24 countries. https://nationalsurvivornetwork.org

Nordic Model Now! is a secular, feminist, grassroots women's group based in the UK that is campaigning to abolish prostitution and related practices. Abolition is defined as a new social consensus that recognizes the harm and violence intrinsic to prostitution, both to the individuals caught up in it and to the broader society, and the adoption of concrete measures to bring about its eradication while helping those caught up in it to make a new life outside. Their website offers a large range of articles and papers.
https://nordicmodelnow.org

OSCE: Organization for Security and Cooperation in Europe is the world's largest regional security organization working for stability, peace, and democracy through political dialogues about shared values. OSCE published (June 10, 2021) a major report in support of combatting human trafficking: *Discouraging the demand that fosters trafficking for the purpose of sexual exploitation.* https://osce.org

Polaris Project is a data-driven social justice movement that works to reduce sex and labour trafficking and support survivors on their paths toward freedom and healing. Regular blogs are posted for education and awareness. https://polarisproject.org

Prostitution Research & Education (PRE) is a non-profit organization founded in 1995 by Dr. Melissa Farley to conduct research and offer education and consultation to the public and policymakers. PRE's goal is to abolish prostitution while advocating alternatives for women. PRE collaborates with other organizations whenever possible. https://prostitutionresearch.com

Rights 4 Girls was founded in 2014 by Yasmin Vafa, a human rights attorney and advocate. The organization works to address federal policy on gender-based violence and human trafficking in the U.S. They educate lawmakers, provide training to judges and service providers, launch public awareness campaigns, conduct research, and build partnerships with other youth-serving groups. https://rights4girls.com

Space International: Survivors of Prostitution-Abuse Calling for Enlightenment is a Facebook page formed by Rachel Moran in Dublin in 2012. Group members worldwide raise awareness about the realities of commercial sexual exploitation.

Stop the Traffik was founded in 2006 in the United Kingdom as an informal coalition dedicated to raising awareness of human trafficking and generating the political will necessary to stop it. It developed into an independent charity and continues targeted actions worldwide through education, advocacy, fundraising, and technology. https://stopthetraffik.org

Survivors for Solutions (S4S) was created in 2104 by Autumn Burris in Denver, Colorado to advocate for peer-led services and programs, survivor-informed policies at all levels of government, and provide best practices consultation to government, non-profits, and institutions. https://survivors4solutions.com

The Lanier Law Firm, with offices in Houston, Los Angeles, and New York, has prepared a guide about the connection between the trucking industry and human trafficking. https://lanierlawfirm.com/trucking-and-human-trafficking/

Truckers Against Trafficking (TAT) began in 2009 as a ministries initiative and became its own anti-trafficking movement in 2011. TAT believes that prostitution is inherently exploitive, victims deserve to be treated with dignity and respect and presented with meaningful options, and traffickers and buyers need to be brought to justice. Its mission is to develop a mobile army of transportation professionals to assist law enforcement in recognizing and reporting human trafficking. https://truckersagainsttrafficking.org

World Without Exploitation is a community of organizations and individuals who share a vision to end human trafficking and sexual exploitation. It was founded in 2016 by Coalition Against Trafficking in Women, Demand Abolition, National Organization for Women/New York State, Sanctuary for Families, Survivors for Solutions, and The Voices and Faces Project. It has 200+ member groups. https://worldwithoutexploitation.org

INDEX

ABOUT THE AUTHORS

ANDREA HEINZ is a Socialist Feminist who spent seven years in Edmonton's licensed sex industry, exiting in December 2012. She holds a diploma in Correctional Services and is presently completing a Bachelor of Professional Arts in Governance, Law, and Management. Andrea is a peer-reviewed scholar on commercial sexual exploitation, has written for several professional publications, participated in a number of interviews, and appeared as a witness for the parliamentary review of Canada's prostitution laws.

Andrea enjoys long distance running and lives in Edmonton with her husband and three young children. While co-authoring this book, she also spent three years as Executive Producer for an eight-episode docuseries titled *Labeled*. In 2020 she was honoured with a Woman of Courage Award by the Centre to End All Sexual Exploitation (Canada).

KATHY KING is a retired clinical social worker (BA, BSW, MSW) with over five decades of professional employment and volunteer advocacy. Her first book was *Child Sexual Abuse: The Search for Healing* (1990) co-authored with Christopher Bagley. In 1997, her passion became more personal when she lost her only daughter to drug addiction, mental illness, and exploitation. Kathy has contributed to many articles and, in 2018, launched a website, MissingCara.ca, where she shares her story.

Kathy lives in Edmonton with her husband, whom she met in 1993. Both have stepped back from their respective careers and enjoy spending time with friends and family. Kathy received a Stars of Alberta Volunteer Award in 2020 for excellence in volunteerism and was recognized as a Daughter of the Year by the Canadians for a Civil Society. In 2021 she was honoured with the Joy Award from Soroptimist International Edmonton and in 2022 was gifted with the Indigenous name "Spirit Woman" on her 74th birthday.

Milton Keynes UK
Ingram Content Group UK Ltd.
UKHW011310300424
441994UK00034B/739